Leading Financial Sustainability in Theological Institutions: The African Perspective

Leading Financial Sustainability in Theological Institutions: The African Perspective

EMMANUEL O. BELLON
Foreword by Tite Tiénou

PICKWICK *Publications* · Eugene, Oregon

LEADING FINANCIAL SUSTAINABILITY IN THEOLOGICAL INSTITU-
TIONS: THE AFRICAN PERSPECTIVE

Pickwick Publications
An Imprint of Wipf and Stock Publishers
199 W. 8th Ave., Suite 3
Eugene, OR 97401

www.wipfandstock.com

PAPERBACK ISBN: 978-1-4982-9188-0
HARDCOVER ISBN: 978-1-4982-9190-3
EBOOK ISBN: 978-1-4982-9189-7

Cataloguing-in-Publication data:

Names: Bellon, Emmanuel, O.

Title: Leading financial sustainability in theological institutions: the African perspective
/ Emmanuel O. Bellon.

Description: Eugene, OR: Pickwick Publications, 2017 | Includes bibliographical refer-
ences and index.

Identifiers: ISBN 978-1-4982-9188-0 (paperback) | ISBN 978-1-4982-9190-3 (hardcover)
| ISBN 978-1-4982-9189-7 (ebook)

Subjects: LCSH: Theology—Study and teaching—Economic aspects—Africa. | Theol-
ogy—Study and teaching—Africa—Finance. | Sustainable development--Africa.

Classification: BV4140.A35 B25 2017 (paperback) | BV4140.A35 (ebook)

Manufactured in the U.S.A.   04/24/17

Contents

Foreword

IN *LEADING FINANCIAL SUSTAINABILITY in Theological Institutions: The African Perspective* Emmanuel O. Bellon addresses a very important aspect of the need for the renewal of Christian theological education. His reflections, rooted as they are in his own journey in leadership, offer insights and present possibilities for long-term solutions to a problem known to the various families of the Christian church. Indeed, over much of the twentieth century, they have devoted considerable energy and resources to the renewal of theological education. With awareness to the abundant literature documenting the conversations and solutions of the past, Bellon's book offers an African scholar and practitioner's contemporary articulated contribution.

The main point of the ten chapters of this book is that the "struggle for training institutions to maintain financial sustainability" represents the core challenge for building the leadership capacity needed for the growth of the Christian faith in Africa. The author makes the case that African theological educational institutions suffer from "limited financial resources." While this is true, my experience in the leadership of theological schools in three schools, two in Africa and one in North America, would suggest that the situation may apply to other continents also. For this reason, Bellon's book should not be viewed as an "interesting" African perspective on a particular phenomenon. It examines a general problem and, as such, deserves careful reading by anyone interested in the current state of Christian theological education and in its future. Bellon's treatment of the issue of financial sustainability illustrates the value of the book for a wider audience.

Based on the 2002 report of the University of the South Pacific's Johannesburg World Summit on Sustainable Development, Bellon defines financial sustainability as the "ability to meet the needs of the present generation without having to compromise the ability of future generations to meet their own needs" (p. xii). Using this definition as a test of the financial health and viability of theological education institutions everywhere, one wonders how many would be considered financially sustainable. The specifics of the financial conditions of institutions may vary. One may not see "carcasses of struggling institutions littering every corner" of every continent as is the case for Africa, according to Bellon (p. 3). Nevertheless, many theological institutions around the world face financial circumstances requiring them to find appropriate and creative solutions. The ideas expressed by Bellon in chapters 6, 7, 8, 9, and 10 provide helpful suggestions to leaders of such institutions.

Bellon recognizes that the financial sustainability of institutions of theological education cannot be the ultimate goal. He emphasizes the essential role of these institutions in the training of leaders for the quantitative and qualitative growth of the Christian faith. The institutions must be viable and sustainable if they are to make the contributions the Christian public expects. They require renewal in multiple areas. Bellon's book represents a needed voice in the worldwide conversation on the renewal of Christian theological education.

Tite Tiénou
Research Professor, Theology of Mission; The Tite Tiénou Chair of
Global Theology and World Christianity; Dean Emeritus.
Trinity Evangelical Divinity School, Deerfield, Illinois

Acknowledgments

IN A JOURNEY TO fulfill one's call in leadership, there are many stops, challenges, and moments of deep reflections. There are people and circumstances that shape and form one in ways seldom expected. The high and low seasons, the joys and tears, commendations and rebukes, celebrations and failures are all part of my experience as a leader of theological institution. Through these situations, I have grown to understand my leadership more and to appreciate every single circumstance and people that has been part of this journey. I am grateful to many people who positively contributed to my reflections without even knowing that they are doing so.

I am particularly thankful to the Global Research Institute at Fuller Theological Seminary that offered the fellowship for me to unplug myself from the busy schedule of institutional leadership to reflect and write at the Pasadena Campus, CA. My warmest gratitude goes to faculty and leaders from various theological institutions, colleagues like Evan Hunter and Jason Ferenczi who shared their experiences and deliberated with me on a number of issues in this book. I recognize Overseas Council International for allowing me to draw insights from their research data and ScholarLeaders International for their support to finish the manuscript.

Finally, I am indebted to my family who has been a great source of encouragement, support, and partakers of my leadership experiences. To my children Josephine, Gifty, Caleb and especially my wife Leticia, I salute you all and dedicate this book to you.

Introduction

THE TASK OF BUILDING leadership capacity to spearhead the growth of Christianity in Africa has been plagued with myriad challenges. At the core of these challenges is the struggle for training institutions to maintain financial sustainability. Although Christianity in Africa has grown forty times since 1910 from a mere 11.5 million believers to over 490 million Christians by 2010, there has not been a corresponding growth in the training of leaders empowered with strategies to shepherd new believers coming to faith every day. The fulfillment of the Great Commission through leadership development is a gargantuan task that requires prodigious resources. Therefore, to achieve this task requires the mobilization of all God's resources. Of course, that is the challenge for theological institutions.

Although the growth of Christianity in Africa is a blessing, the corresponding challenges cast a dark cloud over the future. It is to be seen whether the continent will indeed taste the fruits of this spiritual blessing. Of course, through faith the blessing of transformed lives can be realized if African institutions are able to draw upon grace to develop strategies for financial sustainability and to develop leaders who will nurture a changing society. Our Lord Jesus Christ appreciated well the task at hand, the difficulties on the horizon and the great rewards that await all who labor in his vineyard. Looking ahead, he warned of the plenitude of the harvest but dearth of laborers. Indeed, he commands we pray that the Lord of the harvest send more laborers.[1]

One of the greatest challenges theological institutions face in Africa today is limited financial resources for the development of Christian leaders who constitute a vital part of the Great Commission. The problem of adequately funding programs is not new, however. During his earthly Ministry, Jesus was himself called upon countless times to prove the availability of

---

1. Luke 10:2.

God's spiritual resources for the fulfillment of his aims. His life and manner offer critical object lessons to all who labor in the field.

Christian leadership capacity building is inextricably linked to Christian discipleship. Unfortunately, both of these areas of development have eluded the African church for centuries. The result has been a gulf between faith and practice among believers who identify with Christianity but have not been discipled. The gulf between faith and practice in turn has nurtured nominalism, which is slowly transforming faith merely into one's spiritual outpost. Consequently, the shallow depth of discipleship in many African communities is facing strong competition for attention. Competing interests in Africa's rapid economic development and opportunities to raise one's standard of living are distractions flooding believers with concerns of this world.

In particular, the rapid growth of industrialization and development in many cities, coupled with economic pressures has made recruiting potential leaders for leadership training difficult. Becoming a leader to disciple the church is increasingly becoming an unattractive pursuit among younger generations. Fewer and fewer people are considering theological training as a worthy career for themselves or their close relatives. Theological education which was once held in high esteem and honor is now inconsequential.

The clarion call for discipleship begs the training of leaders, the kind who are grounded and rooted in the word of God and capable of developing other leaders to disciple the church in Africa. Theological institutions built on a Western paradigm, scattered all over the continent are crucibles for developing such leaders, because these training grounds for Christian leaders are struggling to survive. The formal mode of training Christian leaders for the church has suffered a major blow ever since Western missionaries started returning to their home countries. Many Western missionaries teaching in seminaries in Africa have returned to their home countries because of family challenges, insufficient financial support and more importantly the realization that it is now Africa's turn to train its own people.

There are fewer missionaries teaching in our theological institutions today than ever before. The church in Africa is totally unprepared for this gradual but certain change of events. Denominations and non-denominational institutions alike, which formerly depended on Western teachers, now have to fill empty staff positions. Many institutions caught in this web have overloaded the few African faculty available with nearly unmanageable course loads to teach. Hence, teachers have little time, if any to reflect or research to sharpen their skills. This state of affairs is gradually watering down the quality of leadership capacity building for those seeking to serve the Christian church and society. Others have to develop their own financial support locally or abroad to hire teachers so they can keep their training programs afloat. Obviously, these measures are hardly sustainable but that is where African theological institutions are in terms of financial sustainability.

Many students who manage to enroll in these programs often have no financial resources to cover the cost of tuition and therefore need scholarships to remain enrolled in these programs. This growing inability among students to pay the cost of tuition, has resulted in fewer students enrolling in training programs. Hence, small classes now make it difficult for theological institutions to cover their operational costs. Innovative leaders in institutions who perceive this spiraling decline as detrimental to the very existence of theological institutions in Africa are transforming their institutions into universities and offering market-oriented, online courses to raise revenue. Market-oriented courses in the social sciences such as business administration, psychology, communication, computer science and others are successfully attracting students. Regrettably, theological and Bible-based programs are shrinking in size by comparison.

For many, what were once vibrant theological institutions known for training church leaders are now great Christian universities emphasizing everything but the Bible or theology. The Western model African seminaries were built on is now crumbling and doing so very briskly. These theological institutions were not initially established on a paradigm of financial sustainability. Therefore, a growing dearth of theology departments in expressly Christian universities pose a significant conundrum with regard to training Christian leaders for the church and society.

When the multitudes thronged Jesus looking for not only physical healing but spiritual nourishment, his disciples felt cornered. In feeding the multitude, Jesus proved an unequivocal way of overcoming material limitations. At other times, he chose to bless others by accepting their gifts, freely given for ministry. On other occasions, such as in Gethsemane when soldiers came for him, Jesus willingly sacrificed his own safety, not call forth the legions of heaven that were at his service. Rather, he demonstrated a perfectly balanced response, deploying his divine resources according to need and strategy.

Therefore, victory, it seems, lies in structuring strategies with proper balance in perspective. Apostle Paul in his letters to the Corinthians validated a biblical application of fundraising for different purposes of Christian mission. He elucidated the conditions for which that should be encouraged while sounding caution on when to refrain. Like Jesus, the apostle balanced the approach of fundraising for missionary service with tentmaking as an equally viable means of fulfilling the great commission. Theological institutions in Africa must strive to employ all biblical principles to achieve desired financial sustainability.

Unfortunately, there is widespread misunderstanding among many Christian leaders today regarding provision for the needs and purposes of theological institutions. Many Christian leaders are unresolved on how to define appropriate steps to achieve financial sustainability for African educational institutions. Building leadership capacity for the church in Africa cannot be over-emphasized. It is critical to now develop a system for training leaders through a culturally relevant mode of sustainability upon African standards.

So, what is financial sustainability? Broadly defined, it is the ability to meet the needs of the present generation without having to compromise the ability of future generations to meet their own needs.[2] However, for this to happen, the present generation must accrue enough benefits now and into the future. Douglas R Snow, a professor in The Sawyer School of Management, Suffolk University indicated that for institutions, sustainability is achieved when social benefits exceed total costs and where viable functional networks exist with other local institutions.[3] This goes beyond an institution's financial viability or focus on the bottom line, but rather to its capacity to engage the external environment It is the ability to generate net social benefits to improve the welfare of society.[4] For theological institutions, financial sustainability is the ability to fully meet operating costs while effectively fulfilling its organizational mission with an emergency financial reserve that ensures operations for at least one year, while maintaining an institutional capacity that attracts funding for capital projects.

It is absolutely essential that theological institutions achieve a level of sustainability that allows them to meet operating costs annually. This means institutional debt has to be reduced to the barest minimum and managed closely. In this regard, the use of emergency reserves would not only reduce an institution's financial risk, but make it healthy by demonstrating an important component of institutional capacity to attract capital funds. Institutional capacity is broader than simply having access to emergency financial reserves. It includes among other things, a qualified faculty, administrators, communicators, developers, strong leadership team, efficient structures and systems, networks, strategic partners, and high-caliber students. Achieving financial sustainability is inevitable if theological institutions in Africa are to make a social impact that secures the future of theological education.

2. "USP WSSD Team Report."

3. Snow, "Microcredit."

4. Ostrom and Schroeder, *Institutional Incentives*.

The Overseas Council International has a rich history through its Institute for Excellence, a training program for leaders studying at theological institutions affiliated with the council. In December 2010, the council conducted an online survey in an effort to identify current challenges regarding financial sustainability. The results, reported in August 2011, offered vital information for future theological institutes concerning the financial sustainability of theological education. Reports from published findings will be discussed in this book.

This book is divided into three main parts: history and financial challenges of theological institutions; biblical foundations of financial sustainability; and pathways to financial sustainability. The history of financial sustainability is discussed in chapters 1 to 3 and addresses historical initiatives, training opportunities, and matching financial resources with needs of today's institutions. Biblical foundations for financial sustainability will be explored in chapters 4 and 5, with a discussion of biblical principles for charitable support versus tentmaking as viable alternatives for generating income. The third and final section in chapters 6 to 9, reveals suggested pathways to financial sustainability for theological institutions, and covers church ownership, institutional governance, third stream modes of delivery, strategic collaborations, and leadership development. An overview in chapter 10 reviews the current state of theological education and the pathways that have contributed to creative responses to financial challenges faced by twenty-first-century African theological institutions.

PART ONE

History and Financial Challenges of Theological Institutions

Chapter 1

The Historical Initiatives

In Africa, the focus upon theological education to develop leadership capacity has been a hot topic for decades. Through time, different initiatives aimed at achieving quality scholarship were established. Yet, more than eighty years after the debate began, the prognosis under various prescriptions is that endemic financial challenges will continue to negatively impact theological education in Africa. The carcasses of struggling institutions littering every corner of the continent bear witness to this prognosis. Yet, these ailing institutions are still hopeful that somehow a contextually relevant remedy will emerge to set them on a path to financial sustainability.

It is noteworthy that theological education in Africa has always been at the heart of African ministry since the era of early recipients of the gospel. African Kings sent their children abroad to study theology in the early 1800s. King Naimbana of the Koya Temne of Sierra Leone was one such king who sent his three sons abroad, sending one specifically to pursue Christian theology. However, it was not until 1814 when the Christian Missionary Society secured a plot in Leicester Mountain, Freetown that the first Christian Institution was built. Unfortunately, five years after its inception, the school was closed; although, later it was converted into a seminary of higher education in 1820.[1] Regrettably, in 1826 the two remaining students were dismissed and the institution shut down for lack of teachers and a lack of interest among the population.

This remained the case until Rev. Charles Haensel opened an institution at Fourah Bay in April 1827. Among reputable theologians trained at

---

1. Sanneh, *West African Christianity*, 132.

that seminary was Bishop Samuel Ajayi Crowther.[2] The institution was later renamed Fourah Bay College and thrived for almost a half-century before it was upgraded into an institution of higher learning. That was the beginning of African theological education as we know it. There are earlier models of theological education in Northern Africa that date back to the first century. However, for this discourse we will focus on sub-Saharan Africa, and use a snapshot of the Fourah Bay model, which has been replicated in many places across Africa.

In 1938, the International Missionary Council held at Tambaram described theological education as the weakest element in the entire enterprise of Christian Missions.[3] Although significant gains had been made over the years, the prevailing situation at that time left much to be desired. Even many of the resolutions at Tambaram remained dormant until after World War II when research published between 1950 and 1962 gave hope to the dreams and aspirations of the council. Specifically, research regarding the mission field was published and provided an impetus for the International Missionary Council meeting which was held in Ghana in 1957–58. The Ghana meeting established the Theological Education Fund (TEF) with resources of $4 million USD and a schedule of mandates designed to strengthen theological education in the developing world over a specific period of time.

The first mandates focused on ways to better train and educate ministry workers to meet the demands of the growing African church. The goal was to educate African Christian leaders to embrace scholarship for academic excellence in ministry.[4] "Major grants of more than $2,800,000 USD were distributed to twenty-five strategically situated institutions. These schools were considered the best options for qualitative growth in the future. Over $1,000,000 USD were eventually spent towards the development of school libraries and the publishing of theological textbooks.[5] Unfortunately, that mandate period—the first step in transforming the landscape of Africa's theological education—ended in 1964 with marginal progress.

The second mandate lasted from 1965 to 1969. At that time a number of scholars were intently focused on the nature of ministry and the constituencies theological education sought to serve. The question posed was *Can theological education effectively address the pertinent needs of the church, given the dangers posed by the proliferation of religions?* The answer gave rise

2. Ibid., 134.

3. Webster, *Training of Ministry*, 4.

4. Kittel and Friedrich, eds., *TDNT*, 238.

5. *Report from the Theological Education Fund.*

to a popular idea to describe the aspirations for Africa's system of theologi-cal education. The idea was "Rethink." Nevertheless, this second mandate ended without conclusive or comprehensive resolutions; although, it did pave the way for a third mandate.[6]

The third mandate, which caught the attention of the world was not without its critics. It lasted from 1970 through 1977 and focused on con-textualization. As a form of renewal, contextualization was meant to shape theological education into a training platform focusing on the following is-sues: the urgent need of renewal and reform confronting the church, the role of justice in human development, theology that is authentic and appropri-ate within the context of prevailing needs, and dissecting non-authoritarian elitist pedagogy devoid of practical application.[7]

Following the end of the third mandate, a number of sporadic and uncoordinated initiatives and models of theological education sprang up across different regions in the developing world during the 1970s with the aim to upgrade and popularize theological institutions in the region. Asia Theological Association was established to advance theological education in Asia as theological education by extension gained significant steam. The As-sociation of Evangelicals of Africa and Madagascar was formed to provide accreditation to post-secondary theological institutions. These initiatives, which were financially supported by Western churches, contributed to get-ting the wheels of theological education rolling in Africa and other parts of the developing world. Nevertheless, the fundamental challenges on how to sustain theological education over the long haul remained enigmatic.

Part of the third mandate to contextualize was also to determine the viability of theological education in the developing world. As Zorn noted, the question of viability itself was a complex but central part of the discourse concerning theological education:

1. Can theological education as it has developed in the Third World—with encouragement from the Theological Education Fund and others—be self-supporting in the areas of finances and personnel if working in conjunction with local or regional resources?

2. If theological education in its present form is financially unviable, what are the alternatives?

3. To become regionally viable, can theological education continue to depend on stultifying foreign assistance or find substitute resources?

6. Coe, "In Search of Renewal," 235.

7. Kittel and Friedrich, eds., *TDNT,* 239.

4. How can theological education be viable in those areas where poverty and sparse populations make full-time ministry financially unsustainable?

5. Is it possible that Third World theological education is an unsupportable method of producing an unsupportable and/or irrelevant ministry?[8]

One may like to know whether plausible answers were found to these questions or whether they generated any debate that resulted in positive breakthroughs over time. However, it is difficult to find resolutions or deliberated initiatives that respond to these questions arising out of the third mandate. After several decades, reflecting on these questions even now spawns more questions, but few great answers. So, is there any light at the end of the tunnel? Are there contextually relevant solutions to which we can address ourselves?

This is the pathway of our discourse from a biblical as well as contemplative standpoint. In reality, theological education in Africa can glean profitable lessons from what is working and what has not. Ultimately, collective experience can provide a framework worthy of active deliberation as we move toward more comprehensive approaches.

THE ROLE OF THEOLOGICAL INSTITUTIONS

Theological institutions serve as training organizations primarily devoted to the advancement of theological education. They are established to educate individual Christian leaders with biblical, theological, and ministry skills necessary for effective service in both church and society. Yet, there are myriad perspectives regarding what theological institutions should be doing based on theology, traditions, doctrines, and preferences.

There is a need to provide adequate technical skills within historically familiar skillsets for those who wish to serve as pastors. Graduates will endeavor to meet the needs and demands of congregants as they seek to individually achieve both desirable societal transformation as well as spiritual growth. Leaders must be formed in their dedication to religious life and witness in the community. Therefore, a theological institution is the place where the formation of intellectual, practical, and professional leadership skills must happen to ensure that Christians grow deeper in their relationship with God and fully grasp biblical truths.

---

8. Zorn, *Viability in Context*, vii.

The four main areas of theological education have been Bible, Church history, theology and practical application of dogma for engagement with society. Edward Farley, outlined four historical types of theological education as follows:

1. The life wisdom or *habitus* model (the earliest model exists in the monastic movement);

2. The scientific model (science developed from philosophical schools in Alexandria and later developed in the Middle Ages);

3. The university model (the "crown of science" in which theology becomes the focus of fourteenth- and fifteenth-century theological faculties);

4. The "professional" training model (the inner ecclesiastical needs of the Christian community in terms of ministerial formation).[9]

David Kelsey perceived the role of theological institutions as following a twofold core mandate: the *paideia* and *Wissenchaft*. *Paideis*, modeled after the ancient Greek vision of education, emphasized formation. The Berlin university system approach in the nineteenth century was named *Wissenchaft*, which referred to mastery of a body of knowledge and demonstration of core competencies.[10] Kelsey discussed the advantages and disadvantages of *paideia* and *Wissenchaft* and demonstrated the difficulties in keeping the two in dynamic balance.

Another dual perspective has been the pure education versus the pure vocation model introduced by Alison Le Cornu. Pure education is characterized by communal, face-to-face mentoring/learning; whereas, pure vocation emphasizes training. Pure education emphasizes content and knowledge proficiency in order to gain mastery of the "truth." Pure vocation focuses on informing and performing to develop skills for ministry tasks.[11]

Kelsey and Le Cornu are on the same page with regards to using these two paradigms to define the role of theological institutions. However, it is noteworthy that there has been an on-going tension between both of these ideological perspectives for decades. Theological training at advanced levels is geared toward preparing student scholars for research and for the ministry. However, a standing preference in many African institutions has been to

---

9. Farley, *Theologia*, 42–80

10. Kelsey, *Between Athens and Berlin*, 6–19.

11. Le Cornu, "The Shape of Things to Come," 13–26.

focus predominately on the vocational aspect of ministry. Very few African institutions advance a purely academic line.[12]

Although a vocational focus has been the norm for some time, the need for balanced instruction cannot be overemphasized. Africa needs to allow more vocational ministry leaders to develop as scholar leaders, too. Therefore, the issue is not just an either/or argument. Rather it is an issue best served by both approaches. Consequently, how Africa will develop leadership capacity to address multiple areas of need is still to be discovered.

Ultimately, developing leadership capacity is to equip an army of men and women with advanced vocational and scholarly research skills and competencies in order to influence church, society, and academia. The role of theological institutions will be meaningless if they fail to prepare men and women with the necessary knowledge and skills to be quality leaders needed in this era. To adequately meet this objective, theological institutions must engage in biblical values-based leadership training, because leadership training devoid of values is a mere cosmetic dressing lacking the capacity to effect change in individuals or society.[13]

The need for competent leaders with values has been reiterated by many African authors because it is so central to the purpose of theological education. Scholars argue that new and alternative frameworks for theological education in Africa need content that will produce church leaders who are competent to meet contextual challenges facing the continent. The extent to which theological institutions can impact the Church, society and academia will be solely determined by the quality of leaders these institutions produce.

Theological Formation

Pioneers of theological education in Africa were preoccupied with existing models and could not grasp African contextual factors critical to the success of the education they provided. Over the past three hundred years, theological formation has become content and process that can be categorized across five types of institutional environments:

1. Non-residential extension programs affiliated with church-based theological centers such as Bible schools, or through catechetical courses and de-centralized regional training programs;

---

12. Cole, *Training of the Ministry*, 2.

13. Bellon, *Transforming Leadership*, 55.

2. Residential church-based academic and ministerial formation programs in denominational or inter-denominational seminaries or theological colleges;

3. Academic theological programs taught by theological faculties at publicly funded, secular universities or divinity schools (i.e., where both the curriculum and teaching staff are still church-affiliated);

4. Academic theological programs offered by divinity schools and administered under privately funded Christian universities;

5. Academic theological programs available in religious studies departments in publicly funded state universities; theological education programs independent from church-related influences.[14]

African theological institutions closely follow the Berlin school of thought as described by Kelsey. The Berlin model emphasized mastery of knowledge and the intellectual pursuit of the same. Learning is teacher-driven and instructors are custodians of knowledge who must be revered. Students have the responsibility to absorb everything from their instructors during classroom lectures. Simply put, missionaries who championed theology instruction in African institutions essentially replicated what they had experienced in their own countries. Much of what missionaries understood of the African cultural context was inaccurate. Additionally, missionaries did not have a factual grasp of any contextual sociology influencing the local culture, nor vice versa.

MODELS OF THEOLOGICAL INSTITUTIONS

African theological institutions are for the most part administered by one of the following: non-denominational mission agencies, or Western Christian denominations (in collaboration with a specific mission agency), or indigenous African Christian denominations. Since these institutions are established to operate within the same philosophy of ministry, an institution founded by a mission agency closely resembles that agency.

Therefore, faith mission agencies typically profess a heavy focus on faith alone as the sole means for obtaining key provisions and sustenance. All affiliated institutions will also follow suit. Likewise, if an agency relies on donations, so too its theological institution will rely mainly on donations from the West—supplemented by student tuition. That approach to funding

---

14. "World Study Report," *Challenges and Opportunities*, 14:17.

will not necessarily exclude attempts to generate local funding but any additional fundraising efforts would likely be a lower priority.

Institutions started by Christian Western denominations to support their missionary endeavors are designed to meet the leadership needs of the denomination in a manner that safeguards the ethos of the denomination. The institutions are led by qualified denominational leaders and the students and faculty are recruited only from the school's founding denomination. These institutions are also financially supported by donations. In this case, the money is provided by members of the denomination and other partners affiliated with the denomination.

Of course, the administration of these schools are inextricably tied to the theological disposition of the denomination, making the institution an extension of the church. Students enrolled in this style of theological institution are often recruited from denominations sharing the same or similar basic doctrinal beliefs. Yet, although these institutions were started and often run by Western missionaries, much will change when local leaders take charge of daily operations. However, the philosophy of the ministry will remain the same.

Theological institutions sponsored by indigenous African denominations are similar to those started by Western denominations, except that many are still evolving into full-fledged accredited institutions. African church denominations are part of an emerging church phenomenon that is initiating theological education in response to specific needs of the denominations. These needs have emanated from the lack of value non-denominational institutions place on theology and the exclusivity of Western denominational institutions. Although institutions administered by indigenous denominations have experienced inadequate staffing and subpar facilities over the years, many are newly emerging as strong centers of theological education rivaling older and well-established counterparts because the emerging schools are well-funded by the local church.

As mentioned, each of the three different theological institutions charged with the mandate of developing leaders for church and society depend primarily on donations and then tuition to finance operations. This makes the question of financial sustainability an on-going challenge that institutional leaders must solve if theological institutions are to thrive on the continent. Unlike indigenous African denominational institutions, which depend heavily on distributed learning, the two remaining categories actually constitute a majority of African institutions. The majority of schools with operations based on Western models are experiencing dire financial woes as sustainability strategies are not using local know-how to address the problem.

The three operational models to a greater extent speak to the success and failures African school administrators have experienced so far. This is not to suggest that there is a perfect operational model, but by analyzing operations categorically, we can enhance our understanding of the endemic nature of our current challenges and design a better framework. It is fair to conclude that Western styled operational models for the African theological institution were taken from European and North American educational systems. Yet, even among these regions, world theological education has evolved over many years. Actually, the topic still generates discussions on what constitutes effective theological education.

Seedbed as an Analogy

The Western model gave rise to a seedbed approach to education among African theological institutions.[15] The metaphor of "seedbed" is appropriate in this discourse given the etymology of the word coupled with the function of theological institutions. The word seminary comes from a Middle English word referring to "seed plot," "seedbed" or "nursery." The word comes from the Latin *seminarium*—the Latin root being *semin* or "seed." Therefore seminary is a place where something is developed or nurtured as is a seed in a bed of soil.[16]

The seedbed analogy is almost self-explanatory: seeds are introduced to soil that can provide all the nutrients, minerals, and water needed for germination. In this environment, shoots of the plants are shielded from harsh weather elements and tenderly supported to grow. After tender seedlings have grown to a certain maturity, they are gently taken from the seedbed, still rooted in some of the nurturing soil and transplanted elsewhere to grow and bear fruit. A plant that begins in this manner is expected to be strong enough to weather many external challenges.

Such was the birth of theological institutions in Africa. Schools did well initially in the sheltered garden of Africa when the original soil consistently made nutrients available. However, being left in the garden to flourish like other plants has posed great danger to the African theological institution's survival. So, over the decades efforts have been geared toward temporary provision of the seedbed conditions and rebuilding of shelters in the garden to ensure survival. We are all still in the process of discovering how the plant can survive in the garden together with other local plants.

15. Zorn, *Viability in Context*, ix.

16. *Merriam-Webster Dictionary*, s.v. "seminary," https://www.merriam-webster.com/dictionary/seminary (accessed December 21, 2016).

Such is the predicament of the theological institution in Africa. Poised to meet the need for leadership development in Africa, little consideration was given to the dynamics of the African garden in which theological education was transplanted. Should theological institutions be transplanted at all? Could they have been planted directly into the garden? What implications would that have had on the current model? What has been the experience on other continents? How have African theological institutions weathered the storms following transplanting? Where are they now in terms of their theological education identity? Africa is not the first to have experienced such transplanting, considering that its latter supporters from North America have suffered a similar fate. Only there, even though the transplanting was in a different geographical location, the culture and people were almost the same.

Transplanted Curriculum

In Africa, transplanted theological curricula had little or no relevance to the learning patterns, culture, or prior knowledge of the recipients. It introduced a dialectic thinking process in a holistic context. This inevitably created a parallel model which characterized theological education as a foreign plant that must be left alone.

The third mandate of the Theological Education Fund was meant to rectify this hands-off approach through a campaign to contextualize theology. Since the start of the third mandate, sporadic initiatives have made incursions into the subject matter. Nevertheless, we do not have a comprehensive overview of what was achieved. Except for a few cosmetic dressings in the curricula of theological institutions, the original casts have remained the same, leaving little room for innovation. Unfortunately, efforts were short-lived minimal impact. J. N. K. Mugambi noted, "As long as the syllabi of African theological colleges are imported from elsewhere, pastoral training will continue to be out of tune with the cultural and religious dynamics of African societies among whom the trainees are expected to work after graduation."[17]

The challenge of overcoming the foreignness of transplanted theological institutions has been complicated by different factors over the years. One complication is that teacher training occurs predominantly in Western institutions of higher learning. Graduates who are trained under a Western methodology will later accept positions in African institutions. The transplanted teaching staff will understandably use teaching methodology and

17. Mugambi, "Christianity in Africa," 111.

content based on what they experienced, and mentor Africans to mimic the same.

Inflexibility complicates training when local academic leaders are denied the opportunity to create new, and unique content relevant to the local social, cultural contexts. Even more disturbing is the fact that Africans who studied in Western countries will not think any differently from those who taught them while serving in in the African context. Hence, these issues perpetuate the sheltered garden characteristics of theological formation in Africa.

Western institutions of higher learning that offer advanced degrees insist on certain courses as primary requirements for admission. In some cases, where there is doubt as to whether applicants have fulfilled prerequisites if through alternate but equivalent course work, students are still made to take listed requirements to fulfill the curiosity of admissions boards. Institutions in Africa avoid the risk of losing graduates to advanced Western institutions of higher education by keeping curricula of the transplanted training intact. Therefore, requirements by Western institutions and compliance from African institutions ensure that the transplanted curriculum remains in the sheltered garden.

In reality, to fundamentally transform society, "Curriculum development must begin from the context of the learners and proceed to discern the text that can provide relevant knowledge, skills, and experience appropriate for each particular context."[18] This ensures continuous learning and positively impacts both teachers and learners, as teachers reflect on the dynamics of changing society and implications for what is being taught. Learners apply the knowledge, skills and experience to their ministry spheres of influence.

It is not only the curricula and teachers that are sheltered in the transplanted garden, but also available learning resources, too. Transplanted curriculum is sustained by Western literature and does not incorporate local narrative to communicate local principles as another means of advancing learning.

For many years, theological institutions in Africa depended on Western theological thought and frameworks to provide academic fodder. Consequently, biblical interpretation was done using Western theological systems that are, in reality, completely alien to basic African thought patterns. For example, most of the reflections done on theological education financial sustainability focus on other regions of the world. Not surprisingly, I struggled to find academic resources published by Africans on the subject

18. Bellon, *Transforming Leadership*, 111.

of sustainability. Therefore, African leaders must engage the endemic challenges that threaten the survival of theological education and find African solutions to salvage the downward trend in enrollment we are currently experiencing.

Financial sustainability, as earlier defined, transcends the ability to cover an institution's operating cost, because it involves building institutional capacity that is able to effectively accomplish the following: deliver its core mandate, meet operating costs, build reserves, and attract other funds for capital projects. As much as progress has been made in many areas of theological education, there are no tangible results to show in this particular area. Hence, the sheltered garden facilitated by foreign missionaries is still prevalent. Consequently, the focus on financial sustainability is still limited to donations and tuition despite the obvious need to build institutional capacity across the board. Unlike other disciplines, a sustainable approach to local ownership and support of an institution is a core mandate of its beneficiaries.

Institutional Accreditation

The role of accreditation in the sustainable model was not seriously considered until as recently as the last two decades. It was feared that accreditation would secularize institutions, and force them to lose the original organizational mission as experienced in many Western countries highlighted in James Burtchael's book *The Dying of the Light*. This was a genuine concern and the fear was warranted, considering the numerous examples across the globe.

However, the lack of accreditation has created a perception that graduates of theological institutions are not fit academically to serve in other areas of society. Lower academic requirements for admission have further reinforced the notion that theological graduates would fail in mainstream educational programs. Therefore, they have no option but to pursue lower level and uncompetitive educational opportunities. In other words, theological institutions were seen as dumping grounds for academic failures. This led to the conclusion that such students should not be taken seriously by society.

Graduates were poorly remunerated by the parishes they served because of the financial struggles of many churches. Likewise, poor salaries were based on the perception that theological graduates are poorly educated and merely trained to serve God, not to earn high salaries or live comfortably. Notwithstanding, these perceptions began to change when African theological institutions started securing accreditation from pioneer agencies like Association of Christian Theological Education in Africa (ACTEA). ACTEA has influenced the evolution of evangelical theological education in Africa for over three decades.

Established in 1976, the ACTEA standardized educational requirements and outcomes providing a way for schools to develop a common identity, sense of community, shared values and purpose that has since energized theological education in Africa. Although not all evangelical institutions are affiliated with ACTEA, there are over 30 institutions in more than 20 countries.[19] This demonstrates significant growth in the number of theological institutions seeking accreditation in Africa.

As these institutions venture into public recognition especially after attaining state charter status, government regulatory agencies are demanding that institutions widen their scope of academic instruction to cover other areas in the social sciences. These institutions have been asked to provide training that will serve needs beyond the confines of the church.

Although the features mentioned above do not exhaustively describe the model of theological institutions in Africa today, the discussion was designed to provide an overview of major issues characterizing and impacting theological institutions in Africa today. The discussion is to help us appreciate the past, discern the present and embrace the future. In particular, ensuring financial sustainability for leadership capacity building through contextually African theological scholarship may be the last battlefront for theological education in Africa.

Even African scholarship has moved beyond the delimitations of African identity to offer valued insight as a global voice among theological scholarship. Africans are writing not only for themselves but for the rest of the world. Accordingly, their voices are being duly valued on the world stage. Contextualization continues as sub-Saharan cultures across the continent evolve and blend into other cultures under the pressures of globalization.

Marginal gains have been made in curriculum development but he who pays the piper is still naming the tune. Accordingly, efforts are haphazard and lack the substance to be truly African. Undergirding all these challenges is the dominant issue of financial sustainability.

Sustainability determines the nature of the facilities needed to accommodate instruction, who is hired, how and what they teach. Among available learning resources the level of integration and contextual relevance of the curriculum is also affected. This in turn, influences the caliber of students willing to enroll in a school because of the kind of accreditation an institution can attain. Like the old adage, "cash is king," the war of financial

19. Bowers, "Theological Education in Africa," 19–23.

sustainability if won will significantly change the model of African theological institutions and free these schools to strengthen their prophetic voices of which the world is in dire need. Like the old adage, "Whoever eats at the King's table cannot prophesy."

CURRENT CHALLENGES FACING THEOLOGICAL INSTITUTIONS

There are significant factors that influence the operation of theological institutions besides core functions to train leaders for church and society. Institutional identity, financial pressures, contextual differences, and pedagogical challenges are all critical elements that impinge on the operation of African theological institutions. The temptation to focus on models of theological education like many writers have done is very strong because it is safe and portrays the challenges in a sanitized manner. I have resisted going in that direction with every fiber of my being, because the real issues of financial sustainability are staring me in the face and I cannot help but address them.

Given the astronomical growth of the church, existing institutions are unable to cope with the need. The form of education that requires full-time students is no longer tenable and therefore enrollment into full-time programs is dwindling, as enrollment in part-time and lay-centered programs grow. The need is huge but the structures currently in place were not designed to anticipate this change. Therefore, challenges to access will continue at least for the next two decades if nothing changes to utilize the convenience that technology affords us as a solution.

On the socio-political and social-economic fronts, the emphasis has often been placed on HIV/AIDS. However, we are aware that malaria and non-communicable diseases (NCD) are killing more people on the continent than HIV/AIDs. It is rather unfortunate that very little attention is given to the most deadly killers; but rather significant resources are spent on so-called popular ones like HIV/AIDS.

Theological institutions are too often out of the loop with regards to current trends such as the burden of disease in Africa. Related to this is the lack of political will to change society. Political leaders can be pre-occupied with self-aggrandizement and do not enact legislation that will create jobs for the African youth bulge (biggest demographic category), reduce mortality or improve education. The ability of our political leaders to responsibly govern our nations by increasing public good is in great doubt. The multiplication of social ills, an increase in violent crime and the breakdown of family systems speaks to the desperation. The prophetic voice of theological institutions through their graduates in places of authority must be heard, loud and clear. In reality, theological institutions have been marginalized and their prophetic voice muted for lack of relevance or substance that could awaken the conscience of hearts and minds. This is partly because theological leaders are participants in the same ills that they claim to condemn.

Finally, the biggest of all the challenges is lack of resources, which is the focus of this book. Africanized scholarship and curriculum have seen great improvement with the emergence of many associations and societies. There are a growing number of African originated journals published by institutions of higher learning and associations creating the platform for academic discourse on controversial issues in society. However, theological scholarship is not speaking to the daily challenges of the common people. Likewise, the level of cross-disciplinary research leaves much to be desired. Hence, theologians are sidelined from the main social science domain and almost labeled as non-scientific.

African theological scholarship must engage other disciplines using a biblical worldview to provide an empirical rationale to the many social problems. To drive this agenda, the curriculum of theological education must be transformed from its current Western paradigm to an indigenous theological thought that is contextually relevant. So long as the current curriculum prevails, the struggle to respond to African problems through a theological grid will be elusive. Therefore, Africanized scholarship should not only be considered as an avenue for theological contribution but as a platform to engage every niche of society.

Part of the reason theological education took off in the early 1970s to 1990s is because of huge financial investments from the missionary community, Christian foundations and other mission focused groups like the Theological Education Fund. When that era ended and the funds started to dwindle, the institutions began to struggle.

Houston clearly pointed out that training takes place in the midst of poverty, wars, economic chaos, digital divide, erratic electricity, lack of library facilities, and lack of trained personnel.[20] This list may sound overwhelming, but I have experienced a combination of many of these needs in a single institution. Sometimes, the situation is so complex that it is difficult to know where to begin a mitigation process.

Many African theologians with advanced degrees who were trained in the West with scholarship funds are not actually serving the church or theological institutions. They are working to develop non-governmental

20. Houston, "Missiological and Theological Perspectives," 716.

organizations (NGO) because neither the church nor theological institutions can afford to match the competitive salaries offered by NGOs. The campus libraries are outdated and those striving to subscribe to electronic databases are unable to keep up with subscription fees. In this book we shall address all of these challenges and others using biblical, theological, and practical perspectives as we seek to establish how leadership capacity can be developed in light of the role of financial sustainability.

Chapter 2

Opportunities for Training
The Call to Christian Ministry

THE CALL TO CHRISTIAN ministry is understood in various ways depending on church tradition and denominational tenets. Nonetheless, there are fundamental features of every call that are common regardless of the tradition. It is foundational that God is the caller and he calls all his children to serve him through service to his people. Often the emphasis is placed on the ministry but really God calls people to himself. Our Lord Jesus Christ did not call the disciples directly to ministry, but rather called them so they might be with him and he might send them out in due time (Matt 10:1–3).

Os Guinness, a social critic and author of the popular book, *The Call: Finding and Fulfilling the Central Purpose of Your Life*, described a calling as "the truth that God calls us to himself so decisively that everything we are, everything we do, and everything we have is invested with a special devotion, dynamism, and direction lived out as a response to his summons and service."[1]

The first step is to be with the master. Next, we walk in obedience in whatever the master bids us to do. It is only when we respond to the call that God gives us responsibilities in his ministry. Even before any church or denomination recognizes a believer as called by God into a particular kind of ministry, it is possible that the person has already received a call to service in the ministry from God privately.

---

1. Guiness, *The Call*, 4.

What does it mean to be called? "The call to the ministry emerges in the consolidation of events, experiences, and persons seen retrospectively."[2] It is the inner conviction that God is leading you to pursue a particular ministry function whether in a capacity as a career or as the master passion that drives life's decisions and activities. Although many narrate their dramatic encounters with God in ways similar to biblical characters like Moses and Paul, the call does not need to be dramatic at all. Many of God's leaders have received a genuine call from him without any burning bush or flashing light experiences.

Are there occasions when one can doubt a calling or when others question the authenticity of one's calling? There are countless biblical characters who had similar episodes including Moses, Elijah, David, Peter, and others. One's doubt or the doubt raised by others does not negate God's call. Similarly, affirmation of an individual or community vision does not necessarily authenticate God's call to service in a particular ministry. If God has indeed called you to serve in a particular ministry, he will give you the giftedness as well as the assurance you need to function in that capacity.

It is generally believed that those called into ministry are to serve God's people and not themselves. God's call is not to fleece the flock but to feed the flock; although, corruption can happen in ministry situations, sadly. Yet, those called by God should show themselves capable by learning on the job or applying themselves to any form of learning that will help them execute their duties in a credible manner.

People in this capacity are considered full-time, meaning they are employed in the ministry on a full-time basis. Sometimes if they are to serve as missionaries, they are required by their mission agencies to raise ministry support for their endeavors. Similarly, there are many people who have been called by God to serve him in the church, but instead make their livelihoods in other professions. Likewise, there are still many professionals who have been called by God to be ministers within their professional careers. Many of these people are already serving as elders, deacons, board members, and others in their local churches and are using a significant amount of their time and effort to support the growth of the ministry. A number of these professionals are also lay preachers and share ministry responsibilities with the full-time pastors under which they serve. We refer to these "lay" personnel as laity. Regardless of the amount of wages paid for their livelihood, the ultimate reward is from God.

Ironically, the dichotomy of clergy and laity has clouded our understanding of God's call, making one group dispensers and the other the

---

2. Kemper, *What Every Church Member Should Know*, 65.

recipients of ministry. We have lived with this myth for years and our theological institutions have reinforced the myth that if one is really called, then one needs to have formal training to serve in the ministry. The inherent danger of this notion is that what really qualifies one to be called by God is solely training. Rather, God's call is unequivocal and he provides the needed gifts and abilities. The reality is that many have been called to be ministers, although functions will differ (1 Cor 12:4, 7; 1 Pet 2:5, 9; and 4:10). Training merely equips those who are called with an understanding of how to use their gifts and abilities effectively.

The different functions of ministry leadership do not distinguish between specific offices. Otherwise, if this were true, then would training through theological institutions still be necessary? You bet. Who must have the training? All of God's people must be trained so each can serve the body of Christ with knowledge and skill. The primary responsibility for those called to the pulpit to minister as pastors, teachers, evangelists and prophets is not to do the work of the ministry but to equip the saints of God to do the work of the ministry. This is the way to provide leadership, in this regard (Eph 4).

Training programs for professionals exist in other fields. Churches emphasize theological education. However, many unfortunately have made it a requirement for ordination. This has created a kind of specialized club for those who pursue formal training. There is a growing number of professionals serving in the local church who need theological education but really have no desire to be ordained. All that is needed is for the individual to be equipped to serve. Yet, African theological institutions are unable to meet this need.

Among those who are called to ministry, training should not just be conceived as vocational but also academic with the aim of equipping men and women to serve the church, society and academia. Those participating in extended-learning programs like all seminary students must learn to think about their ministry theologically as they integrate faith in every aspect of life. Understanding a call to ministry is significant to theological education because it determines who is able to enroll and the kind of environment and curriculum to be applied to the training process.

The inherent problem of a call to Christian ministry typifies traditional pastoral training in an African seminary. From the start, one must resign from jobs or whatever the livelihood to enroll in a training program, which often spans two to four years of study—depending on the level of academic training and entry requirements. Standard features of who should serve as ministers also limits other professions: identifying who should be equipped to effectively serve as ministers in a local church or as missionaries in their respective fields. Sadly, this emphasis on clergy as the only people who can serve subtly reinforces the secular and sacred debate creating a chasm excluding other professionals from serving in the church as pastors.

Over the past decade, the number of full-time students preparing for ministry has dwindled. As the need for ministers grows as the African church experiences record growth, the continent is experiencing an inverse trend among the ranks of individuals training for the ministry. The number of ministers in training is low and constantly dwindling. This is a very dangerous situation, indeed.

The Theological Education Fund (funded by Western sources) provided significant financial support in 1957. As a result, theological institutions in Africa were established to enroll a certain number of full-time students in order to meet the needs of the church. Sadly, today dwindling enrollment and the drastic drop in support from Western countries are grinding the entire training process to a halt. Yet, there are many people who have been called from all walks of life to serve the church and society. They just need the requisite training.

TRAINING LEADERS THROUGH THEOLOGICAL EDUCATION

Leadership development through theological education in Africa is meant to equip those who have been called by God to serve him in the church and society. The training has evolved in form and shape; however, the enduring institutions so far have been those associated with formal academic programs. These are certificate, diploma, and undergraduate Bible college programs sponsored by mission agencies and churches across the continent. They are either offered as residential programs or in modular form where students spend two- or three-weeks studying during a quarter or semester system on a school campus. The curriculum is patterned after Western theological frameworks, using mostly library resources from the West.

Few modular courses are ever added to address African challenges like poverty, traditional religion or even African church history. Students receive a lot of practical Bible instruction and theology but most often very little training in the application of that knowledge to actual church and social leadership issues. Students spend a majority of time learning leadership skills after completing their theological education because the core curriculum lacks practical information or assessment of leadership competencies specifically designed for the African church. A majority of instructors are

Western missionaries transplanting Western skillsets. This is particularly true among denominational institutions whose missionaries are likely to come from the country where that denomination originated.

In non-denominational institutions, there is often a mixed-bag of theological traditions in one school. The differences are not intentionally created to provide a robust academic environment. Rather, the eclectic environment accommodates the availability of an eclectic teaching staff. Sometimes theological differences and presuppositions among missionary teachers are clearly evident in theological institutions in Africa.

African institutions started offering masters' degrees in the early 1980s and doctoral programs were introduced beginning in 2008. The master's and doctoral programs were mostly sponsored by mission agencies such as African Inland Mission, Association of Evangelicals of Africa, Campus Crusade for Christ, and Southern Interior Mission, among others. There were some theological institutions that had affiliations with state universities and as a result, graduates from the colleges could pursue advanced degrees in religious studies at affiliate universities. Ghana's Trinity Theological Seminary established in 1942, had such an affiliation with the University of Ghana until it recently secured a charter from the National Accreditation Board.

The goal of each program has been to provide leadership training for church leaders. More specifically the graduate programs were meant to develop teachers to instruct lower level programs, and introduce academics to engage in theological and missiological discourse as well to inspire writing for publications. The training format at the graduate level of many institutions started by independent mission agencies was not any different from the prevailing paradigm of standard Bible courses, except that since these institutions were few, they attracted people from different countries on the continent making it expensive for students as well as institutions because of housing and traveling costs.

Theological Education by Extension

The Theological Education by Extension (TEE) program was started in 1962 as a new training model to develop leaders for the growing Two-Thirds World Church.[3] This model of theological education has been very effective and is worth mentioning here because of its impact on church leadership in developing countries. It started in Guatemala and spread to other parts of Central and South America, Asia, Africa, and North America.

3. Snook, *Developing Leaders*, 94.

TEE is an adult theological correspondence program featuring a customized learning program. The program materials are comprised of printed content supported by teacher instruction at a location where the program is headquartered. The focus of instruction is the Bible and theology for individuals who are not full-time students, but work for a living. Therefore, participants who are mature adults, spiritual and accepted by their peers can enroll in the program without abandoning their jobs and livelihood. Materials are provided for students to study at their own pace, while assignments must be completed for grading. In addition, teachers meet with students occasionally to discuss difficult issues and offer further tutoring.

An independent-study program challenges students with rigorous instruction in a supportive framework, by offering them practical opportunities to participate in church ministry activities, seminars, and spiritual formation activities. Meetings are often held at a local church, where students work in groups and the training program is supervised by local church administration. Theological institutions are affiliated to provide program accreditation and authentication of satisfactory student completion.

Moreover, an institute can offer transferable credits for participants who have completed the training and want to pursue further study in an institute of higher learning. Robert Ferris noted, "Through TEE, thousands—perhaps hundreds of thousands—of Christians in the 'Third World' have received ministry training which would otherwise have been inaccessible to them."[4] There are many people who would never have had an opportunity to serve in the local church as teachers or preachers, had it not been for a TEE program. Therefore, TEE has played and continues to play a significant role in training for church ministry.

TEE has provided an affordable model for developing countries, a relatively cost-effective distributor of theological education. This model makes learning accessible to full-time working participants, too. Yet, apart from time commitments, pulling together the finances to regularly pay tuition and support a family can be almost impossible for most students. Of course, in many cases tuition is subsidized and sometimes there are scholarships to reduce the burden of fees.

Historically, cost effectiveness was the justification used to support the launch of a TEE program, because this kind of satellite-instruction would be significantly less expensive than a boarding situation such as is used at residential seminaries.[5] However, most of the funding needed to start a

4. Ferris, *Renewal in Theological Education*, 15.
5. Snook, *Developing Leaders*, 40–41.

TEE program (including materials preparation, and so forth) require out-side funding.

Despite all the benefits and cost effectiveness of TEE, there are still many financial challenges. Snook explained that administrators frequently complained about the lack of program funding as churches grappled with ownership of and responsibility for the program.[6] Over the last two de-cades, challenges such as runaway inflation have plagued many developing countries in the Global South, making materials too expensive to produce and distribute. So, as beneficial as this program can be to churches, it has not always been high on most budgetary agendas. The financial responsibil-ity of paying administrators and African writers has been a burden the local church has not been able to shoulder.[7]

In Kangwa Mabuluki's paper on TEE in Zambia, he highlighted a number of successes enjoyed by the program, as well as challenges. Among the three key challenges encountered during the Zambian TEE program was competition from church theological colleges and lay training programs; financial sustainability; and staying focused on growing needs. He high-lighted three important solutions that served to mitigate these challenges at that time: lay formation; supporting churches with gifted ministers; and financing theological training.[8]

In spite of all these important solutions, tuition at Bible colleges and seminaries is still unaffordable for many people despite the availability of subsidies and scholarships. For that reason alone, everything must be done to ensure that the program grows and reaches more people who need theological education. The overall financial challenges impacting theologi-cal education are not unique solely to theological institutions, but similarly impact training programs that are meant to be affordable.

One way forward is to strengthen the financial sustainability of cost-effective educational programs and make appropriate, effective leadership training accessible to a diverse population of learners. TEE has been a driv-ing force in leadership development education in different parts of Africa. Over the last forty years theological education has made great gains and has graduated a number of leaders who are currently serving the church and society in different capacities. A number of influential Christian leaders in Africa benefited from the earlier efforts of theological education. Some of these leaders are denominational heads, principals of Bible colleges, faculty

6. Ibid., 41
7. Ibid., 94.
8. Mabuluki, "Theological Education," 34.

at different levels of higher education and leaders of local and international para-church organizations.

African theological institutions have contributed significantly to the growth of the church by producing graduates who understand the mission of the church and are able to teach God's people to pursue that mission. Through effective biblical teaching and preaching, these leaders have reduced the prevalence of syncretism, which used to be a characteristic hallmark of African Christianity. The numerical growth of believers, the growing depth of discipleship, the development of discipleship materials and proliferation of church Bible study groups along with spiritual renewal experienced by the African church over the last three decades can be attributed to sound biblical teaching. The interaction between trained and untrained leaders has motivated untrained leaders to go to Bible colleges or enroll in short courses to improve their biblical competencies and sharpen their leadership skills.

Over the last ten years, graduates whom I have mentored through seminary have planted several churches with some congregations numbering thousands of people. Others are leading para-church organizations. Other graduates, while not directly serving in ministry are employed in leadership roles at national banks, microfinance organizations, and cooperative initiatives. In Nairobi City, over the course of two years, one graduate multiplied small Bible study groups from 25 to 120 groups with each group having a minimum of 15 members. Trained African missionaries are serving across the continent as church planters and tentmakers. I have observed how pulpit ministry has evolved from mere story-telling to biblical exposition. The impact of theological education over the last decade has been phenomenal and one might hope that this trend will continue and even surpass the expected targets set by earlier proponents of theological education in Africa.

Nevertheless, there has been a significant decline in enrollment across theological institutions. Although Africa is reaping the rich benefits of theological education in the church now, the strong voices that advocated theological education in different forums during the 1980s and 1990s have since gone to be with the Lord, and the current generation has had other ideas. The current generation is not as passionate as the previous one had been in advocating theological education. The passion and urgency that drove theological education over the last three decades is dwindling in intensity. Instead, the growing desire for affluence in many Africa countries is discouraging people from pursuing theological education.

Are we really losing the passion and urgency in this generation? Is the value placed on financial gain from a career in ministry worth the loss of devotion and sacrificial service? Has the church and theological leaders in Africa become complacent? Have we been socialized to place our faith in materialism to the extent that training leaders for the church, society, and academia has lost its glittering attraction? Why are we so unalarmed by our current state and future perils? Why are many people coming to faith every day in Africa but fewer and fewer leaders are training to shepherd the church and equip those newer saints? What will the future hold for African church leaders? What will be the quality of pulpit ministry be if this trend continues? These and many provoking questions deserve our attention and full engagement.

It will be helpful to evaluate the impact certain factors have on enrollment today. Specifically, the factors at hand include the following: the Holy Spirit as replacement for training; theological students stigmatized as academic failures; inadequate finances for fees; and the lack of accreditation for theological institutions. These represent some of the factors associated with the challenge of pursuing theological education in furtherance of ministry objectives.

The Holy Spirit and Theological Education

Dependence on the Holy Spirit was considered a substitute for theological education. The idea was that theological education is unnecessary when one can depend on the Holy Spirit to teach believers all things. This has been a prevalent belief among Pentecostal churches—a denomination which in fact dominated church affiliations among the majority of believers in Africa. Yet, this understanding of ministry and training has changed significantly as many leaders who did not learn theology as the result of this former understanding are now encouraging emerging leaders to pursue education. Many church leaders and their congregations can now differentiate between the quality ministry coordinated by trained leaders versus that of untrained leaders. There is a general awareness that believers can no longer use the Holy Spirit as an excuse not to plan, research and prepare for preaching and teaching.

As much as dependence on the Holy Spirit is encouraged in every aspect of life, we have a responsibility and a biblical mandate to study in order to show ourselves approved unto God as workers who need not be ashamed, but who can correctly expound the word of truth. This mandate must inspire a great shift in thinking. Theological education should be recognized as a viable means to accomplish this objective. It is a necessity in preparing for the ministry across the continent.

Yet, if this is so, why are classes in theological schools not full? Understanding that something is good or necessary is not a strong enough motivating factor, apparently. Rather, the decision whether to commit to education to undergird ministry nowadays seems to be influenced by weightier factors than a shift in thinking. Given the strong downward trend in enrollment, there must certainly be more compelling reasons we should address in order to wisely discern a prevailing rationale underlying this current phenomenon.

Stigmatization of Graduates

It used to be a popular saying that if you fail your exams and are unable to progress farther in the national academic system, you could become either a teacher or attend Bible college to become a pastor. These Plan B career options were stigmas, which discouraged many from intentionally pursing pastoral ministry as a career. Even Christian parents and relatives may discourage family members from pursuing pastoral training. In reality, society's influence in this regard has been more powerful than one could imagine. Of course, this is because most of us are not above caring about what other people think and say about us.

In this case, career choices can be negatively or positively influenced by peers and relatives. As might be expected in a society where aspirations are impacted by prestige, and income, competitiveness begins with performance early on in school with the youngest members of a family and reflects upon the ability of a family unit to acquire all the social accoutrements of success. Traditionally, vocations and professions with gatekeepers restricting easy access are valued highly, because of the high level of competitiveness required to succeed. The strong, the skilled, and the best win these roles: engineers, medical doctors, architects, lawyers, and so on.

Typically, family members and relatives are proud to say that a son, daughter, sister, brother, nephew, or niece is studying—or competing, to earn a place in highly esteemed professions. However, there is little social value assigned to a career in ministry. Consequently, negative social opinions about ministry as a career can be a deflating blow to the self-esteem of potential theological students and their families.

Specifically, in situations when one successfully passes national exams and gains admission to a state university but instead opts to go to Bible college, an entire family can express such strong opposition the pressure can be traumatizing. A family can intentionally or inadvertently discourage a family member from attending a Bible college under the onslaught of rantings about all the money spent financing private elementary and high school education. Obviously, this disappointment would be a reflection of material considerations including social prestige, but never a consideration that the call of God on this person's life might be a factor in the decision.

Of course, a decision to enter Bible college can actually have something to do with lower entry requirements. Many perceive that admission into any theological institution is easy and that one does not have to accomplish much in high school to gain admission. Actually, entry requirements were set low by pioneering missionaries to attract students in the initial stages. Unfortunately these low standards continued for many years until recently. One missionary lamented in a conversation, that we are not here to train academics, just pastors and we do not want to deny anyone who has been called into the pastorate an opportunity to train. The essence of this statement is admirable.

Nevertheless, it does reduce the social capital of all who lend themselves to training in a community when the stigma of Bible college is still fresh and prevalent. For years, pastors have been respected for their spiritual insight and fervor but not for their academic training. They might be given the benefit of the doubt by congregants that they have a call from God, but are not equally acknowledged for strong academic intellect. This notion asserts that one cannot be a pastor and an intellectual at the same time.

However, due to government requirements and accreditation agency standards for enrollment, Bible colleges and seminaries have raised standards to match state university entrance requirements. This to a greater extent is slowly changing the age-old stigma of theological education in Africa. Better still, there is a growing number of professionals and other academicians who are pursuing theological education not necessarily to be pastors but rather to positively impact not only their local churches as deacons, elders, but society at-large as Christian leaders in the marketplace and political arena. Many leaders are now combining professional expertise with theological knowledge in the pulpit to preach and teach.

Considering that few people with lower qualifications continue to enroll in preparatory classes and programs, generally the standards of admission have significantly improved and are almost comparable to the same in any institution around the world. Still, as perceptions are changing and the stigma of Bible college is fading, why are these social shifts not translating into higher enrollment in theological institutions?

If admission standards and academic discourse are to be comparable to academic rigor in any other university department, then why are not many more people pursuing theological education as a career or even as an enrichment program for effective ministry in the church? If theological education is no longer confused with the role of the Holy Spirit in personal spiritual development and likewise, if theology education is no longer stigmatized (or at least not as much as it once was), why are not the seats filled in our theological colleges and seminaries? Perhaps the answer lies in the final factor—the availability of resources to finance tuition.

Lack of Finances

For years, institutions of higher learning in Africa were state-owned; therefore, an aspiring scholar only had to pass entry exams to gain admission. Tuition and boarding fees in these institutions were free and sometimes students were even given stipends for books and other living expenses. Similarly, many church denominations supported students emerging from their congregations by covering costs for students entering theological institutions. The current situation of an aspiring scholar attending a Bible college and not paying tuition or other fees is not a familiar situation.

Operations in theological colleges are not the same as those in state universities. Non-denominational colleges and seminaries depend on external funding from donors to bridge the competitive gap in what institutions offer in the full-spectrum of their programs. Some church denominations even cover the full cost of their leadership training programs by using funding from donors to attract more students.

Sadly, unlike state universities, the low-cost of education at Bible colleges and seminaries for students was perceived negatively, fueling long-standing mistrust of the objectives of Bible colleges. The population perceived the objective of church sponsored leadership training as a conspiracy to Christianize Africans. The real cost of providing this education was never disclosed and neither was it appreciated by the surrounding communities. Neither was the value that a trained Christian leader added to the intellectual and social capital of the economy esteemed.

Parents and relatives in the past perceived graduates from theological institutions as burdens rather than assets to the community. Many who graduated from Bible colleges and seminaries were poorly paid by their parishes and often had to depend on assistance from family members to survive. They were unable to contribute financially to the well-being of other family members and their own children struggled through their education for lack of finances. To go to Bible college or seminary is to take an oath of poverty and Christian parents are unable to support their children who take this path. Many parents were reluctant to invest in theological education because they perceived the benefits in monetary terms.

On the other hand, if one graduates from a state university, there can be many prospects in the marketplace. Graduates are likely to be offered competitive salaries. This is not necessarily true of graduates from a Bible college who become pastors, and accept salaries well-below those of peers graduating from a variety of other degree programs. This awareness of low-earning power for pastors has translated into a fear of a less than financially rosy livelihood in the future among those considering this career. Across many societies in Africa, therefore, many do not see the benefit of investing in theological education.

Today, a lack of finances can no longer be a reason for supporting theological education—especially since many who graduate from state universities are not getting jobs as readily as before when the economy was more vibrant. There are many private colleges that are not state owned and parents are spending a fortune to educate their children, despite no guarantee of well-paying jobs after graduation. The high subsidies provided for state universities still partially exist and in some places governments are demanding that students pay tuition and boarding fees for the duration of their enrollment in a university. Consequently, many are realizing that a lack of finances is no excuse to ignore educational opportunities and that one must invest if one is to realize personal goals and dreams.

The global shift at the center of Christianity and the astronomical growth of believers in the African church presents an incredible opportunity for those who want to serve in the church. The church is now one of the largest employers in many African countries with employees paying taxes to the government. Apart from the economic benefit for the government, the church is growing in numbers.

Hundreds of new churches are planted everyday across the continent and each will need leaders to shepherd the flock. Many pastors serving in churches today are professionals in other fields who received a call from the Lord and because they are educated, they studied the Bible independently and are able to teach doctrines from the Scriptures. Nevertheless, why have enrollment numbers at theological institutions not increased over the years?

Others have been lay leaders in churches for years and therefore have learned how to lead and feed the flock through experience. Since these individuals have developed a reputable name, they are given oversight responsibilities to pastor congregations despite not having any academic theological background. If theological education does make a difference in one's ministry as earlier alluded to, then why are these leaders not considering theological education even after they have taken their pastoral leadership roles in the churches?

There is seemingly a gulf between theological institutions and individuals serving in leadership roles in need of training. Professionals earning a living through their expertise in other ventures, but are still assuming ministry positions have the resources to pay for part-time training programs if offered conveniently and effectively. Churches that professionals attend also have resources to adequately support leadership in training more so than pastors in rural communities. There are more national missionaries today in many African countries than there have ever been before in history, and they are all supported by national churches. However, even these missionaries do not have basic theological education. So, again, why are theological institutions struggling to fill seats in classrooms and train leaders when such a market for training exists?

Institutional Accreditation

Accreditation has always been the sore thumb in theological education and many have indicated this as a primary reason not to enroll in certain institutions. Many have been frustrated after transferring from a theological institution because the few credits earned were not transferrable. Students were required to pay for and re-enroll in the same type of course at another school. The institutions are recognized by the denominations that established them. Those that are non-denominational are often on the periphery of the education system. People have known that these institutions exist but no one took them seriously because gaining admission into these institutions of higher learning for an advanced degree was easy. Students found themselves spending more time and money spinning their wheels to earn a credible academic degree.

The most notorious among these institutions were the non-denominational missionary supported institutions. These completely neglected the accreditation discussion and only met the barest of minimum requirements set by the government to exist as institutions while their graduates struggled in the community to gain credibility. Ironically, leaders of these institutions who were often missionaries saw accreditation as an attempt to take away their autonomy and to be forced to comply with standards that are unbiblical. Simply put, they believed accreditation would destroy their institutions. It was perceived as the evil which must be avoided at all costs.

Incongruously, Christian workers and missionaries who served in these institutions all had credentials from accredited institutions, and thus they were given permission by the government to operate the schools. Efforts from graduates and other members of the community to push such institutions to secure certain kinds of accreditation were met with indifference and often lackadaisical efforts. Ultimately, very little was done given the minimal or even zero commitment to secure accreditation at all by these institutions.

On the other hand, denominational institutions sought accreditation from theology schools of member denominations domestically and abroad. Usually, these affiliate institutions were already accredited with a national board under the governments in their host countries. These accreditations have allowed graduates from denominational institutions to pursue advanced studies in their affiliate institutions when an affiliation exists with a local university. In that case, the university allows them flexibility to pursue their vision and mission under certain legal restrictions. This accreditation arrangement has worked very well for many African denominational institutions so long as they maintain their end of the bargain.

However, are there dangers with accreditation? Definitely. Institutions must tread with caution when applying for accreditation since the result could be loss of mission and direction for the institution. Some accreditation may result in a change in the following areas: program offerings, the background and caliber of faculty, enrollment standards, and a potential demographic requirement among those enrolling. Yet, should we avoid accreditation? No, because there are forms of accreditation that are globally accepted and sympathetic to the mission and vision of theological institutions. We must pursue those standards for accreditation, by all means. We must pursue them for the sake of the institution's credibility, and that of graduates to benefit the communities for which institutions exist to serve.

Today, many theological institutions have earned accreditation either through an existing university or accrediting agencies like Association for Christian Theological Education in Africa (ACTEA), which was founded in 1976. The ACTEA alone represents over 30 institutions in more than 25 countries across the African continent.[9] The inauguration of ACTEA was a great blessing to theological education in Africa because it provided an identity, removed a significant stigma and created a platform for global acceptance at a time when very few theological institutions had any accreditations. The peer review process of ACTEA was comparable to any peer review accreditation process in the world and the credibility of this process has been maintained over the years. In reality, ACTEA has had its challenges regarding resources, personnel, and rebranding, but overall it has kept its core mandate and continues to advance theological education in Africa.

9. Bowers, "Theological Education in Africa," 1.

With the problem of accreditation solved, this has not in turn solved low enrollment in theological institutions across the continent. Evidently, crossing over into other disciplines with theological education degrees can pose some difficulties; although, this is not a problem unique to Africa. There are several places in the world where pursuing a PhD in a particular field requires preparatory course work or a master's degree in that field, if one has not previously done any work in that area. Otherwise, that a degree from an ACTEA accredited institution is recognized globally is very impressive. Still, such changes are yet to improve the number of people seeking theological education in African institutions.

In spite of the significant progress made in changing the mindset of many African Christian leaders regarding the balance of credible training with the Holy Spirit as key to effective church leadership, and the removal of social stigmas attached to theological education through accreditation and standardization of curriculum, institutions are constantly battling to improve enrollment. A lack of finances perhaps is contributing to fewer people opting in for a theological education. Still, the dwindling numbers are disastrous to the financial position of these institutions, as well as to the future of Christianity in Africa if there are too few graduates to significantly bolster the intellectual as well as spiritual depth in the leadership ranks. This is a matter we will address in the next chapter.

There are various obstacles including obstacles to full-time employment that prevent enrollment in a formal program. Yet, such programs can still improve accessibility to a wider population among those wanting to train to serve the church and society. As mentioned earlier, a biblical understanding of God's call to ministry goes a long way to establishing that ministry is not the sole reserve of pastors.

Therefore, theological institutions need to change their requirements for training and should craft programs that will both equip pastors in the pulpit and other professionals serving as laity in the church. Training programs for ministry can take shape differently such as in the form of correspondence courses (i.e., TEE program) or distance learning. This will help those who desire to enroll but cannot, to gain access to formal instruction.

Factors that have impeded the advancement of theological education in the past are still prevalent and therefore every effort needs to be made to reverse declining enrollment in theological education. To achieve financial sustainability, institutions are offering non-theological courses in order to remain financially viable. Currently, the more established and financially endowed denominations do not want to support theological institutions, but instead are turning their Bible colleges into universities. The challenge of financial sustainability and the conversion of theological institutions into universities will be discussed fully in Chapter 3.

Chapter 3

Matching Financial Resources

THE NEED TO DEVELOP financial resources for theological education and other missional activities has existed since time immemorial. Propitiously, missionary contributions and various local partnerships made the hope for Christian leadership development programs a reality over the centuries. It is noteworthy that persecutions from national governments and sporadic outreach activities characterized Christian missionary activities until the 17th century. The Great Awakening came about in the 18th century. This was when Protestant mission societies—founded and staffed by intra-denominational volunteers belonging to the sponsoring mission body started the work. The voluntary nature of Protestant mission activity made promotional work and fundraising a necessity if a society were to raise money and recruit volunteers for the mission field.[1]

During the 1700s, the raising of funds to support missionaries became very popular since potential missionaries needed funds to finance long-haul overseas travels that they could not personally afford. Missionaries and officers of mission societies raised support by visiting churches, delivering sermons, and encouraging interested church members to start local mission support groups.[2] These individual believers, churches and their support groups provided prayer and monetary support for missionaries and mission societies.

The 19th century evolved with local mission-minded pastors preaching sermons about missions, organizing annual local mission conferences

---

1. Robert, *Promotion of Missions*, 563.
2. Ibid.

and regular mission study groups to keep the missionary interest high across local churches. Although the 20th century started with national Christian group partnerships removing the need for general mission volunteers, many denominations, independent churches, and para-church organizations were actively involved in evangelism to unreached people groups and therefore, heavily engaged in mission promotion. The voluntary mission paradigm driven by missionary support through various agencies was the foundation for almost all theological institutions in Africa. These learning centers were simply considered part of a mission organization's outreach project because the institutions were financially supported by the organizations and their donors. Financial sustainability or the cost of providing theological education was never a consideration and neither was there any hint that this would become an issue in the future.

UNDERSTANDING THE COST STRUCTURE

It is impossible to discuss financial sustainability of African theological education without close scrutiny of the cost structure that determines the total cost of education. The real cost of providing theological education in Africa has not been fully calculated nor communicated to students or the communities that could benefit from the training. As often noted, theological education is an expensive enterprise and institutional leaders are fully aware that the cost of operation always outstrips the revenue generated.

The apparent difference between the cost of training and the bottom line is not evident in denominational institutions where the commitment to train ministers overshadows the cost of operation. This skewed understanding of operations undermines any effort to strive for financial sustainability thereby making it very difficult for theological education to be a contender in the competitive arena of higher education in Africa.

It takes funds to train leaders and an understanding of cost centers and revenue streams is crucial. The following are some of the costly items needed to provide theological education: faculty and administrative staff; learning resources (library, classrooms, offices, and halls, furniture, equipment, student housing, utilities), and program management (accreditation, fundraising, marketing, legal expenses).

Faculty and Administrative Staff

Over the last forty years, theological education in Africa has depended on missionary faculties. These faculty members raised their own ministry support through home churches and mission agencies for salaries and living expenses. About 90 percent of faculty members in African theological institutions have been missionaries. This means that 90 percent of faculty salaries and living expenses have been raised from outside the continent as missionary support provided through mission agencies.

Missionaries often handle their salary related issues under their sending churches or mission agencies. The hourly time missionary faculty spend on the job has generally been considered ministry—a gifts in kind donation at institutions and therefore not captured anywhere in the financial records of the institutions. In other words, the cost of providing services was not generally quantified nor factored into tuition or an institution's overall cost of operation.

Often the salaries actually recorded were non-missionary salary expenses and therefore for many years the cost of hiring faculty in many African theological institutions was a mystery. This neglect was made possible because in most cases, the leaders of institutions as well as administrators were all missionaries and did not see the need to include themselves as costs in financial records. Moreover, in the spirit of religious freedom, African governments have been lenient with churches, para-church organizations, and Christian colleges regarding financial records, filing returns, and subjecting their operations to necessary scrutiny. A particular theological institution operated for decades without honoring their statutory tax obligations. They later negotiated with their government for a repayment plan, as they improved their financial position.

The cost of faculty is not only salaries but also medical, accident and life insurance. Long term benefits such as pensions and social security must also be factored into the equation. Most missionary faculty serving in African theological institutions often take care of these needs individually through their sending churches and mission agencies. Many of these are statutory requirements, but because about 90% of faculty are missionaries some of these staff expenses are not considered costs to the institution. With the exception of a few denominational colleges and seminaries, almost all the Bible colleges and seminaries were started with this faculty model. Quite a number still enjoy these benefits.

This anomaly significantly falsely portrays the cost of theological education as lower than it actually is. In turn, this false picture results in very low tuition required from students who enroll in the programs. Of course, students are happy because their fees are comparatively cheaper than their counterparts in non-theological institutions. Tuition falls way below realistic budget thresholds because schools fix rates on the ability of students to pay rather than on actual calculations of the cost of operations. Tuition is usually about 25–35 percent of the total cost. Consequently, 65–75 percent must come from other sources of revenue.

The call for a moratorium on Western involvement in African missions by theologians in Africa and the West in the 1980s introduced challenges that were not carefully investigated. It was a blessing that the response had been weak and somehow adherence to the moratorium had been rather gradual than sudden because it would have grounded many initiatives, especially those involving theological education. Compared to other areas of missions in Africa, outreach to unreached people groups, translation of scriptures in other languages, and theological education may be considered among the last frontiers.

Over the last decade, there has been a growing exodus of missionary faculty from Africa returning to their home countries. In one particular graduate school, about four families left an institution in one year, and there are countless stories of similar departures from other institutions. Four families in some cases can mean eight members of faculty since many spouses also serve as teachers. For an average teaching staff of 12 to 16 per institution, this is a big loss, since some double as teachers and administrators. The departures are triggered for various reasons including relocation of young adult children to colleges, aging parents who need care, retirement, health challenges and so on. As faculty leave their staff positions, the courses they had been teaching are left unattended. Of course, classes in theology, missions, and other ministry fields must be taught because they are part of a bigger program for which students have enrolled.

Closing programs as faculty departs would be detrimental to an entire institution. The loss of 60 percent of total faculty would mean closing more than half of the programs offered at a school. Such a situation would certainly lead to slowly closing a school. Yet, closing a school would send a negative message to the community about a theological institution's ability to sustain its programs and keep its doors open. Instead, campus leadership would be well-advised to hire African faculty members, who are not missionaries but paid staff, unlike missionaries whose volunteerism is essentially supported by donations. Of course, suddenly a school's payroll budget would inflate and create a financial crisis that in reality had always existed like an unattended time bomb waiting to explode.

This has been one of the major sources of financial crisis among theological institutions in Africa today. Did we not know that one day volunteer missionary faculty members would be substituted by paid African faculty to fill positions vacated by missionaries returning home? Did we not know how much donors were contributing to an institution so that it is reflected on balance sheets? Where there any particular preparations made to forestall this crisis? Was the financial structure and institutional framework not sustainable from the onset? Evidently, a quasi-faculty cost structure operated for years that was not at all sustainable. As a Christian leader once stated, "Theological education is a lousy business everywhere." Yet, the response to this crisis may partly lie with African faculty development.

Faculty Development

Over the last three decades, a number of bright African students were given scholarships to study abroad, mostly at the alma maters of their local missionary faculty. The intention was to train a new generation of educators who are Africans but cut from the same mold as their former teachers. These young new scholars would be poised and ready to replace the aging missionary staff. The intention was for these graduates to become missionaries but in their local communities and to continue the work of the foreign-born missionaries. The anticipated benefit outside of maintaining the school's standard of education was to train missionary instructors who would be available in the future to teach at relatively the same cost as their former instructors.

Different kinds of scholarships were secured for these graduates, some better than others. Although, many of these students had to find two, even three other jobs to cover their living expenses. For some of them, there were no particular provisions made to support their family's living expenses during their studies. Neither were there specific job placement programs to absorb them into any of the African institutions after their studies. The mere fact that they were to return to Africa and serve as missionary faculty without any structure or system to support them during their studies was a major disincentive to their return.

For those students who did return to Africa, there were no competitive salary structures that would allow them to live an average life and take care of their families. Although all manner of vows and bonds were signed between students and their institutions, the reality was that they were not agreeing to a fair trade off. The scholarship agreement did provide students with opportunity but whether inadvertent or not, took advantage of their unawareness of their future value in the marketplace. When they were asked to commit to a future earning rate that would not be comparable to a livelihood they could earn otherwise, the reality was they were committing to contractual/bonded servitude. Graduating students were qualified to earn a reasonable livelihood given the work they accomplished in the program.

Yet, the program was asking them to commit to a future that promised so much less than they could earn otherwise.

The need for survival overshadows any contractual commitment that holds no bright future. Consequently, many of the students completed their studies but did not return to their institutions. The trained African graduates could not have imagined when they began their journey that they would be in a situation in which they might end up with the same qualifications as their missionary faculty friends, but be offered a standard of living far lower than their counterparts. They could not have imagined how they might afford living expenses once they began their individual commitment to study abroad but with family in tow. The kinds of primary and secondary schools suddenly available to their children are the kind only expatriates, missionaries, African businesspeople, and those working in international NGOs, or multi-national organizations could afford. The new array of expenses forced some of these faculty-in-training students—especially those located in the USA, to stay a bit longer after their studies so that their children could at least complete their high school education.

However, the longer they stayed the more they got absorbed into the Western system. Consequently, while waiting for their children to complete school terms, many found full-time employment and opportunity in personally fulfilling workplaces abroad. Accordingly, these African graduate students never felt the need to return to their African institutions. Moreover, the institutions had no plan in place to help their scholars reintegrate into the institutions that sent them to study abroad. In the case of those scholars without young children, they likewise opted to work a while to raise enough money to resettle in Africa. Yet, many found well-paying jobs elsewhere and never returned.

In addition, some graduates did not attempt to return to Africa for fear that a weak economy would not provide sufficient opportunities. Instead, these individuals availed themselves to whatever employment opportunities could be translated into a stable livelihood abroad and settled into those positions. Therefore, the reality was that initial educational contracts and agreements with funders and contracting theological institutions alike were constantly broken. Graduates learned to live with the guilt while struggling African institutions grew bitter about students who abandoned them.

In response to this troubling trend, some Western institutions decided to accept students for advanced studies if they promised not to travel with their families. However, that proved to be disastrous since the consequence of that arrangement resulted in marriages and family units falling apart under the emotional strain of extended separation. Ultimately, that style of faculty development failed in many cases because the entire development process did not include a system of care or support for graduates.

The hope to shape an African faculty into a corps of missionaries was entirely flawed because to do that would require students to successfully raise money abroad where they would study in residence for just a short time. Or alternately, raise money locally, from home where people with advanced education would not be expected to still ask for charity after earning a degree that should enable them to earn a profitable livelihood.

The cultural gulf between institutions and their African trainees comes from not understanding that people with advanced degrees in Africa are supposed to provide for their less fortunate siblings and support relatives who are struggling to acquire basic education. It is inappropriate for teachers who have completed their education to challenge friends and relatives who are less educated with less opportunity for social advancement to be their benefactor. A faculty member who cannot support the family's educational aspirations or living expenses, but must depend on friends and relatives to provide assistance is a poor reflection on the entire theological education enterprise. For this reason, parents will often ask their children, "Why attend theology school, when all you can do after you earn your highest degree is ask for charity for your livelihood from those who need your help?" This indeed has discouraged many from pursuing theological education in Africa.

Leadership serving as missionaries could not promise salaries and benefits for returning graduates because it is not part of the cost structure of the institution. Many graduates who earned advanced degrees as promised resign from the program due to poor, indifferent, and haphazard faculty development programs with little if any promise of a stable livelihood upon graduation and beyond. For this reason, today we have serious faculty shortages in theological institutions. Many of these faculty members have been recruited into international para-church and development organizations, where their mandate is do everything but teach theology.

These international organizations are attractive because they offer theologians reasonable salaries that can translate into a livelihood. Theological institutions at all levels are facing severe financial problems with the departure of missionary faculty, mainly because current faculty costs were never factored into the cost to operate these institutions. These institutions were meant to build leadership capacity for the church and society at-large in Africa. Faculty development is not just about sending African trainees to Western countries to study with the hope that somehow they will miraculously complete their studies and return to their institutions to teach. There is more to the process than focused education of the faculty. Yet, until these incidentals are carefully addressed, the number of trained African faculty who are not teaching in theological institutions will continue to grow.

Administrative Staff

It was not only faculty costs that triggered financial crises but also the expense of administrative staff payroll in different sectors of the institution. The cost of support staff has added to the financial burden of theological institutions: librarians, technology staff, accountants, human resource staff, deans, chaplains, communication staff, janitorial and repair people, and security officers, among others. A number of these positions were held by missionary staff, who raised their own support to serve in the institutions. Other tasks were the responsibility of spouses of missionary faculty who supported their husbands or wives by serving alongside in the institution.

Consequently, the departure of one married faculty missionary could actually be the departure of two full-time staff whose salaries were paid through missionary support. The gap increases if more missionaries across departments return to their home countries. Apart from the contribution of missionary spouses, funds utilized for paying the administrative staff come from foundations, churches, trusts, and individual efforts by missionaries mobilized to support the institution. Sometimes the departure of a missionary faculty meant the end of support to the institution if a prior relationship between the donor and African leadership had not been established.

The departure of missionary faculty, the high cost of hiring local faculty, the drop in financial support from friends of missionary staff and low salaries among the administrative staff adds up to a financial nightmare. The combination of faculty and administrative staff costs are not a determinant of tuition or whatever amount if raised from other sources. Yet, due to operational shoe-string budgets, staff members are often poorly paid, as mentioned before. They have no benefits apart from pensions and social security from the government. Many African institutions that have tried to cut staff to reduce costs have undermined the quality of service for which they were once greatly reputed. Moreover, the rate of turnover among administrative staff in theological institutions is very high. Institutional history is lost because of these staff departures and the Christian testimony of treating workers well is often left in jeopardy.

Learning Resources

Learning resources provided by an institution that are limited in availability to students or are of substandard quality can negatively impact instruction. Collectively, learning resources refers to libraries, classrooms, meeting halls, computers, furniture, student housing, and utilities. Although a number of these items may be considered fixed assets, one must first raise the funds to purchase them and maintain their continued usefulness. However, once the funds are raised which is often done by a missionary staff, the ability to maintain and keep facilities operational becomes an overwhelming task.

Library and Digital Materials

It is almost like a maze. Just when you think one problem is solved, another emerges with no end to the twists and turns. It is one thing to build a library. It is a whole new responsibility to maintain and keep it functional. Although raising money to start a library is difficult, it is much more difficult to raise funds to upgrade a library, maintain subscriptions, and hire qualified staff. Many of the libraries in African theological institutions mostly circulate old books and lack current resources that would enable students and faculty to wrestle with current global debates in their various disciplines. Other institutions had old donated computers in their libraries that kept breaking down every now and then. Unfortunately, maintaining learning resources over the years has been done through missionary and faculty connections. Often when missionaries returned to their home countries, donors supporting those specific missionaries and areas of particular interest discontinued supporting these areas of the institution.

A few years ago, the idea to subscribe to different electronic databases to update library resources was floated around and many institutions bought into the idea. However, over time links to databases were cut off when some institutions could not maintain their annual subscription. Conversely, those who managed to keep their subscriptions had difficulties maintaining reliable connections to the Internet, vital to accessing databases. Still others could neither provide reliable access to the Internet nor pay subscription fees.

In addition to these challenges, many libraries did not have electronic detector systems to assist librarians in reducing theft. Therefore, if important books were stolen from library shelves, no one was able to detect it. In a rather sad story, a librarian started selling newly donated books to outside bookstore owners to make extra cash to supplement his income. He was later caught and his appointment terminated. As to how many books the librarian stole before he was caught is a mystery still to this day.

Physical Facilities

The situation is the same for classrooms, computers, furniture, student housing, and utilities. In some parts of the continent where electricity is erratic, classes are cancelled seasonally; because, for example, when it is so hot it becomes too hard to concentrate without air conditioning in hot and humid classrooms. Likewise, the threat of power outages in the evening is an issue, because it is difficult to schedule evening classes without lighting. Scarcity of potable water flowing on campus and lack of electricity become major distractions. Lack of power generators and water reservoirs to keep business running can undermine the core mandate of an institution and frustrate institutional leaders.

Once built, student housing is expected to last for years; although, the cost of maintaining these facilities far outweighs what students pay as rent. Therefore, housing becomes more of a burden than a blessing to the institution. When students are unable to pay even the subsidized rent, the result can be the eviction of students and their families. The most difficult evictions occur among international students who do not have relatives residing locally. For these students their options are severely limited.

Theological education with student housing complications is a messy affair that the most experienced real estate agents would find difficult to crack. One is confronted with costs and related challenges on a daily basis and these can be so intense in nature that the future becomes a hazy obstacle of discouraging challenges. Similarly, the grind of maintaining an institution is enough source of stress to institutional leaders to cause all manner of distractions, emotional stress, and strain to compromise their ability to provide quality services to students. The bottom line is that these bread and butter concerns central to operational management do affect the quality of education at an institution.

Program Management

Program management ensures whether an institution stays open or closes. It is an uncompromising responsibility that requires significant resources to implement. Although certain aspects of the overall program, such as learning resources, faculty and administrative staff salaries could be considered part of program management, I want to categorize these based on their direct relationship to the core business. All in all, management is the grease that keeps the machine of theological education running.

The new trend to gain accreditation comes with a high cost. Whether it is ACTEA or government accreditation, one must remit annual payments to keep academic programs accredited. In some cases, institutions must pay accrediting agencies for the programs as a whole and then additional charges are levied on every active student enrolled in the program. Although these payments are annual, they can be difficult to meet, depending on the financial strength of the institution. Accreditation is great so long as an institution can afford it. Yet, if an institution is struggling to pay faculty and staff salaries or to provide electricity and water on campus, accreditation will likely be put on the back burner for a while. This financial sustainability crisis perhaps explains why many institutions are behind in their annual remittances toward accreditation.

Institutions should be built to last and flourish. Therefore, poorly managing resources such as those earmarked for accreditation to meet daily operations, for instance, robs an institution of the opportunity to grow and establish itself. A typical example often involves fundraising and marketing. For instance, most of the funding that theological institutions receive is for student scholarships and specific capital expenditures. Most charitable funding is not often meant for institutional development.

Fundraising has been the forte of many theological institutions. Unfortunately, these schools do not regularly receive support to build their fundraising capacity either for local campaign drives or to appeal to international partners. On the other hand, forward-thinking institutions are able to add value to their operations and grow while weak institutions receive funding but exhaust their resources, stagnate and eventually die due to poor management of funds. Repeatedly, I have observed theological institutions struggle to raise money, often spending more money than they are able to raise, because they do not have strong, well-established fundraising offices.

Institution building for fundraising and marketing cannot be overemphasized in this discussion. Generally, fundraising and marketing offices of theological institutions are very weak. Yet, they are expected to raise 65–75 percent of the entire budget. Sporadic fundraising efforts result in a few trickles which disappear so quickly. It is as if zero funds had been raised, ultimately returning the institution back to square one. Administration therefore should not solely rely on special programs such as commencement ceremonies and other public engagements to market the institution for fundraising.

Financial challenges from legal actions can have also a grave impact on an institution's ability to advance its core mandate. Theological institutions are vulnerable to all manner of legal maneuvers because if do not manage strong representation protecting them from lawsuits in matters affecting their interest in property—ranging from workplace issues to other industrial actions.

FINANCIAL STAKEHOLDERS' ROLE

The need to understand stakeholders cannot be over-emphasized because theological institutions do not exist to serve themselves but others. The stakeholder concept is broader than identifying mere consumers or beneficiaries of a product. It includes everyone who has an interest in the establishment and delivery of the core mandate of theological education. Stakeholders can include donors, mission agencies, churches, accrediting organizations, foundations, trusts, government, students, faculty, administrators and the general community. Even those who are remotely influenced by theological education are credible stakeholders in the fulfillment of this important mandate.

The divine commission for disciple-making has a "teaching them to obey all that I have commanded you" component which is fundamental to the entire process (Mt 28:19–20). The "teaching to obey" implies that there is going to be a teacher and student or "disciple-maker" and disciple. It underscores the importance of preparing those called with the responsibility of equipping the saints for the work of the ministry. God the ultimate stakeholder cares about the preparation of teachers as well as students, because this is fundamental to disciple-making, as charged in Matthew 28. Although there is no direct command to go and build theological institutions or plant churches, theological institutions are necessary to accomplish the command of Jesus Christ. Jesus demonstrated the importance of teaching and mentoring through his relationship with the disciples.

Jesus spent a considerable amount of time teaching and answering their questions to prepare them for the challenges and hardships they would face after he released them into the world (Mt 10). Jesus therefore called the disciples to be with him with the intention to train and equip them that he might send them out to do the work of the ministry. We have a model in Jesus to follow in forming the hearts and minds of those who respond to the call to teach and train God's people. The shepherding of the flock in general requires training and mentoring so God's leaders will show themselves capable of handling the word of truth (1 Pt 5:2; 2 Tm 2:15). One important way of preparing these leaders is through theological education.

Church

The African church existed long before theological education became a serious business on the continent. Hence, the church to a greater extent does not owe its existence to the institutions. The use of the term church in this discussion is the institutional body or organized body of believers belonging to a denomination or fellowship. In Africa, the church refers to all denominational and non-denominational organizations of believers. The early history in Africa indicates that the church has a great appreciation for training leaders to direct the affairs of worship.

However, the former training was not the kind that theological institutions provide today. The church had an informal training program that ensured that those who felt called to serve the church were first attached to the pastorate or parish and then given informal training on how to interpret the scriptures, preach, and administer the sacrament and other ordinances of worship. In other words, the church had its own internal training program before the institutionalized curriculum that we call theological education today became a reality. When churches in Africa switched to this mode of training, it was perceived as a continuation of the existing informal training programs except for a few situations when the institutions were established by mission agencies.

Initially, the church participated in the establishment and determination of curriculum, because it was considered the primary stakeholder of theological education. Nowadays, doctrinal information was informally held in the church. Today it is harbored in a separate institution that will oversee the full responsibility of its maintenance and growth. Over the years, as institutions became more autonomous, curriculum slowly drifted from the core and dynamic needs of the church. Eventually, instead of the church's needs informing the curriculum of institutions, the curriculum has become the determinant of what should happen in the church.

The astronomical growth of Pentecostalism over the last thirty years paints a completely different picture of the African church as a primary stakeholder of theological education. Unlike the early churches planted by missionaries from the West, many Pentecostal churches emerged from local leadership that had no association at all to theological education whether formal or informal. Leaders called by God in this tradition depended on the Holy Spirit and also learned from their spiritual leaders how to lead a church. The acceptance of theological education as a mode of training for church leadership is a recent phenomenon and therefore theological education is an external resource to be engaged in when necessary. It is not a key player in deciding the core activities of the church.

The biggest population in the African church is the Pentecostals, who as a group did not take part in the early discussions regarding theological education. So, many of them do not have established theological institutions as did the early missionary denominations. The leaders of Pentecostal and other indigenous independent denominations had no access to theological training established by the main missionary churches. It was believed that the doctrine and practices of these Pentecostal and other indigenous churches were incompatible with those of the early missionary churches and therefore were not allowed to enroll in those established institutions.

The growth and rapid expansion of Pentecostal churches over the early missionary churches made theological education in these early missionary churches less attractive. The assumption was that attending any of the theological institutions during Africa's early missionary movement would destroy one's fervor and passion for the Lord. The belief had been that this would render one's church stagnant. Therefore, the concept of the church as a primary stakeholder of theological education was tempered by various extenuating factors. There are few non-denominational theological institutions started by mission agencies such as SIM, AEA, CCC and other associations, because interestingly Pentecostal churches were not primary stakeholders in these institutions either.

Again, the majority viewed Pentecostal denominations as outsiders who needed help but not ownership of the training institutions. Today, many of these non-denominational institutions are still directed by the mission agencies that established them. Unfortunately, a bigger constituency of the African church remains at the periphery of theological education.

However, this situation was obviously bound to be short-lived among Pentecostal churches. Many experienced the benefits of theological education through some of their leaders. For this reason, Pentecostal denominations and other independent indigenous churches initiated their own denominational training programs within their churches, ignoring institutions created by the early missionary churches and those started by mission agencies.

The proliferation of theological programs across every denomination and church has raised a number of questions. Will these smaller but proliferate programs located in many communities across the continent follow the example of the early missionary church institutions, and only provide limited access to their programs? Will their programs be exclusively designed for a particular group of people or will instruction be made available to all? Moreover, how will all these mushrooming institutions find qualified faculty to lead their programs? Where will they get the resources to establish the facilities needed for theological education? What will happen to the quality of theological education they provide? What will happen to the non-denominational institutions already established by various mission agencies?

The graduates of theological institutions are trained to serve in church and para-church organizations. The preparation is meant to make them marketable to the denomination that established the institution or other churches started by a mission agency. However, they are often employed by the church to fill vacant positions in the denomination. Sometimes graduates are challenged to plant their own churches within the denomination.

The church also establishes student internships available to those still in pastoral training. These internship programs provide a platform for theological leaders to test theological thought, different models, and evaluate the current status of the church. Nevertheless, as has been shared, theological institutions whether denominational or non-denominational, both struggle for lack of financial support. But just as importantly, these programs also struggle with lack of relevant feedback from the churches. This may be the real challenge. Still, this negligence does not absolve the church from its role as primary stakeholder of theological education.

Of course, if training church leaders is considered full-time ministry like any other church activities, then the resources needed should be made available. Since churches are the primary beneficiaries of theological education, one can only hope that the church will fully support theological institutions that provide trained personnel for the church. Perhaps, this is not just about understanding theological education but about ownership and a willingness to commit resources to make theological education succeed.

Mission Agencies

Missionary organizations have been on the forefront regarding the establishment and support of theological institutions. After several years of evangelism and discipleship in various parts of the continent, and after facilitating the establishment of churches, it has been apparent that the sustainability of their work depends on the continuous training of leaders to shepherd the African church. Churches were initially led by missionary staff and provided primary level education for the local communities. This was the main preoccupation of many missionary leaders. Later, as more people came to faith in Jesus Christ, missionaries started informal training of lay ministers to facilitate worship in the churches. These selected leaders through mentoring were given basic exposure to the teaching of Scriptures and how to conduct worship services.

Mission agencies were the driving force behind many theological institutions, especially those established by the early missionary church and later the non-denominational institutions. However, missionaries led these institutions for years before they turned them over to their local counterparts. This was because there were very few qualified personnel in churches to lead the schools. The agencies were actively engaged in raising financial support, personnel, and learning resources from their home countries to operate the institutions. Although this was lauded in the beginning, it became the paradigm of ministry in that many of these resources for the development and growth of theological education were from outside the continent. The departure of missionaries representing various agencies significantly affected the way theological institutions were operated and managed. There became a growing need to re-invent theological education in Africa, with the full cost of doing business clearly outlined to the stakeholders.

What role should mission agencies play in line with this re-organization? How strategic should that plan be so that past mistakes are not repeated along current modes and strategies? Mission agencies both local, and international still have a role to play in the delivering of theological education. However, the delivery has to be proactive, purposeful and strategic as we shall see in Chapter 6 of this book.

Donors

The establishment of denominational and non-denominational institutions was all supported by generous donations mainly from the West. Generous support has been one of the reasons theological education in Africa has come so far. Many donations went towards building classrooms, dormitories, offices, libraries. Other charitable contributions were made to ensure that furniture, computers, and personnel would be available. The plan was to make theological education take root and grow.

More importantly, there were those who gave towards scholarships so that those students who might not be able to afford the education could still have access to training opportunities. Sometimes gifts were designated for specific projects that a donor wanted to support. Other charitable gifts have been given based on the expressed needs of the institutions. Financial gifts from individuals, foundations and trusts played a critical role on how far an institution could progress over the years. Donors and other financial stakeholders often influenced the agenda for the operation of theological education in many respects.

What they were willing to fund and how quickly they wanted to see something done, indirectly moved the waters of change in that direction. The emphasis on HIV/AIDS, theology of work, children at-risk among others issues, were typical agenda items African theological education was called to address. This emphasis to some extent influenced the African agenda but at the expense of other core areas of social struggle. The original mandate of deep biblical and theological engagement that the church must have with itself and its neighbors as it seeks to train leaders to influence society is still at a developmental stage. Although, some of these newly funded initiatives are romanticized endeavors that require scholars, courses, library resources and even facilities exclusively devoted to that engagement.

This subtle but important agenda setting for theological education demonstrates how important stakeholders are to beneficiaries. To a large extent, it explains the giving culture of stakeholders in the West and those in Africa. Stakeholder preferences and goals are important. However, they need to be aligned with the real needs of theological institutions, which sometimes require more probing to truly identify and define solutions to problems. This level of engagement de-emphasizes the power of the funds in order to focus on the shared mission between financial stakeholders and institutions. It provides support in terms of expertise to leadership and drives solutions that are long term and sustainable for the institutions concerned.

As much as progress has been made on many fronts in theological education as a result of generous gifts, institutional capacity for sustainability remains elusive and isolated at the bottom of the problems-to-fix list. Funds have been utilized for the purposes they were designated based on perceived needs but random projects such as popular academic programs in no way contribute to the development of institutional systems in theological education.

The Achilles heel of many theological institutions in Africa is a weak network of institutional systems. This is not an attractive project to fund because the results are difficult to report. When you give toward student scholarships, you can count the number of students who benefited from the scholarship and the number of courses they took and what they are doing with their subsidized opportunity. All of this can be objectively evaluated. On the contrary, building strong institutions takes time, commitment, expertise, and other resources that do not often yield immediate results. However, institution building is an almost guaranteed path toward creating financial sustainability.

It has not been a priority to develop consistent channels of income beyond limited donated funds from individuals, foundations and trust funds. Stakeholder responsibility has been limited to providing resources. At the same time, the appetite for sustainability has remained low among theological institutions. Sometimes the effort to plan forward thinking sustainability is misrepresented as avoiding the task of securing funds from those with a history of giving. A prudent financial strategy to explore sustainability options by leaders of theological institutions is deemed as a lack of faith. Sometimes such forward thinking leaders are punished for their actions depending on the ownership dynamics of the institution. Nevertheless, sustainability should be considered an integral responsibility of financial stakeholders and leadership.

Government

In many of our discourses, consultations and conferences, the state is not considered a stakeholder of theological education. Yet, we are cognizant that no institution can operate without state approval. Schools started by missionaries many years ago were later handed over to the state in many African countries. So, in reality, the state is now the sole custodian of these institutions. Although, mission agencies and churches that initiated these programs are allowed by the state to continue to contribute to their development and to freely propagate faith through them.

Theological institutions are categorized by the state in many ways as human capacity development agencies. In fact, the contribution of theological institutions goes beyond developing leaders. They are recognized for transforming society in spiritual, physical, social, financial and emotional areas of life. Graduates of theological institutions serve as chaplains in the state house, armed forces, and many other areas in government. These leaders are invited to state functions to participate in special events that involve the entire country. Government leaders attend the services led by graduates of theological institutions. Likewise, the decisions and policies they pursue are often influenced by these spiritual leaders. In some African countries, graduates of theological institutes are special advisors to heads of state. Currently, I know more than six graduates of African theological programs who are serving in different advisory capacities to presidents.

In some African countries, government leaders who are sympathetic to the Christian faith have contributed generously to events hosted by theological institutions. Moreover, there are many business-oriented social links between theological education and African governments. Regrettably, these links have not been thoroughly developed or explored to benefit sustainability of theological institutions. The government most often benefits more from a relationship with theological institutions than the other way around.

Theological institutions contribute to the government agenda of building and sustaining a good and just community through leadership development. Leaders with a background in theology serving in government roles are at the forefront of social justice and act as the voice of reason on behalf of the community. Although many have lost their lives at this particular level of political participation, the voice of the church in Africa through its leaders has continued to grow ever stronger.

At the 2011 African Forum for Religion and Government (AFREG) held in Accra, Ghana a presenter clearly delineated how the church in Ghana is one of the largest employers in the country and therefore contributes immensely to taxes and other development levies. Though we cannot attribute all these gains to theological institutions, they have nonetheless contributed to the training of some of the leaders pursuing change in society. The government is undoubtedly an important stakeholder of theological institutions and more effort must be made to bring this understanding to bear on how institutions can strategically avail themselves to resources that support financial sustainability.

Community

The role the community plays as a theological institution stakeholder is rather amorphous. It is true the community is comprised of government, church, donors, and others. However, there is a large portion of the community outside of these areas who are stakeholders in the institutions. These may include other schools, businesses, families, professionals, social groups and associations.

Other non-theological schools recommend theological education to their graduates and also accept graduates from theological institutions as either teachers or administrators. Facilities such as libraries and classroom space at theological institutions are shared with external groups. Local businesses sometimes support school events during fundraisers; likewise, professionals who are experts in a variety of disciplines often offer their services at discounted prices to theological institutions.

Family members in a community support their children who are pursuing training to be involved in ministry while social groups seek counsel, guidance, and direction from leaders of theological institutions. These are all important stakeholders who are often left out when serious discussions regarding theological education are held. Their participation in the process of developing leaders for the church has been haphazard. Theological institutions partner with these stakeholders only when convenient but not to fulfill the core mandate.

Theological institutions need to be accountable not only to donors, faculty, churches, and other immediate partners, but to the community in which it resides and to those it seeks to serve. Representatives of the community should serve on governing boards to guide the direction of the institutions because the community is a strategic stakeholder. This stakeholder relationship needs to be more clearly defined and harnessed by the institutions for more effective outcomes.

Other stakeholders such as students, faculty, administrators, and accrediting agencies have already been discussed in previous chapters and for all the reasons already mentioned, should be included. It is critical to acknowledge that these are important stakeholders in African theological education and should contribute to the viability of theological institutions.

THE OVERSEAS COUNCIL INTERNATIONAL SURVEY REPORT

In December 2010, the Overseas Council International (OCI) conducted a global survey on the state of financial sustainability among its affiliated institutions and reported the study's findings in August 2011. The population sample was drawn from OCI member institutions with the following geographic distribution: 32 from Sub-Saharan Africa, 12 from Asia, 30 from Southeast/East Asia, 22 from Europe, 30 from Latin America including the Caribbean, and 10 from the Middle East including North Africa, all totaling 136 institutions across the world.

The survey was completed by leaders of the institutions with the substance of their answers supplied by campus leadership teams. Accordingly, responses represent the true state of the institutions at the time of the survey and not merely the impressions of institutional leaders. Although this survey was nearly global, our analysis and discussion in this chapter will focus mostly on data from 32 institutions located in the Sub-Saharan region.

Four main variables represented the core of the survey: student enrollment, sources of income, financial viability, and organizational changes. The questionnaire was developed around these four variables to ascertain their impact on financial sustainability at each respondent's theological institution in Africa. The term "financial viability" was utilized in the questionnaire and later labeled data results. Notably, it was the term adopted by the researcher. So, the use of the phrase financial viability in the session represents the researcher's terminology in the data report and not a shift from the phrase financial sustainability, which is the theme of this discussion.

Student Enrollment

The OCI data on 32 theological institutions in Africa revealed that the average enrollment in theological institutions in Sub-Saharan Africa was 150 students in 2011, and had been increasing steadily over the next five years with a steep growth among part-time students. They out-numbered full-time students by a ratio of 2-to-1. Respondents indicated that enrollment of full-time students had increased by 75 percent, compared to figures representing the previous five-year period.

This strong upward trend is anticipated to continue, as 54 percent of enrollment concurrent with the 2011 survey represented part-time students. The percentage of part-time enrollment around the time of the survey (compared to figures previous to 2011) reflected a remarkable increase of 62 percent. On the other hand, there was also a dismal decrease of enrollment by 19 percent in some institutions. Considering that part-time enrollment is a fairly recent phenomenon, the future of part-time enrollment seems most promising given that 70 percent of the respondents predicted that part-time student enrollment would continue to increase at least five years beyond 2011—perhaps even farther into the future.

A change in enrollment trends can alter the entire financial landscape of a theological institution and have great implications for its financial outlook. Projected growth of part-time student enrollment is a great opportunity that calls for new strategies in the way materials are presented to resonate with the new demography. This is because, to continue offering full-time courses while the bulk of student enrollment is shifting to part-time status could escalate the cost of operations negatively impacting budgetary outlooks.

In particular, changing the delivery of current materials to accommodate part-time students should be designed to increase enrollment but reduce costs. Of course, operating a part-time program would mean adjusting the number of full-time staff, since fewer hours would be needed. This adjustment could reduce payroll and overall operating costs, as well. Moreover, this may have significant impact on the use of physical facilities and their development.

The cost of engaging part-time faculty to teach part-time students could be much more affordable than employing a full-time faculty. Yet, the most critical question to consider when weighing the benefit of part-time versus full-time staff is just how the shift in accessibility to faculty would impact the quality of theological education and more specifically spiritual formation of students. These are questions we can only address after we have considered the implications of a shift in student enrollment.

Part-time students by definition are those who are not taking a full academic load and who are usually employed full-time by day (or in the evening). Fewer credit hours mean less tuition to pay compared to full-time students who are expected to complete a specific minimum number of credit hours to graduate within a pre-determined window of time. Part-time also means limited contact and interaction with faculty, staff, and other students on campus. Part-time students may appear on student rosters as active students but may not be taking any class, which means no tuition payment to the institution.

These students traditionally take longer to complete their programs, as they skip semesters from time to time to address other concerns in their lives. Consequently, institutions need a huge number of part-time students consistently taking a certain minimum number of credit hours every semester to cover their budget. Therefore, an average enrollment of 150 students—54 percent of whom attend part-time, is a highly inadequate enrollment structure to support full-time faculty and administrative staff.

Requiring full-time faculty to meet the needs of part-time students under these circumstances can be very expensive unless the mode of delivery is significantly altered. The choices are limited as they are determined by the number of the respondents; therefore, a change in the instructional mode is inevitable. There is a need to re-define the quality of theological education as we know it today, and explore feasible educational strategies to enhance learning and enrollment of students in a part-time context.

A re-thinking of curriculum design can ensure that only the essentials are taught to enhance the quality of instruction for part-time students. They have less time to learn components of classical theological education that many graduates never use in their ministry. Such offerings could be categorized as optional electives, instead.

Institutions will also have to consider the impact of a part-time student population on support services such as housing and other physical resources. Student enrollment is an important factor in the level of revenue generated. Consequently, budgeting for such issues requires different budgetary and deployment strategies than those used in a traditional full-time student framework. Therefore, schools must find effective alternatives as they grapple with these foreseeable changes to enrollment.

Where Revenue is Generated

Regarding sources of revenue, data from the OCI survey aggregated around tuition and fees, donations and gifts, revenue from operations, and similar sources. Everyone recognizes that tuition and fees generate revenue for a school from student enrollment. Donations and gifts are funds received from partners, churches, foundations, businesses and individuals. Miscellaneous revenue channels include income from investments and government grants. Lastly, operational revenue refers to rental income, sales of goods and services.

Tuition

Revenue from tuition and fees covered, on average, 35 percent of total operational costs for 59 percent of the institutions. On opposite ends of the spectrum, 10 percent of campuses generated enough revenue to cover 80 percent of their costs of operation. At the other extreme, 21 percent of campuses generated enough revenue to cover only a meager 14 percent of operational costs.

On average overall, tuition covers about a third of the total operational costs of theological institutions surveyed in Africa. Respondents reiterated that this was an increase by 75 percent compared to five years ago and anticipated a marginal increase of up to 79 percent over the subsequent five years. If the proposed increase over five years would occur, tuition and fees would contribute to up to 45 percent from the then current state of 35 percent of operational costs in 2011.

However, such an increase would require exponentially higher enrollment figures of full-time students, which would seem unlikely given enrollment trends at the time of the survey. Reaching that threshold with part-time students who comprise 50 percent of the total enrollment population would even be a bigger task, considering that it would take a two-fold or three-fold increase in the number of part-timers to meet the projected overhead. Therefore, an increase in enrollment of part-time students, a new trend, would not necessarily translate into additional revenue because of the inconsistent enrollment levels each semester. The tuition situation as it stands is unlikely to change even if institutions should change their delivery modes to accommodate part-time students. Other sources of revenue must improve dramatically to render revenue from tuition a significant contributor to financing overall operational expenses.

Local and Foreign Donations

Donations have been the most consistent source of funding for theological institutions in Africa. The inception and development of theological education in Africa survived on donations from churches, individuals, foundations, trusts and businesses. For 52 percent of existing institutions, donations constitute 40 percent of revenue needed to cover operational costs, while for 48 percent of institutions donations cover 60 percent of budgetary costs. Therefore, donations play a significant role in the financial sustainability of theological institutions in Africa.

However, compared to 2011, donations especially from foreign sources have decreased by a whopping 40 percent. As might be imagined, this has created a financial crisis in many schools. Institutions are divided on whether this downward trend will continue or improve over the next five years. Extraneous factors indicate that the situation may remain the same or decline further as the economic environment for many partners struggles to regain momentum. In other words, donations are not as forthcoming as they had been. In reality, an aggressive fundraising agenda would greatly improve an institution's chances to enhance familiar contributor relations and develop new partners. The role of an effective institutional department dedicated to facilitating fundraising cannot be over-emphasized.

Beyond Charitable Donations

Donation and gifts are from individuals and organizations but revenue from operations is what can be associated with goods and services such as rentals or sales that an institution can provide or coordinate. Other sources of revenue can be investments and government grants. Notably, half of survey respondents reiterated that their operational expenses were covered through a variety of revenue channels beginning with the most obvious—tuition and fees (50 percent), donation and gifts (30 percent), and operational (20 percent) or other activities.

Despite revenue from operations and similar resources being marginally low, it is anticipated that diverse revenue streams will rise in the coming years. About 40 percent of operational revenue is covered by foreign sources; yet, more than half of the respondents indicated that income from foreign sources had been declining and 70 percent of the respondents predicted this decline would continue. Revenue from operations had not been thriving as anticipated at the time of the survey with 61 percent of institutions claiming that this income contributed to only 19 percent of operational expenses, while 39 percent of the institutions underscored that the income covered 20 percent.

Threats to Financial Viability

The OCI data revealed that there are apparent threats to the financial viability of theological institutions in Africa. The most significant among them is the increase of operational costs as services previously rendered by missionaries and other agencies for free are now shouldered by institutions. The 52 percent increase in operational costs over the five years previous to the 2011 survey points to fundamental concerns associated with the lack of a financial sustainability model for theological education as indicated in Chapter 2. This to a greater extent means that faculty and administration payrolls are major factors in the cost structure of theological institutions.

Therefore a shift in faculty demography poses a significant threat to institutions than might have otherwise been anticipated. Next to the high operating cost is the unanticipated 50 percent decrease of income from other sources. Although these other sources are not structured gifts, they contribute to the overall income of the institutions. Other factors that pose significant threats to the financial viability of the institutions are decreasing full-time student enrollment, tuition, and gifts from local and foreign sources.

Notably, tuition and foreign revenue streams have the most impact on budgets compared to other revenue sources. Respondents asserted that financial viability could be achieved with the increase of full-time students in current and new programs, part-time students, operational revenue, and revenue from foreign or other sources. The preferred path to financial viability among the above mentioned sources is to increase the strength and variety of revenue streams, as well as decrease operational expenses. As much as this may be considered ideal, 76 percent of all the respondents agreed that increasing full-time student enrollment in current programs is very significant to attaining financial viability. The apparent misunderstanding as to the cumulative impact of tuition on financial viability is rather disconcerting, though. But it also describes the confusion over what will actually provide financial sustainability for theological institutions.

With anecdotal answers regarding the potential (or actual) experiences theological institutions have faced in achieving financial viability, respondents shared that a decline in tuition as a result of low enrollment was a major threat since their core business is to train leaders for church and society. The issues raised as threats to financial stability in the survey were not very different from those already discussed in this chapter, except that the explanations in the survey were very vivid. For instance, the impact of the global economic crisis on donations, including high inflation, devaluation of currency, and increased costs in educational materials provided a sharper focus on the issues undergirding the financial threat. Others include general donor fatigue resulting in decline of gifts to theological institutions.

The inability of local churches to support their leaders in training has perpetually been a bone of contention for theological institutions both among denominational and no-denominational. It is an enigmatic question whether churches actually have the resources but simply fail to support students or do not have the resources to support students who are unable to pay tuition. This, together with other factors mentioned presents a threat to the financial viability of theological institutions across Africa.

Overcoming Financial Threat

The respondents had several ideas demonstrating their commitment to overcoming financial threats in their institutions. The three main areas respondents identified to strategically focus efforts in a battle over financial threats included donations, educational programs, and income generating projects. Although reducing dependence on foreign donations and increasing local donations was favored among respondents, they also acknowledged the fact that many people who could support theological education locally are unaware of what the institutions do. Therefore, creating a general awareness among churches and in society regarding the need to support theological education would be well-advised.

As an example, some institutions were originally opened by mission agencies as non-denominational facilities. These same non-denominational campuses perceived the mushrooming of denominational and unaccredited institutions as competition which could kick them out of business. However, standard business strategies such as marketing and promotions are often negatively perceived by faith-based organizations as a conflict with the very idea of faith.

Consequently, strategic marketing and branding efforts to promote schools to specific demographics have not been utilized because of the negativity and lack of expertise with marketing. Though such strategies could initially improve the visibility of theological institutions to the public, increasing local donation requires more sophistication in managing gifts. Such strategies require an institutional fundraising infrastructure and qualified personnel. It also requires an organized alumni association that is committed to supporting the institution and creating public awareness of the benefits of theological education in their spheres of influence. Yet, this is so often nonexistent in theological institutions.

Respondents noted that diversifying academic courses could increase enrollment and subsequently revenue for their institutions. Others focused on online courses and providing training consultancies. Diversifying academic programs holds promise for increased enrollment and revenue, but at a very high cost by potentially changing the entire ethos of an institution. It takes a significantly higher enrollment in courses to achieve financial sustainability but at the expense of relatively low enrollment in theological courses according to market demand.

The danger is that an institution can risk stifling and choking theological instruction if program diversification is pursued as a means of achieving financial sustainability. Online courses appear inexpensive but in actual fact are as expensive to manage as regular face-to-face programs. The investment required for set-up and management of online versus traditional classroom courses is a formidable obstacle for many theological institutions. The situation is not any different from setting up satellite campuses and providing training consultancies. These programs all depend on the availability of faculty to facilitate delivery.

Respondents also noted that revenue-generating projects are neglected strategies that could raise a school's financial viability. Various projects were cited that could provide additional monies for theological institutions. Those cited included developing property or building rental facilities for offices, or housing, including guest housing. These all could reasonably increase revenue for institutions and reduce financial burdens. Respondents noted that rent from existing facilities for conferences and seminars would likely generate revenue if institutions were able to coordinate several of these activities each year.

As much as these income-generating projects are viable, they require a form of leadership and management that is totally different from current institutional structures across the continent. Many theological institutions are structured to manage income-generating projects. The business and managerial acumen it requires begs the establishment of parallel legal entities that could manage income-generating projects on behalf of theological institutions.

Notably, none of the respondents identified the reduction of operational costs as a means of overcoming the potential threats to the current lack of capacity. Yet, the inadequacy of faculty, administrative staff, facilities, or learning resources should defy any notion that reducing these is an adequate measure of addressing financial threats. Rather, respondents are not only cognizant of the threats to financial viability of their institutions but have creative ideas on how such could be curbed.

ORGANIZATIONAL CHANGE

Fundamental to organizational progress and growth is change, and leadership is all about change for the better. It is the inevitable movement to new paradigms and shifting away from what was expected to happen without leadership. Be it revolutionary or not, change will eventually happen, but the best changes are those which will carefully guide an organization toward desired goals and aspirations.

Therefore, a willingness to embrace change as a means of development must characterize institutional efforts for financial sustainability. When change is required, an institution has limited choices to change or to be changed, since doing nothing is not an option. Pursuing organizational change is not necessarily for the sake of change. Rather, it is the pathway to survival. More importantly, improvements can trigger growth for financial sustainability.

Willingness to Change

In anecdotal responses, many respondents indicated their willingness to change, although some qualified the kinds of changes they desired. Institutions accept the fact that they are evolving from traditional training models to innovative methods that include the exploration of e-learning and m-learning technologies. A willingness to change is critical for the implementation of these new ideas. Notably, there is growing flexibility among denominational institutions to accept students from other denominations while at the same time exploring ways to make training affordable.

Other respondents expressed how well-qualified faculty and administrative teams are evolving by using curriculum that responds to the needs of local evangelical communities in design and content. Many respondents cited the influence of its board and the ability (or inability) of members to take responsibility for making changes as a fundamental path to progress. However, many noted that their governing boards were most cautious about these changes. As much as many are open to change, many are equally committed to a singular vision, mission and values. Some boards would not support any change that would significantly impact the organization's identity. However, overall, there is a palpable openness to change and growth as long as the results will strengthen the advancement of an organization's vision and mission while easing the financial strain being experienced.

Agents of Change

The study focused on seven agents of change in an institution. The change agents included the following: students, church leaders, a governing board, administrative staff, teaching staff, accrediting agencies, and government regulations. The most significant agent of change among the seven was the teaching staff, according to 68 percent of respondents. Next, 61 percent pointed to a governing board and 54 percent saw students as primary change agents.

The faculty is the direct custodian of an institution's core mandate and therefore their opinions hold sway over the operations of an institution. They have the capacity to bring an institution to its knees and frustrate efforts to train leaders for church and society. A qualified and united faculty poised to build a lasting legacy for an institution is an asset that every institutional leader would like to have.

Undoubtedly, the extended influence of faculty is primarily through students. Therefore, it is not surprising that students were also selected as one of the top three agents of change in an institution. Faculty interacts with students more than any other group and wields influence over student perceptions, ideas, and behaviors. Likewise, the action of students with faculty can be reactive to new or existing policies or a particular cause of action introduced by management of the school. Therefore, the combined efforts of faculty and students can present an overwhelming force for change that is difficult to resist.

Faculty and more importantly students who drive change are expected to utilize established peaceful channels to manage grievances. However, in many cases they are confrontational as aggressive demands and ultimatums are launched back and forth on specific issues at stake. Although one may not associate such actions with theological institutions, there are countless examples of such confrontations on the African continent.

Sometimes, faculty instigate students to action while appearing neutral to avoid being branded as violators of institutional policies and regulations. As professionals, instructors cannot lose their reputations—even on the mere perception that they are contradicting the values and virtues passionately propounded in class. Therefore, how institutional management handles faculty and student change initiatives is critical to other change processes a school may be pursuing or wanting to pursue. Carcasses of many important change processes litter African theological institutions due to unsuccessful management of faculty and student initiatives.

A governing board has the potential to minimize student and faculty conflict by adequately addressing issues through effective management of a school. Among respondents (61 percent) affirmed the role of a governing board as an institution's second most significant change agent. Yet, although identified as the second most significant agent of change, a board should actually be considered the most influential source of change in every institution. Otherwise, this begs the question as to whether governing boards are actually leading institutions to make desired changes.

Sadly, many governing boards are poorly constituted and among those that have qualified members, there is a basic lack of understanding regarding effective operation of theological institutions. Perhaps the cost of leading change in theological institutions is too much to bear, requiring time, finances, and energy that members of the board are not prepared to pay. It is puzzling that the hands-off approach to governing or lack of understanding of core business principles can so undermine a board's significance and stifle real action. Governing boards serving theological institutions have yet to realize their full potential and the impact they can have in moving an institution toward a sustainable financial position. Every institutional leader in theological education is craving for such proactive leadership to support the fulfillment of core mandates effectively and inexpensively.

Despite church leadership, administrative staff, accrediting agencies, and the government having some influence as agents of change, according to survey respondents, these specific groups were not voted among the top three change agents. Of course, accrediting agencies and government regulations are influential change agents because of their real ability to pressure institutions to accomplish as much. However, the survey data from the OCI study does not support this position. Since the extent of change from accrediting agencies and government regulations were not explored in this study, the fact should not be lost that accrediting agencies and the government do have the authority to stop academic programs or even shut down an institution based on a breach of stipulated standards. Likewise, church leaders are perceived as having the least real significance in the change process of institutions. The chasm between church leaders and institutions has been growing over the years. Even among denominational institutions, engagement is not as intense as it used to be, lessening the influence of the church in institutions.

Administrative staff is employed full-time but still is not often paid as well comparatively to their counterparts in the public or private sector. Concerning the acute unemployment situation in many African countries, it is understandable that they would rather protect their jobs than rock the boat by advocating changes that might cost them their livelihood. Every effort is therefore made to maintain the status quo until better employment opportunities arise elsewhere. Therefore, administrative staff in many theological institutions can be the least proactive change agents due to their employment terms. One of the fundamental reasons for their poor terms of employment is that institutions were not established to pay staff. Faculty was mostly composed of actual missionaries whose spouses provided administrative support. Institutions were designed to be led and driven by volunteers and missionaries who supported the vision of an institution at any cost.

Obstacles to Change

Leading change is one thing and being an obstacle to change is a whole different ball game. There are consequences to change and therefore some would rather resist or even become an obstacle to change so that no one has to face unknown outcomes. Undoubtedly, an institution's perception as to how far it has sunk and the hopelessness surrounding its current financial situation may lead members to draw the conclusion that change is not possible or better still, not necessary.

The possibility for change and any corresponding opportunity are lost when a large number of staff, faculty, administrators, and key stakeholders consider the financial situation of an institution irredeemable. Oftentimes, obstacles emerge because the reputation of an institution is at stake, should financial sustainability efforts fail. Subsequently, personal attachment to a reputation may result in loss of history and shared experience. Therefore, efforts to retain these precious social elements can also strengthen the determination to resist change at all costs.

Change has an inherent ability to create dissatisfaction and tension in an organization, straining existing relationships and disturbing the status quo. Those likely to be affected might perceive the related loss of significance to their current and future roles in the institution, triggering an abnormal fear that results in strange behaviors. Sometimes these strange behaviors are a direct result of irrelevance and lack of purpose for one's existence that the process may trigger. Whatever happens, it takes trustworthy leadership and perseverance to lead and sustain change toward financial sustainability regardless of internal or external organizational obstacles.

The top three significant obstacles among the seven areas were noted by respondents as government regulation, accreditation and their agencies, and church leadership. Respondents rated these as the most significant obstacles to their organization's viability. Survey participants responded that 64 percent of them on average felt government regulation was a significant obstacle. Next, the role played by accrediting agencies was a significant obstacle to change according to 54 percent of respondents. Finally, 41 percent of respondents felt church leaders created an obstacle to change.

It is true that government regulations provide the standards and guidelines under which an institution can be established and operated. Although, such standards determine whether one sets up shop or not, once an institution is established, very little interference is normally expected from the governments of many African countries. Accrediting agencies are the gatekeepers of academic standards for programs offered in theological institutions. They approve the programs and demand regular reports demonstrating adherence to regulations. However, biased rogue leadership within an accrediting agency could be a pain in the neck for institutions. Unfair bias can result in an agency's refusal to accredit a new academic program that may be needed but seems to be outside the mandate of current institutional planning.

Institutions may run into difficulties with the government if the organization fails to operate within the boundaries of domestic legal regulations. Internal change is often resisted if the benefit of the change violates the tax exemption provision or any other benefit enjoyed by the institution. Changes that warrant financial sustainability may require a separate legal entity with no personal stake in the organization to serve as managers. Otherwise, there are so many avenues for change within an institution for financial sustainability that government regulations should not unavoidably create an obstacle.

The Need for Change

As discussed, there is a need in church and society for change. Academics can change to meet the needs. However, these transitional changes are often met with resistance from agencies that may not share the same views on how a particular program could address such a need. Therefore accrediting agencies provide credibility and direction for a program but could also become an obstacle to change in an institution.

Church leaders were noted as the third obstacle to change in theological institutions. Denominational leaders typically perceive among their responsibilities the need to guard the traditions of the church including those associated with its theological institutions. Personal attachment and the need to preserve history may be a driving force for some church leaders to resist any change that may alter physical facilities or significantly introduce unconventional programs that drastically change school demographics.

I remember a meeting that brought a number of leaders into a facility where leaders studied and worked. At that time, the facility was due for demolition in order to build an ultra-modern facility. Many of those leaders lamented the loss of an iconic structure that represented their history in the institution. At that meeting, they did not consider the current and future needs of the institution at all. From that moment onward, those leaders fought hard to block the construction of the new building and they eventually prevailed. Their egos and personal preferences were satisfied; but, the institution lost an opportunity for change that could have rendered it financially viable in the future. The obstacle to change posed by church leaders could be more than reasonably costly for an institution simply because for some, change is difficult to bear.

BIBLICAL REFLECTIONS

The historical background of missionary support and its application to theological education provides a framework for us to understand why early missionaries, who pioneered theological education in Africa adopted a particular financial model. They could not have done any differently because many of them were under strict obligations from their mission agencies and denominations as to the kind of ventures in which they could participate. The cost structure of providing training became fuzzy and therefore significant cost elements such as faculty and administration, learning resources, and program management were often shouldered by missionary staff or through their fundraising activities.

Financial stakeholders such as the church, donors (local and abroad), government and community were not as engaged as they should have been, while the institutional ability to leverage contributions fell short of expectations. The biblical paradigm of raising support and launching revenue-generating projects that draw from the expertise of stakeholders is critical to attaining financial sustainability. It does not only support the deposition of fundraising and missionary support but opens a whole arena of revenue-generating projects, for which theological institutions have performed dismally.

PART TWO

Biblical Foundations
for Financial Sustainability

Chapter 4

Missionary Support for Ministry

FOR MANY YEARS, FUNDRAISING campaigns have been the most popular way to finance theological education in Africa and other parts of the world. Not surprisingly, the Apostle Paul—who wrote nearly half the New Testament—had more to say about fundraising and missionaries to support the church than any other writer in the New Testament. In his characteristic uncompromising style, he described a clear strategy that may, to the casual observer, seem like a contradiction. Although he constructed a robust defense regarding the right of a minister to either raise funds or make arrangements for direct support of pastoral leadership, Paul also defended and justified the right of a minister to voluntarily refuse financial support.

Insofar as theological institutions have embraced fundraising for decades, misconceptions still abound. We can consider Paul's biblical rationale for fundraising by first looking at some of the examples of when and where he received missionary support. We can apply these lessons to the quest for financial sustainability among theological institutions.

APOSTLE PAUL'S MISSIONARY SUPPORT FROM MACEDONIA

Macedonia and Philippi churches played an important role in supporting Paul's ministry, and he used their fine example to challenge other churches he planted. Macedonia in Paul's time was a piece of land near the gulf of Thessalonica. It was land which stretched from the great river valleys into the Balkan Mountains. As a Roman province incorporated among six Roman colonies of which Philippi was one, Macedonia was famous for its timber and precious metals. Yet, in spite of its social organization along tribal lines and diversity in communities, the area was often referred to in the New Testament as a single unit within the Roman Empire. There were many churches including Philippi, and Macedonia which sometimes in Scripture were referred to simply as the churches of Macedonia. While, in other instances, specific colonies of the province were mentioned because of their unique importance.[1]

The Macedonian church gave liberally to support Paul's ministry, and especially his fundraising efforts for the Jerusalem church. Paul appreciated the grace that God had given to the Macedonians because out of their deep poverty, God gave them the ability to be charitable (2 Cor 8:1–3). The Macedonians gave within and even beyond their ability. Rolston noted, "[T]he abundant flowering of the grace of liberality in the midst of the poverty of the external circumstances of the Macedonia Christians presents to Paul a strong study in contrasts."[2] The earnestness with which the Macedonians gave was overwhelming, for they even begged Paul and his companions to allow them to participate in supporting them (2 Cor 8:4).

> And now, brothers, we want you to know about the grace that God has given the Macedonian churches. Out of the most severe trial, their overflowing joy and their extreme poverty welled up in rich generosity. For I testify that they gave as much as they were able, and even beyond their ability. Entirely on their own, they urgently pleaded with us for the privilege of sharing in this service to the saints. And they did not do as we expected, but they gave themselves first to the Lord and then to us in keeping with God's will. (2 Cor 8:1–5)

It is interesting to note that, despite the Macedonians not knowing Christians in Jerusalem, they were still more than willing to financially support them. They earnestly desired to enter into fellowship with Paul as he ministered to other believers. However, they could not have done this if they had not sacrificially given themselves to the Lord (2 Cor 8:1–5).

Giving oneself to the Lord sacrificially is the beginning of genuine love for God and the saints. The Macedonians seem to have understood and exercised this important Kingdom principle. For they not only supported Paul's fundraising activities for the saints in Jerusalem but they also gave to meet his needs and those of his companions in ministry (2 Cor

---

1. Judge, "Macedonia," 721.

2. Rolston, *Stewardship in the New Testament Church*, 85.

11:8–9). Undoubtedly, the Macedonians were selfless, unflinching, reliable and steadfast in their giving to the ministry, a fact that may both have encouraged and emboldened Paul as he interacted with other believers on the subject of giving. Paul told the Corinthians that he refused to be a burden to them because of the Macedonians. They supplied all his needs through the brethren who visited him (2 Cor 11:8–9). The church at Philippi in particular stood out among many in Macedonia, because of its generosity and fellowship with Paul in all his ministry activities.

Paul's Ministry at Philippi (Missionary Support from Philippi)

Philippi was a Roman colony of Macedonia. The town derived its name from Philip of Macedon, who took it from the Thasians around 360 B.C. He enlarged the settlement and fortified it to defend its frontiers against the Thasians. Philippi was referred to as the leading colony among the four divisions of Macedonia.[3]

Paul's contact with the city began with a vision he had in Troas, when a man in the vision implored him to come to Macedonia to help (Acts 16:9). After this dramatic invitation to visit Philippi, Paul's ministry there was characterized by his preaching, arrest, and dramatic release from prison. Any other contact that he may have had with Philippi can only be inferred from Acts 20:1, 6 and 1 Tim 1:3.

The Philippian church supported Paul and his fundraising activities on many occasions, proving their love and concern for the apostle's ministry. He gave thanks for the fellowship of the Philippians in the furtherance of the Gospel from the first day of his ministry to the moment when he wrote the letter to the Philippians. Paul acknowledged the perseverance of the Philippians in spite of all obstacles when he said, "From the first day to now." They had formed a kind of partnership around the Gospel demonstrated by the gifts they sent to Paul (Phil 1:5).

After Paul and Silas were released from prison for preaching the Gospel, they fled to Thessalonica. Yet, the brethren in Philippi continued to send them gifts (Phil 4:16). Again, while Paul was at Rome, the Philippians thought about him but lacked the opportunity to give. Finally, the Philippians sent their offering through Epaphroditus to be delivered to Paul in Rome (Phil 4:18a). Paul responded by describing the gift from Philippi as a fragrant offering, a sacrifice acceptable and pleasing to God (Phil 4:18b). He did not take the generosity of the Philippians for granted. Instead, he

3. Gordon, "Philippi," 928.

took time to acknowledge their fellowship and partnership with him in the ministry.

Evidently giving to support God's work should be considered an act of fellowship through which the brethren can share their material possessions for the training of church leaders. Theological education is not about the South or the North, developed or developing, or the center of gravity of Christianity or any peripherals. It is about the kingdom of God and that all who are members of the kingdom should be active participants in the sustenance of this important process of leadership development for ministry. Apart from fellowship, the charity of the Macedonia brethren can be described as excellent, spontaneous and sacrificial. If the Macedonian and Philippian examples are to be emulated by theological institutions today, then it is necessary to evaluate the rationale for fundraising activities per Paul's teachings in 1 Cor 9:1–14.

PAUL'S RATIONALE FOR MISSIONARY SUPPORT

Paul's perception of fundraising is a revolutionary one. As he noted, fundraising is crucial for any missionary activity and benefits all three parties involved: benefactors, funders and God. First, the recipients of the funds receive a benefit, which also brings them joy. Paul himself expressed his gratitude and joy after the Philippians sent needed charitable support to his ministry in Rome. The funders are enriched with joy, satisfaction and spiritual blessings which the Lord credits to them for their sacrificial charity. Ultimately, the focus of giving is God, who is pleased with offerings to support his cause through men (Phil 4:17, 18b). Therefore, Paul had a very positive outlook on raising funds for the ministry and defended his position in 1 Corinthians. "Don't we have the right to food and drink? Don't we have the right to take a believing wife along with us, as do the other apostles and the Lord's brothers and Cephas? Or is it only I and Barnabas who must work for a living?" (1 Cor 9:4–14).

In 1 Corinthians 8, Paul discussed the Christian faith and food sacrificed to idols. He indicated that food in itself holds no specific mystery. So, the Christian can eat any food—including that sacrificed to idols. However, if by eating such food he causes his brother with a weaker conscience to stumble, he had better not eat it. Paul applied the principle of self-denial to the example of eating food sacrificed to idols, by posing the question to the Corinthians who were debating his apostolic authority in 1 Corinthians 9.

During his second missionary journey, Paul visited the Corinthians but refused to receive financial or any other material support from them. Instead, he worked with his own hands to supplement the support he received from churches outside Corinth. As might be expected, believers in Corinth did not take kindly to Paul's decision to refuse their support. In the end, Corinthians questioned the legitimacy of Paul's apostolic authority after his departure. In response, Paul defended his apostolic authority to both receive financial support as well as to decline it. As an apostle he enjoyed the widest range of liberty. Yet, for the sake of the people he served, he often ignored his apostolic authority. Lenski noted, "Only in a few instances did Paul weave in such profound apologetic features on a matter concerning his person, for this is an inquiring and yet very effective discussion."[4]

Missionary Support for a Minister and Family

Paul's defense begins with a series of rhetorical questions directly related to his apostolic authority. He asked, "Am I not free? Am I not an apostle? Have I not seen Jesus our Lord? Are you not the result of my work in the Lord?" (1 Cor 9:1). The question, "Am I not free?" is directly connected to the subject he had discussed earlier about food sacrificed to idols (1 Cor 8:1–13). Therefore, if he, being an apostle gave up his right to food for the sake of the weaker brother and his right for financial support in order to work with his own hands, we can emulate him. Although Paul was free as an apostle to use his authority, he considered the weaker brethren. Similarly, if it is expedient for a theological institution to do so, it is advisable for it to explore other options of funding when necessary.

Furthermore Paul asked, "Am I not an apostle?" Definitely, an apostle who proclaims the liberty of Christ Jesus is free and can exercise his authority for the furtherance of the Gospel. Through this question, Paul drives home the point that if he is an apostle of Christ, then his situation should not be any different or worse than that of other apostles.

In his attempt to establish his apostolic position, Paul asks again, "Have I not seen Jesus our Lord?" He wanted to make sure that he was not regarded as an inferior apostle compared to the rest of the apostles. John Calvin observes, "Some people in the church were hostile, jealous and loud-mouthed in their repeated assertion that Paul's Gospel was from men and

---

4. Lenski, *First Epistle to the Corinthians*, 350.

[he had] never cast his eyes on the Christ."[5] Although he did not walk with Christ in the flesh like the twelve apostles, he actually saw Christ in a vision on his way to Damascus. Torrance further noted that Paul is not claiming to have seen Christ before his ascension, for many people saw Christ then, but never became apostles.[6] It was during his encounter with the risen and glorified Lord that Jesus appointed him an apostle. This appointment carried no less authority than the apostleship of the first twelve.

Narrowing it down further, Paul asserted his apostolic authority by asking the very people who had doubted him whether or not they were the fruit of his labor. He asked, "Are you not the result of my work in the Lord?" In effect, the very fruit of his labor testifies that he is an apostle indeed. However, this does not suggest that the person who plants a congregation is an apostle. Rather, this is but an additional qualification to justify his apostolic ministry. The phrase "in the Lord" modifies the entire sentence. Paul is not claiming to have done all that by his own power, but by that of the Lord. Therefore, if to others he is not an apostle, to the Corinthians he is one in the Lord. The Corinthians were the evidence of Paul's apostolic authority and, upon this authority, he declared his right to missionary support.

In view of his apostolic authority and willingness to give up his right, some people misunderstood him. They claimed that he did not deserve to be supported and, since he knew that, he did not request support. Yet, Paul did not flinch in defending his position, instead he asked, "Don't we have the right to food and drink?" This is a question that requires a reflexive negative answer. He declared, "Yes, God forbid that an apostle of Jesus Christ should be denied food and drink" (1 Cor 9:4).

The entire paragraph, except for verse 8, is in the plural, compared to each of the verses 1–3 and 15–27 written in the singular. Because of the use of the plural, it is noteworthy that we are forced to consider Paul's traveling companions—who are not specified in the passage but agree with his stance on missionary support. Basically, he included the views of his ministry colleagues in his own personal defense.[7]

Lenski observes that the phrase indicates the right of the apostles to be supported with material provisions by the congregations they founded and served.[8] By food and drink, Paul was not referring merely to eating and drinking, necessary for survival, nor solely to foods sacrificed to idols

---

5. Calvin, *The First Epistle of Paul to the Corinthians*, 183.

6. Ibid.

7. Robertson and Plummer, *1 Corinthians*, 179.

8. Lenski, *First Corinthians*, 355.

as mentioned in Chapter 8.[9] This is the first of a series of questions that argue for the right of missionary support. And despite Paul personally refusing entertainment at the cost of those he ministered to, he had the right to receive missionary support to enjoy entertainment. The use of the phrase food and drink now moves the argument from the arena of food (sacrificed to idols in Chapter 8) to material sustenance for God's servants. This is the responsibility of every believer, whether strong or weak in the faith.

Furthermore, Paul asked the Corinthians, "Don't we have the right to take a believing wife along with us, as do the other apostles and the Lord's brothers and Cephas?" (v. 5). Like the preceding question, this one is connected to the issue of missionary support. The phrase used can literally be translated "a sister, a wife," but is commonly taken to mean a believing sister in Christ, as in a wife; although the expression is the common use of a predicate accusative indicating a sister who is also a wife. Surprisingly, the Vulgate translates the word as "women" versus "a sister or wife."[10] Paul was indicating that the apostles have a right to marry and to take their wives along with them in their travels. However, the fact that Paul was not married and that none of his companions traveled with their wives except Aquila with Priscilla, this argument he raised makes his point unclear.

The argument here is not that Paul needs to marry and bring along his wife in order to receive missionary support. The Lord's brothers—James and John—and Cephas (Peter) were married and traveled with their wives. However, Paul's argument was not made because he was jealous about the support they were receiving in their ministry. Instead, Paul was claiming that they had a right to support at the expense of the Church, and that if they were married, the wife who feels comfortable to travel with her husband shares the same privilege. Peter's name here is significant because it proves that he—the leader of the apostles—and Paul have the same level of apostolic authority to share the same privileges.

Perhaps what worried the Corinthians most was not that Paul worked, but that the kind of work he did was not worthy of an apostle. The Corinthians considered manual work demeaning, which should not be associated under any circumstance with an apostle of the Lord Jesus Christ.[11] The mention of Barnabas in 1 Cor 9:6 somehow resolves Paul's use of the word "we." The following question throws more light on what had been the custom of Barnabas and Paul: "Or is it only I and Barnabas who must work for a living?" This statement implies that Barnabas and Paul must have agreed dur-

9. Ibid.

10. Robertson and Plummer, *1 Corinthians*, 180.

11. Fee, *1 Corinthians*, 404.

ing their first missionary journey not to receive support from their converts (Acts 13:3).

Although all the questions relate to the same issue, for the apostle and his companions the questions address different areas of their lives. It indicates where they needed missionary support, of which they had the right. They had the right to receive support for their daily needs and to have a wife accompany them in their ministry if they made such arrangements. They had the right to not work at any trade to provide for their own needs. By application, donations to support contemporary missionaries and their families serving in African theological institutions are biblical and totally justified. Paul illustrated this right through many common life stages as presented in subsequent verses.

A Workman Deserves His Wages

Apostle Paul starts the next phase of his argument by justifying his apostolic authority for missionary support through a range of analogies. Although each analogy uses a different illustration, each nevertheless progressively strengthens his argument regarding a missionary's right to charitable support. Paul used an analogy of soldier, farmer, and shepherd to support his point.

> Who serves as a soldier at his own expense? Who plants a vineyard but does not eat of its grapes? Who tends a flock but does not drink of the milk? Do I say this merely from a human point of view? Doesn't the Law say the same thing? For it is written in the Law of Moses: "Do not muzzle an ox while it is treading out the grain." Is it about oxen that God is concerned? Surely he says this for us, doesn't he? Yes, this was written for us, because when the plowman plows and the thresher threshes, they ought to do so in the hope of sharing in the harvest. If we have sown spiritual seed among you, is it too much if we reap a material harvest from you? If others have this right of support from you, shouldn't we have it all the more? But we did not use this right.
>
> On the contrary, we put up with anything rather than hinder the gospel of Christ. Don't you know that those who work in the temple get their food from the temple, and those who serve at the altar share in what is offered on the altar? In the same way, the Lord has commanded that those who preach the gospel should receive their living from the gospel. (1 Cor 9:4–14)

The Soldier, Farmer and Shepherd

As a rule, soldiers work for pay or they can be given rations financed by the public. The key word in this first analogy is wages, primarily denoting rations in lieu of pay, but also military stipends in general.[12] It is important to note in this context that the use of the word applies to the soldier's food, uniform and any other expense he may incur while discharging official duties. In this instance, again, Paul started his question with the phrase "at any time?" which is a hypothetical particle common in classical Greek but rarely used in the New Testament.[13] Consequently, the sense here is that no soldier actually serves at his own expense, but earns wages drawn from the public treasury. However, there is no way the Corinthians could have paid Paul from any public treasury for his spiritual ministry to them.

Paul raised the principle that a man who devotes his life to work for God by serving his people should be able to live by that work. Analogously, if a soldier leaves his trade for war, support is due to him from the community in whose service he fights. Drawing parallels with a soldier is Paul's higher calling to a spiritual ministry as an apostle to the Gentiles. The word rendered as "wages" indicates that the Corinthians owed their very lives to Paul's ministry. Therefore, donating material provisions to him would certainly be the least the congregation could do in return for the saving benefit he provided to them.

Paul also used an analogy of a farmer who spends all his life sowing and caring for his crops. Paul asks rhetorically whether the farmer should not taste of the fruits of his labor. Referencing the Law of Moses, Paul reminds them that those who planted vineyards but had not tasted of its fruits were exempted from going to war (Deut 20:1–9). This law exempted such people from war for fear that they might die without tasting the fruits of their labor. Therefore, if a lowly farmer was not expected to face the danger of war because he had not tasted the fruits of his labor, how much more the minister of the Gospel and the fruits of his labor? Was it too much for Paul to expect and receive material provisions for spiritual services rendered to the Corinthians?

Paul drew these analogies from common but universally accepted customs in life. The analogy of the shepherd illustrates how he who tends a flock by right must also partake of the milk or anything made from the milk. Calvin remarks, "[W]hen natural justice lays down this as the fairest way of doing, will anyone be so unjust as to deny the necessities of life to

---

12. Findlay, *1 Corinthians*, 847

13. Ibid.

the pastors of the church?"[14] To deny a farmer or shepherd basic provisions is to destroy their motivation and deprive them of the joy and satisfaction their labor undoubtedly brings to other people. However, in 1 Cor 9:8, he makes it clear that his right or authority for support does not solely depend on analogies drawn from the law. Instead, he contrasted the analogies of daily life with his divinely vested authority from God as enshrined in the Law of Moses.

The Law of Moses

Paul did not appeal to the Old Testament in his letters to the Corinthians except in the passage relating to missionary support in 1 Cor 14:21. Again, Paul started with a question, "Doesn't the Law say the same thing? 'Do not muzzle an ox while it is treading out the grain.' Is it about oxen that God is concerned?" (1 Cor 9:8–9). Paul quoted from Deut 25:4 to support his claim of the right to receive missionary support from the Corinthians. By this quotation, Paul is saying that the law is only abolished as a means of obtaining salvation as indicated in Rom 3:19. However, it remains the revelation of truth and right. We can therefore draw guidance from the law for our Christian conduct. Findlay indicated that the ethics of the New Testament are comprehensively those of the Old Testament, enhanced by Christ. Therefore, Paul is referring to a distant incident, but one which nevertheless is very close to the law of Christ.[15]

In Deut 25:4, God expressed his concern and respect for animals used in a working situation. Historically, one method used in threshing grain in the Middle East was the harnessing of oxen to pull a sledge while trampling grain on a hard threshing floor to separate ears of grain from the stalk. Peter C. Craigie noted that the prohibition against muzzling oxen was in order reward the labor of the animal. Oxen could eat from time to time while threshing. The animal should under no circumstance be denied sustenance while working on behalf of man.[16]

Consequently, as a sign of love and kindness, which was to be shown to all creatures, no man was to muzzle an ox. "It is argued that if one legislated for a lesser matter, then in a matter of the same general type but which concerned bigger and more important issues, the legislation for the greater could be deduced from that for the lesser."[17] Paul therefore argued

14. Calvin, *The First Epistle of Paul to the Corinthians*, 187.

15. Findlay, *1 Corinthians*, 483.

16. Craigie, "Deuteronomy," 313.

17. Thompson, *Deuteronomy*, 251.

that those who toil to produce spiritual food for believers should receive adequate compensation for their labors in terms of material benefits.

Rabbis, like Christians, are able to distinguish the spiritual as well as the literal sense from much of scripture. It is likely that Paul was doing something like that here by applying the principle to the spiritual sphere, which was once originally applied to the material sphere.[18] Inasmuch as the passage shows God's care for animals, Rabbis took interest in the metaphorical meaning to consider it an argument regarding "the lesser to the greater."

Paul's method of interpretation here is radically different from that of others, such as Hellenistic Jewish philosopher, Philo of Alexandria. While Philo often destroys the historical sense of a text, Paul extracts its moral principle.[19] For instance, Paul's use of the word "us" intentionally includes all ministers working in the vineyard of God, including himself. As if this were not enough, the apostle indicated that the person who plows a field and threshes the grain is working and must do that with the hope of partaking of the fruits of labor, which is the right reward. As humane as feeding hard working oxen may seem, Keil and Delitzsch indicate that the issue with oxen is not supposed to be taken literally. Instead, it must be understood in the general sense in which the Apostle Paul uses it in 1 Cor 9:9 and 1 Tim 5:18. It means that a laborer should not be deprived of his wages.[20] Findlay notes that the expression "because of us" is emphatically repeated. "It is not for men as against oxen but in analogy to oxen; the right of Christ's ministers to eat and drink is highly safeguarded by the principle."[21]

Material Harvest for Spiritual Seeds Sowed

Again, Paul opens his argument with a powerful set of questions: "If we have sown spiritual seed among you, is it too much if we reap a material harvest from you? If others have this right of support from you, shouldn't we have it all the more?" (1 Cor 9:11–12). By comparing physical things to spiritual things, the familiar argument "from the lesser to the greater" is highly effective here. The question implies that other Christian teachers received continuous support from the Corinthian Church, and this makes Paul and his companions' claims very relevant. It also implies that if the Corinthians granted this kind of support to others after Paul left them, how could they deny it to him, who had been the first to bring them the salvation message?

18. Ibid., 250.

19. Findlay, 1 Corinthians, 483

20. Keil and Delitzsch, "Deuteronomy," 422.

21. Findlay, 1 Corinthians, 848.

As Frederick Louis Godet noted, Paul raised the comparison by saying, "We have the right, and we do not use it; they do not have the right and they use it."[22] Whereas the farmer and the shepherd partake of the fruit from their labors, it is not completely so with the preacher. The wages received by the preacher are far inferior in value to what he has given to the congregation. So, guided by the analogies given, the principle of support is more indisputable than it actually appears. As noted during his defense of his apostolic appointment, Paul again used the pronoun "we," referring to himself, companions and other apostles. Paul claimed that he and his companions did not redeem the right, but chose to put up with everything to avoid being a hindrance to the Good News of Christ. This points to the apostle's strategy to be somewhat neutral whenever any controversy might impede the clarity of the Gospel.

Power and Authority for Missionary Support

Apostle Paul used the words "power" and "authority" five times in his argument for missionary support. These were the most significant words in this argument because the entire passage hangs on whether Paul was really an apostle. If he was, whether in the same sense as Peter and the other apostles who actually interacted with Jesus or otherwise, he shared the same spiritual authority. A deviation in the meaning of the words, power and authority can lead to a misunderstanding of Paul's entire argument about missionary support. Interestingly, English theologian George Wigram translated all the words as power whereas the Greek and English interlinear translation puts it as authority.[23] Wigram's use of the word power or ability ". . . is different from *power* and *authority*." Power (or ability) is latent in form and does not designate the source or the object of action. When power or ability is used, the word has to be qualified regarding its source and the object receiving the action.

This kind of authority could be granted by a government, master, owners, and parents. Although it can be misleading with regard to power, it is expedient to note that one refers to external power, while the other denotes inward power. It denotes the freedom to act, permission or liberty of doing as one pleases and then the authority to take the action.

Paul uses every available means possible to describe the source of his apostolic authority and the privileges that go with it. He principally uses different analogies, because his argument about missionary support is closely

22. Godet, *Commentary on First Corinthians*, 447.

23. Wigram, *The Englishman's Greek Concordance*, 166.

tied to the authenticity of his authority. According to English theologian W.E. Vine, Paul has been given authority as an apostle called by Christ to perform certain duties in ministry. He (as a missionary) also has the right by divine authority to receive charitable support.[24] The context therefore suggests that just as the Corinthians have authority to eat with liberty of conscience, but curtail some choices for the sake of the weak, so Paul has the authority to eat and drink but can give it up for the sake of the Gospel.[25]

Support for the Preachers, and Temple and Altar Workers

The argument is far from over since Paul adds some more vivid and compelling illustrations to support his right for missionary support. He added two more reasons why he deserves missionary support from the Corinthians. He used an example regarding the temple to illustrate his point and thus drove home the message with the most significant analogy of all. Paul asked the church the following: "Don't you know that those who work in the temple, and those who serve at the altar share in what is offered on the altar?" He answered his own rhetorical question: "In the same way, the Lord has commanded that those who preach the Gospel should receive their living from the Gospel."

By beginning his question with the query, "Don't you know?" he was asking the Corinthians whether they were knowledgeable regarding the practice in the temples they had attended before the Gospel came to them. Paul was addressing a mixed multitude of Jews and Gentiles and therefore his rhetoric navigated cultural cues regarding both the pagan temple practices, as well as Old Testament temple practices. His audience was perfectly acquainted with both.

Those who worked in the temple were fed from the temple and those who fulfilled altar duties shared in what was offered on the altar. The second part of the question "those who serve on the altar" is not an additional part but simply repeats the first half in a more definite way. It was the Jewish practice for priests who offered sacrifices together with their sons to eat the leftover portion of the sacrifice. The Lord mandated that the leftover portion be given to them as their share of the offerings. These were offerings made to God by fire for generations to come (Lev 6:16–18).

The Corinthians needed to be told that this was God's arrangement long before the Gospel of Jesus Christ was preached to them. As Godet correctly put it, "[I]t is well-known that the Levites lived by their employment,

24. Vine, *Vine's Expository Dictionary*, 81.

25 Fee, *1 Corinthians*, 482.

by means of the tithes and offerings paid by the people, and that in like manner the priests lived by the altar, first by means of the tithe which the Levites paid to them and then specifically by the portion of the [offerings] which was reserved for them."[26] Paul did not need to explain this further because Christianity had superseded the temple ritual and the arrangement for support was made by God (1 Cor 9:13). It would therefore be erroneous to assume that this arrangement as well as the Lord's command has no bearing on New Testament believers.

The phrase translated as *the Lord has commanded*, refers to the command of Christ. This is a direct reference from the passage in Luke 10:7–8 where Jesus Christ elaborated on missionary support: "Stay in that house, eating and drinking whatever they give you, for the worker deserves his wages. Do not move around from house to house. When you enter a town and are welcomed, eat what is set before you." The statement both establishes the Lord's command as an undeniable historical fact and also makes a qualitative announcement referring to those engaged in proclaiming the Gospel—those primarily being the apostles and preachers.[27]

Therefore, both the Old Testament and the New Testament combine a strong assurance of missionary support for God's workers. Although Jesus stated these words in Luke 10:7–8 as an admonishment, to Paul it was a command because of its effect on tradition. The casual way in which Paul introduced the last part of his argument confirmed the prevailing tradition of his days in some ways. With that, he draws his long argument regarding apostolic authority for missionary support to a convincing conclusion.

RATIONALE FOR REFUSING MISSIONARY SUPPORT

Through examining Paul's philosophy of missionary support, one tends to run into a conundrum. In one instance, he defended his right to receive support, while at another time, he refused support. For instance, Paul boldly told the Ephesians how "his own hand" had worked hard to provide for his own needs in Acts 20:33–34. Paul's refusal of missionary support in Corinth was probably necessary because of the numerous false apostles preaching there as a way to fraudulently enrich themselves.

However, his refusal to accept missionary support did not necessarily mean he never received any support for his personal needs from other churches. It is evident that the brethren from Macedonia brought provisions to supply his needs, as recorded in 2 Cor 11:9. He received missionary

26. Godet, *First Corinthians*, 450.
27. Lenski, *First Corinthians*, 367.

support for his own needs, and when he was raising funds for the saints in Jerusalem, he challenged the Corinthians to give generously.

Many have interpreted Paul's refusal to receive missionary support as a biblical precedent encouraging unpaid volunteer ministries. For this reason, we need to examine Paul's rationale for refusing support. It is important to note that Paul's fundamental interest was to proclaim the Gospel. He was primarily concerned with the souls of men and not their possessions.[28] When it was necessary, he received financial support from some of his maturing churches. However, he also asserted that he robbed other churches to serve others, putting his passion for souls above passion for possessions.

Avoiding Hindrances to the Gospel

Paul's primary obligation was to preach the Gospel, not to gather financial support. Thus, for the sake of the Gospel, he sometimes renounced his right to missionary support. In Corinth, he perceived that receiving support for his needs would hinder effective preaching and therefore he refused support. Exactly what this hindrance or obstacle might have been is not immediately clear.

The word rendered "obstacle" does not appear in the Septuagint or in any other place in the New Testament. Theologians, Robertson and Plummer observed that the word is rare even in classical Greek. It is often rendered as "an incision, interruption or a violent break," while another literal use in English refers to breaking bridges or roads to stop the march of an enemy.[29] Taken in perspective, Paul was willing to do anything to avoid becoming a hindrance to the Gospel. He wanted his audience to know the free nature of the Gospel and at the same time opposed itinerant philosophers and missionaries who preached the Gospel for material gain.[30] If Paul also exploited the message, there would be no difference between Paul or false teachers. Accordingly, he would be guilty of hindering the spread of the Gospel, which brings salvation to all.

Paul refused the use of his apostolic authority in order to avoid becoming an obstacle to the Gospel or jeopardize his relationship with fellow believers in Corinth. Therefore, when Paul had the opportunity to sincerely proclaim the Gospel with power, he used his authority to refuse missionary support. He wanted to clearly convey that the Gospel is about salvation of souls, not material wealth or possession.

28. Rolston, "Stewardship," 106.
29. Robertson and Plummer, "1 Corinthians," 186.
30. Fee, 1 Corinthians, 24.

Offering the Gospel Free of Charge

It was evident that Paul did not in any way want to burden the Corinthians. As a spiritual parent in Christ, he wanted to give to them rather than receive from them, if that would be helpful. Despite the numerous privileges he had as a result of his apostolic right, Paul stated that he had not used any of these rights and had no intention of using them in Corinth. From this point, his refusal of missionary support and apostolic right becomes the main subject of the rest of 1 Corinthians 9.

> But I have not used any of these rights. And I am not writing this in the hope that you will do such things for me. I would rather die than have anyone deprive me of this boast. Yet when I preach the Gospel, I cannot boast, for I am compelled to preach. Woe to me if I do not preach the Gospel! If I preach voluntarily, I have a reward; if not voluntarily, I am simply discharging the trust committed to me. What then is my reward? Just this: that in preaching the Gospel I may offer it free of charge, and so not make use of my rights in preaching it. (1 Cor 9:15–18)

Paul's use of the expression, "I did write" may refer to the whole letter now completed or the words just written about missionary support. Following that phrase, it is interesting how he expressed how much better it would be for him to die rather than for anyone to deprive him of the opportunity to boast. Godet explains, "It is far from being the desire of the apostle to induce the church to financially support him, for he would rather be deprived of his ministry by death than to discharge it for material gain."[31] Examining why Paul should make such a statement, it becomes clear that the act of preaching in itself contains nothing to furnish him grounds for boasting, because preaching the Gospel is a necessity and he must do it without any complaint. Actually, it is important for us to explore whether Paul's commission to preach the Gospel applies to all believers.

It would appear that his situation is exceptional—unique to his specific circumstances, since he switched to the first person point of view at this point. Though others may find preaching a cause for self-aggrandizement Paul's case is different, for in a real sense, calamity would befall him and his life would end if he refused to preach the Gospel. Findlay noted, "[H]ad Paul disobeyed the call of God, his course from that time onwards must have been one of condemnation and misery. His calling was a *necessity*

---

31. Godet, *First Corinthians*, 453.

and to fight against 'necessity,' the Greeks conceived as ruin; theirs was a blind, cruel fate, but Paul's necessity is driven by Sovereign Grace."[32]

The verse found in 1 Cor 9:17 seems to partly sum up Paul's explanation: "For if I preach voluntarily, I have a reward; if not voluntarily I am simply discharging the trust committed to me." Paul's awareness of the subtle levels of stewardship reflected his submission to God and gratitude for the trust he had been given. Therefore the expression implies no other reward except the trust given to him (Acts 26:16; 1 Cor 4:1). Consequently, Paul shared the Gospel free of charge to the Corinthians. He was motivated by a reward linked to his calling. Although some may interpret this reward as something to be received on the Day of Judgment, this is not necessarily so, because the judgment motif is completely foreign to the discussion. The reward Paul received was the glory of preaching the Gospel freely without charge and seeing lives changed upon the knowledge of Christ's saving grace as indicated in his letter to the Corinthians. Paul in this regard is not just establishing a partial but rather total claim of his apostolic right and calling.

Using Missionary Support of One Church to Serve another Church

It is likely that the false apostles, who came to Corinth after Paul's visit, took all they could from the Corinthians and claimed that it demonstrated their love for them. Ironically, Paul was depicted as the one without love for the Corinthians. He therefore started his defense in 2 Cor 11:7 by asking the Corinthians whether he committed a sin by lowering himself so that the saints could be exalted. This question has been discussed earlier, but it now receives a sharper focus by the implied accusation that since he preached his message without charge, he was not a true apostle.[33]

One of the significant expressions in this passage is the idea of the Gospel of God being offered for nothing. While the Judaizers did not preach the true Gospel but nevertheless received missionary support for it, Paul preached God's message of salvation without charge. This position is significant for two reasons. First, the Sophists justified taking money as payment for teaching. The logic was that if instruction were given freely, there would be no value attached. Second, among Greek attitudes, Paul's strategy to be self-supporting through a trade was a cultural statement—a loss of social

32. Findlay, 1 Corinthians, 852.
33. Martin, 2 Corinthians, 344.

esteem. So, while both of these worldviews were significant, neither explains why Paul used the support of one church to serve other churches.[34]

In response, some may say that Paul's behavior displayed a lack of trust in God's provisions. It is apparent that Paul received assistance from the Macedonians and therefore his refusal of missionary support from Corinth was not the norm. The rule he consistently kept was to accept support from churches he had founded–particularly when he was away from them. He enjoyed very good relationships with the churches he had founded and the Philippian church was a good example of this. He raised this point again in both 2 Cor 11:21 and 12:13.

Paul went ahead to declare that he would rather rob other churches. Here he admitted that he drew funds from other churches such as the church at Philippi (Phil 2:25; 4:10–20). The verb he applied is used in classical Greek to describe stripping a dead soldier of his armor on the field of battle. However, this verb may be used equally to draw a contrast between the Philippians and the Corinthians.[35]

What Paul took from the brethren in Macedonia is sometimes translated as wages, which refers to provisions sufficient to take care of his needs. However, this is sometimes considered sustenance, not regular pay or wages. Still, he felt like he was robbing those churches, especially the Macedonian assemblies who by their generosity gave above their ability. Yet, this does not suggest that support from one church to serve others was an abnormal practice. "Paul's insistence on strictly abstaining from taking supplies from the Corinthians implies that it is possible he brought some supplies with him from Macedonia, and when his own work could not meet his needs, the Macedonians came to his rescue."[36]

Considering Paul's practice, it appears that he did not accept missionary support from any church when he was actively working in that church. However, though he expected churches to support the furtherance of the Gospel, he never gave fundraising higher priority than the Gospel. In the case of the Corinthians, he depended on support from Macedonia and his own trade making tents.

---

34. Ibid., 345.

35. Ibid., 346.

36. Robertson and Plummer, "1 Corinthians," 304.

PAUL'S BOAST IN REFERENCE TO MISSIONARY SUPPORT

Paul used the word "boast" on four different occasions directly referring to specific missionary support under the context of his authority. The word is usually used in a negative sense. We find several warnings in the Scriptures against it. The word is related to a noun that is translated as glory, glorying or boasting.[37] However, the verb is most of the time intransitive and means "to boast," the context indicating pride, positive boasting or the negative sense of bragging.[38] Theologians Balz and Schneider state, "[T]he object determines the sense of use and therefore the form of boasting and the reason for boasting is very crucial in this matter."[39]

In Hebrew the terms refer to self-praise and while the Old Testament finds a place for justifiable pride, there are many proverbs against boasting (Prov 16:31; Ps 52:1). Judaism maintains the same tension between false and true boasting, but it eventually stresses the law as the reason for boasting. It is conceivable that rabbis find a source of boasting in the law or even in its fulfillment.[40]

> But I have not used any of these rights. And I am not writing this in the hope that you will do such things for me. I would rather die than have anyone deprive me of this boast. Yet when I preach the Gospel, I cannot boast, for I am compelled to preach. Woe to me if I do not preach the Gospel! If I preach voluntarily, I have a reward; if not voluntarily, I am simply discharging the trust committed to me. What then is my reward? Just this: that in preaching the Gospel I may offer it free of charge, and so not make use of my rights in preaching it. (1 Cor 9:15–18)

> As surely as the truth of Christ is in me, nobody in the regions of Achaia will stop this boasting of mine. Why? Because I do not love you? God knows I do! (2 Cor 11:10–11)

Paul did not exclude self-boasting from his ministry, because he boasted about the faith of the churches, their love for God and for his own authority as an apostle. Such boasting did not further exclude Paul from a valid boasting in his apostolic work (2 Cor 7:4, 14). Overall, Paul boasted because of the churches he had founded and because boasting within the

---

37. Vine, *Expository Dictionary*, 127.
38. Balz and Schneider, eds., *Exegetical Dictionary of the New Testament*, 276.
39. Ibid.
40. Kittel and Friedrich, eds., *TDNT*, 424.

confines of his work expressed God's grace at work through him. For as much as Paul boasted, he did not do it to compare his work with that of others (2 Cor 10:12). More than once, he boasted about self-examination, with results expressed as thanksgiving and joy in the knowledge of the grace of God.

The Corinthians' resistance to Paul's apostolic authority moved him to self-boasting; but, recognizing how dangerous this could be, he instead began listing his sufferings (2 Cor 10:8–13; 11: 22). The motif of trust is very much inherent in Paul's boasting, for in boasting he declares what he relies on for ministry and for life. He adhered to the principle in Jeremiah 9:22–25 that whoever boasts should boast in the Lord. Paul concluded his argument by saying that he is not inferior to others and that boasting is not necessary, because he is nothing in himself. He ended with boasting about that which is due to him because of his refusal to use his right for missionary support. Boasting in God should therefore be seen in the spirit of God exalting the lowly and humiliating the rich in order that all would trust in God alone.[41]

Dealing with False Apostles

Until now, Paul has been dealing graciously with his enemies. He now comes out strongly to say what he thinks of his opponents by calling them false apostles in 2 Corinthians 11:13: "For such men are false apostles, deceitful workmen, masquerading as apostles of Christ. And no wonder, for Satan himself masquerades as an angel of light."

The use of the phrase "false apostles" appears only here in the New Testament, and some believe that Paul got this term from false prophets, or false christs as listed in Mark 13:22 and false brethren as noted in Galatians 2:4. Bernard observed, "[T]he speedy appearance of false teachers was one of the most remarkable features of the Apostolic Age."[42] Paul considered these false apostles as crafty workers who fashioned themselves into apostles of Christ. Just like the Judaizers in Corinth, they were deceitful men working for their own interests. They were workers, but their devotion to Christ was a sham that wreaked havoc, for they worked for their own profit.

The New International Version uses the word "masquerade" to describe the false apostles, since the present middle participle means, "transforming themselves" (2 Cor 11:13).[43] In Philippians 3:21, Paul uses the word to describe the transformation of our present bodies into the likeness of Christ's

41. Ibid., 425.

42. Bernard, *Corinthians*, 103.

43. Hughes, *2 Corinthians*, 394.

glorified body. This use can be defined as the effort of someone to assume a true nature while remaining unchanged. Paul poured scorn on their claim to be Christ's apostles and clearly explained how the masquerade happened.

He urged the Corinthians not to be surprised, for Satan himself masquerades as a messenger of light. The transition from a false apostle to Satan depicts the full irony and appeal of Paul's case (2 Cor 11:14). Consequently, these charlatans adopt the role of their master Satan. According to the Lord Himself, Satan is the father of all lying, and there is no truth in him (Jn 8:44). As Hughes rightly puts it, "Nothing could be more incongruous, therefore, than for Satan to pose as an angel of light; but he can do so only by falsehood, that is by the contradiction of God's word. . .by his lies he murders the souls of men."[44]

There is no need to believe that Paul is alluding to some rabbinical legend, similar to the one about Eve and the serpent, in which Satan is said to have taken the fashion of an angel. The context suggests that Satan habitually does present himself as an angel of light rather than who he really is on any particular occasion (2 Cor 11:14). It is evident that Satan mimicking the role of an angel of light is Paul's own expression. The apostle is explaining that Satan needs to make evil look attractive to tempt the children of God. Therefore, it is no great thing if Satan's ministers do the same as their master, transforming themselves into false ministers of righteousness.

The false apostles erroneously emphasized that work was the key to unlocking salvation—not faith in God's grace alone. The adversaries of Paul were laying claim to the same designation that he had asserted earlier. He needed to warn the Corinthians about these intruders, imposters and perverters of the saving grace of God. Because these intruders, imposters and perverters sowed works of evil, they would eventually reap God's punishment.

Paul lamented as he asked the Corinthians whether he had defrauded them (2 Cor 12:11–13). He urged his audience to listen carefully to him as he explained what seemed to have been an accusation and misunderstanding regarding the men who came to Corinth to collect money from the poor saints in Jerusalem. This was likewise a charitable proposition that was brought to Paul. In 2 Corinthians 12:17–18, Paul asserted that he did not send men to collect support. Rather, he was concerned about whether they thought he defrauded them by doing that. His use of the word translated as "to send" implies that the mission was definite. The men Paul sent did not raise funds under false pretenses. Neither Titus nor the other believers sent

---

44. Ibid.

were conducting fraudulent business since they acted with the same spirit of openness and integrity.

The name of the other brother with Titus was not mentioned, but the expression, "I admonished and sent a brother with him" refers to the mission that was recorded in 2 Corinthians 12:18. It is plain that Titus' first mission had been admirably fulfilled and that the Corinthians had recognized his single-mindedness and sincerity, for he faithfully carried out the instructions given to him. This was a major distinction regarding how Paul established his authority: unlike his adversaries, he did not seek charitable support from his audience although he had the authority to do so. He served them free of charge. He indicated that as an apostle of righteousness, he did not need to defend himself. When it became necessary to solicit support for the saints in Jerusalem, he did it out of a pure conscience with no fraudulent intentions. These activities of his ministry greatly set him apart from all others who claimed to be apostles but were not.

PRINCIPLES FOR THEOLOGICAL INSTITUTIONS

Theological institutions can draw insights from biblical principles arising in the Pauline experience, because these principles speak directly to one of the primary ways of achieving financial sustainability. The following principles can be drawn from Paul's rationale for missionary support and applied to theological education.

Missionary support is a path toward financial sustainability for those who faithfully spend their lives in spreading the Gospel or serving in Christian institutions. The Levites administrated grain, animal and fruit offerings in the temple, which they were divinely authorized to use for their livelihood as they served in ministry as priests to Israel. It was therefore appropriate that they derived their livelihood from those sources. Just as God appointed the Levites to ministry, so should the staff of a theological institution be supported out of the proceeds of missions. The Lord Jesus indicates that a worker is worthy of his wage, and that those who preach the Gospel should live by the Gospel. This expresses a situation of purpose besides source.

Paul argued that it is not only the missionary or staff member but also their families who deserve to be supported. If these people give themselves fully to the task of spreading the Gospel through teaching and discipleship, they deserve financial support. Faculty and staff who work in theological institutions need to be paid for the work they do, whether they be farmers, soldiers or shepherds. However, we are aware from the previous chapters of this book that institutions are unable to support the needs of faculty and staff who serve the Lord through their capabilities.

Missionaries often face extreme challenges in raising support to serve in African theological institutions. There have been times when faculty resigned because their ministry support fell below the required minimum established by the mission agency. Unfortunately, sometimes paid faculty and staff in certain institutions can serve for months without any remuneration. In the meantime, without a sustainable livelihood their children are threatened to be sent home for non-payment of school fees. This is often due to the financial difficulties in our institutions. Paul established that raising support from local donors and those living abroad to support people serving the Lord is a biblical concept and must be done as an act of worship.

Evidently, spiritual blessings cannot be bought with material treasure. Therefore whatever faculty and staff receive as payment is but an appreciation of God's grace. The work of the ministry cannot be quantified because these are spiritual services offered first to the Lord and then to his people. Under such conditions, negotiations for salaries and benefits take a completely different turn, because those endowed with gifts to serve are not deemed to deserve it and those whom they serve cannot pay them. No salary structure or remuneration plan is good enough for these ministers. It is therefore expedient to consider what is due to these servants in terms of expressing appreciation of their loving service to the Lord but sufficient enough to sustain them and their families. Often, institutions tend to stretch the notion that whatever is given to faculty or staff is sufficient because they are not perceived to otherwise deserve it.

Institutions must be held accountable both spiritually and materially regarding how they meet the needs of their faculty and staff. Any financial support, be it from a missionary agency, church or institution is tantamount to exploitation if salaries fall short of competitive salaries in comparable positions elsewhere. Meager salaries will make it difficult if not impossible for staff to earn a reasonable livelihood for themselves and their families. In reality, this blocks God's blessings for that organization, as well.

When donors give, they commit themselves to also pray. The fact that they are supporting an institution makes them spiritually responsible for the work in that field. The people in Paul's time were already aware of what they should do. It was the norm that preachers, philosophers, and teachers were supported—especially if their message and teachings were accepted. All Paul needed to do was to accept their generosity with gratitude.

In our time, many people are still ignorant of what theology is all about—particularly regarding the mission of African theological institutions. We have a responsibility to educate and challenge potential donors both locally and internationally to embrace and support the mission of theological education in Africa. Above all, theological institutions must now trust God to touch the hearts of donors to give generously and pray, as well as trust God for victory.

As a matter of principle, it would be expedient to depend on financial support from a group of believers externally planted outside of the local ministry field. Every believer engaged in sowing spiritual seeds and spreading the Gospel deserves support from fellow believers who share the same concern. This principle enables one to be effective in ministry, exhorting, correcting, rebuking and encouraging. One does not necessarily have to plant a church in order to be supported. One does not have to come from the West in order to find support from the West. Paul received support from the church in Philippi to serve the believers in Corinth. Dean Gilliland noted, "[I]f we serve God, then money is a servant or tool to be used to bring in God's Kingdom if we are workers together with God. Once the offerings are made, this is neither Japanese money nor American money. It is holy money for God to use where he directs his servants to use it."[45]

The task of training leaders to shepherd the church and society in Africa is not only an African affair, it is the responsibility of every member in the body of Christ. Thus, charitable giving from anywhere in the world is acceptable for the work of missions. Therefore, missionary support from one geographical area or church to serve a theological institution in another area is not a characteristic lack of responsibility but a privilege to serve God in what he is doing in different parts of the world. Although Paul had many problems in Jerusalem in the early days following his conversion, he presented a strong case regarding his ministry among the Gentiles. He never started a church in Jerusalem, but worked very hard persuading the Gentile churches he had founded to give to the Jerusalem saints. What a selfless attitude and approach to missionary support worthy of emulation!

In the next chapter, we explore the conditions Paul laid out under which such a partnership in the Gospel should be examined. Therefore as much as this book is about financial sustainability of theological institutions in Africa, the discussion must also include other parts of the globe, bringing to bear all of God's resources toward God's work. Developing a fundraising department in a theological institution is a highly effective start to planning fundraising activities. Such planning is purely biblical and should be open to all, whether a rich Western donor or a not so rich local donor. All are important to God's kingdom and must practice being responsible stewards of resources to strengthen the capacity of institutions so they may operate

45. Gilliland, *Pauline Theology and Mission Practice*, 254.

effectively on all fronts. When donors commit to supporting institutions, they stimulate and encourage those institutions to develop a vision that motivates them toward the fulfillment of the core mandate. Giving fosters a sense of partnership and fellowship that shares with all stakeholders successes as well as failures of the mission.

Theological institutions are often locked in their own small cocoons, bound by their own denominational beliefs and mission policies. Considering that certain institutions have talented and highly skilled people and facilities to raise more support, it would be appropriate if the entire fraternity of theological institutions functioned as a body, supplementing and complementing each other's efforts. There is need to build partnerships to ensure that the ultimate goal is achieved without much concern for who gets the credit. Theological institutional leaders should not only be concerned about raising financial support for their institutions, but also for other institutions and mission activities unrelated to them. Christ's church must be open-minded and grow into maturity in such matters.

Although on many occasions Paul received missionary support from the churches he had planted, he also refused support on other occasions. He never imposed any burden on his new converts to support him if that was going to hinder the Gospel or the work of ministry. As a matter of principle, he did not subscribe to strategies or gimmicks that would cast the Gospel message in a negative light, a situation that is common today in many churches and para-church organizations. There is need to cautiously erase this unfortunate reputation given to churches and para-church organizations as "money-making machines" engaged in all manner of business except to propagate the Gospel of Jesus Christ.

Paul presents a balanced perspective on conditions under which we should turn down donations however good the motives might be. Where any financial support would be a hindrance to the Gospel, it must be completely avoided because the Gospel must always take preeminence. Servants of the Gospel must distinguish themselves from others who claim to be missionaries but have ulterior motives and misrepresent the Christ of the Gospels.

As in all ministry endeavors, there are times when theological institutions must discern whether a particular gift will enrich or impoverish them. There are donations that hurt institutions more than their prevailing financial constraints. However, we need to ensure that refusal of a gift does not hurt the partnership relationship either, and at the same time that acceptance will not compromise existing programs or the missional direction. As earlier identified, donors influence the direction of an institution, especially when the institution has severe financial constraints.

In other words, leaders are bound to undertake a project often bigger than they have capacity to manage. There is a tendency to launch academic programs without referencing institutional history, learning resources, or experts in a particular field. This kind of situation is always dicey because there is a purpose for every donation and there is donor preference as to how funds are to be utilized. There is nothing inherently wrong with donors having preferences and pushing a specific agenda. Theological institutions have the responsibility to say no, when the purpose of the donation will distract and hinder them from fulfilling their mission.

When financial support, especially from churches and donors results in control of the institution and its activities through policies and regulations, support can stifle an institution's creativity. Institutions must endeavor to amicably address donor straightjacket policies that hinder the school's growth and development. There is a place for "No, thanks." Although, perhaps not under the same circumstances experienced by the Apostle Paul, who had to address his authority, freedom, and rights. Ironically, support had the potential to hinder the spread of the Gospel in Paul's day. It is possible that support can, in a sense, hinder progress and growth of the kingdom as support almost did from the church in Corinth. The acceptance or refusal of support should be done in a boastful and arrogant way, especially when the institution has adequate capacity for donations. At the same time, humility as God's stewards responsible for the tasks assigned is also appropriate.

Chapter 5

The Ministry of Tentmaking

WHEN DONATIONS ARE INSUFFICIENT and/or would hinder the accomplishment of a ministry task, tentmaking is a viable alternative fundraising strategy for theological institutions seeking to fulfill the Great Commission. Tentmaking refers to self-supporting activities to raise funds for ministry. A theological institution's development of income generating projects could be categorized as tentmaking activities—an idea that alludes to Apostle Paul's actual making of tents in Thessalonica and Corinth for income.

In the midst of some serious misunderstandings, the Apostle Paul told the Corinthians that the mission entrusted to him was not given by man. The signs that he accomplished among them were sure proof that he was directly approved and chosen by God. Hughes explained that the signs were confirmation of apostolic work, and therefore depicted the authenticity of the Apostle's mission.[1] By his life and work, Paul allowed God to change the lives of the Corinthians through him and this was the sign and seal of his apostleship. These signs were miracles and mighty works done among the Corinthians.

It is therefore evident from the passages studied in Chapter 4 and in this chapter, that Paul's rationale for tentmaking far outweighed alternative fundraising strategies. In every city however, he had a different reason for his work, depending on the prevailing situation. He made tents while in Thessalonica and Corinth. Overall, he made tents to set himself apart from his opponents who were hawking and distorting the word of God in Thessalonica and Corinth. He also made tents as an example against idleness,

---

1. Hughes, *Second Corinthians*, 456.

to preach the Gospel without charge and to avoid being a burden to the believers. This was unlike his opponents. Although he was misunderstood for his tentmaking, which also brought to question his apostolic authority, his action was to benefit his converts but not in such a way as to demean them. In light of Apostle Paul's arguments, tentmaking is a biblically viable way to raise financial support and should not be considered a secondary option to traditional missionary support.

Tentmaking as alluded to in the Pauline epistles presents a balanced approach to fundraising, which in our situation refers to all manner of donations towards the sustainability of theological institutions. This example does not suggest that we should all literally start making tents, but rather highlights the importance of putting our skills and competences to work in such a manner that generates income for the work of ministry. Apostle Paul went to great lengths to defend tentmaking as one of the viable means of responding to financial sustainability in ministry, especially when other means are likely to compromise the very purpose for which the ministry exists. It is therefore expedient to follow this biblical principle and apply it as each context may determine.

Among other issues, persecution became one of the major factors that contributed to a need for tentmaking ministries in the early years of the first century. After hundreds of Christians had been martyred, many of their peers fled to other countries. In these new locations, they supported themselves through manual labor or as secretaries, physicians and so on, while they shared their faith as missionaries of the Lord.[2] The secret of their power was in the knowledge of the Word of God, and although they supported themselves through tentmaking, their main vocation was as ambassadors for Christ. As a missionary in India William Carey once put it this was, "My business is to witness for Christ."[3] It was during this time he raised financial support by mending shoes.

William Carey learned the Bengali language and after six years was joined by two other tentmakers, Joshua Marshman, a schoolteacher and William Ward, a printer. These three self-supporting missionaries translated and published the entire Bible into six different languages, the New Testament into twenty-three others and thematic collections of the scriptures into ten more.[4] Carey made a significant contribution to world missions and as early as 1833, wrote about tentmaking to share his extensive experiences. Grubb quoted Carey as saying, "We have ever held it to be an es-

---

2. Stewart, *The Nestorian Missionary Enterprise*, 18.

3. Neill, *A History of Christian Missions*, 263.

4. Ibid.

sential principle in the conduct of missions that whenever it is practicable, missionaries should support themselves in whole or in part through their own exertions."[5]

The Basel Evangelical Missionary Society (or the Basel Mission, as it was finally known) greatly encouraged its workers to be self-supporting. Notably, the society established a trading company in West Africa in a region that is now Ghana, where three Swiss farmers who were members of the mission first introduced the cocoa plant to inhabitants in Akropong. From then on, the cocoa plant, which originally came from South America, became the leading cash crop of the West African nation. The Mission sent the first shipment of cocoa from Ghana to Europe in 1891. Twenty years later, Ghana became the world's leading producer of cocoa and her per capita income became the highest in sub-Saharan black Africa.[6]

The Basel Mission society always sought to do everything to show that "godliness is profitable unto all things, having promise of life that now is and of that which is to come" (1 Tm 4:8). In areas where they were not able to open mission stations, the society opened trading posts where its business staff could also witness. Missiologist and author J. Christy Wilson noted, "The mission worked on the premise that the office of the preacher was not the only type of spiritual service. They believed that a person filled with the Holy Spirit is spiritual no matter what branch of God's work he or she is in."[7]

The Basel Mission society formed The Basel Trading Company as a tentmaking venture to combine ministry with secular work. According to pioneering missionary William J. Danker, "The Basel Trading Company has always sought to send out high quality Christians to make its witness in the marketplace. They have not hid their light under a bushel . . . they set it high upon the candlestick of a living demonstration of the Gospel in the factory across the counter."[8] These historical records tell us how God used tentmakers to extend the influence of the Gospel.

PAUL'S EXAMPLE OF TENTMAKING

It is believed that Paul's constructed tents using rough cloth made of goat hair known as cilicium. It's a material that took its name from Paul's native

---

5. Grubb, *The Need for Non-Professional Missionaries*, 11.

6. Wilson Jr., *Today's Tentmakers*, 35.

7. Ibid.

8. Danker, *Profit for the Lord*, 121.

province of Cilicia.[9] Paul may have learned this trade during his youth in Tarsus, as it was required of many Hebrew children to learn a trade. Some believe that cilicium was used for purposes other than tentmaking and so the "patristic interpretations of the Greek word, *skenopoios*, [or tentmaker] point in the direction of leather goods, believing that tents were generally made of leather."[10]

The problem here is that if the tanning of leather among Jews was a despised trade, then any leatherwork would share the same reputation. Furthermore, it is evident that Paul's work was physically straining and this might have also made it unacceptable to the elite in his time.[11] According to Hock, tentmaking was central to Paul's ministry. Moreover, the fact that his trade occupied much of his time indicates that his life was characterized by work in the workshop like a slave, working alongside other slaves. Since work and preaching characterized his lifestyle, Paul must have spoken the Word of God to the people while he worked.[12]

Tentmaking in Thessalonica

During Paul's second missionary journey, he stopped at Philippi and Thessalonica (Acts 17:1–8). Thessalonica was situated in the northwestern corner of the Thermaic Gulf with an advantage of a harbor. This made it one of the commercial cities along with Corinth and Ephesus.[13] The metropolis of Thessalonica was the largest in Macedonia with a population of about 200,000 with the majority of the residents being native Greeks. However, the Jews in the colony maintained their proselytizing influence on a considerable number of the Gentiles.[14] It is not certain how long Paul stayed in Thessalonica. However, Luke recorded in Acts that he spent three Sabbaths there. Other scholars consider the Sabbaths as the time he spent speaking in the synagogues. Therefore, it is possible that he spent three to four months in Thessalonica considering some of his activities there (Acts 17:2; 1 Thes 2:9; 2 Cor 11:14).

Paul was engaged in tentmaking during his stay at Thessalonica to provide for his needs (1 Thes 2:9; 2 Thes 3:8). He worked day and night in order not to burden the Thessalonians while he preached the Gospel.

9. Barnett, "Tentmaking," 926.

10. Hock, *The Social Context of Paul's Mission*, 20–21.

11. Barnett, "Tentmaking," 926.

12. Hock, *Social Context of Paul's Mission*, 67.

13. Hiebert, *The Thessalonian Epistles*, 11.

14. Harrison, *Introduction to the New Testament*, 245.

He reminded the Thessalonians that they were witnesses to his hard work, meaning they saw him working as well as preaching the Gospel. He never ate anyone's food without paying for it, and worked to provide for his own supplies. Paul engaged in tentmaking primarily as an example to the Thessalonian converts who were eagerly awaiting the Lord's return but incorrectly shunned manual work as a waste of time and energy.

Tentmaking in Corinth

Paul traveled from Thessalonica to Athens, and after a brief stop, continued to Corinth where he settled. Corinth was a Greek city in the western area of central Greece. It was a major commercial city that was also known for the Temple of Aphrodite, the goddess of love, whose followers engaged in sexual practices specifically as a form of worship. It was one of the main seaports of Greece which was razed in 146 B.C. only to be rebuilt by Caesar in 46 B.C.[15] Paul arrived in Corinth in A.D. 51 and stayed for eighteen months preaching the Gospel and planting the Corinthian church.

In Corinth, by his own example, Paul demonstrated the importance of tentmaking. Luke recorded in Acts that because Paul was a tentmaker, he chose to stay and work with Aquila and Priscilla during his time there (Acts 18:3). Paul made tents to distinguish himself from the false apostles and to avoid being a burden to the Corinthians. His work ensured that he should not be accused of commercializing the Gospel. He did not use his apostolic right to receive missionary support but rather gave it up and made tents for the sake of the Gospel.

RATIONALE FOR TENTMAKING

Barnett noted, "Greco-Roman culture was familiar with paying fees for the efforts of traveling philosophers and teachers. Similarly, they were given hospitality and other benefits by wealthy patrons."[16] In that context, it may be inconceivable that Apostle Paul chose to be a tentmaker to support himself, since he had planted many churches and had the right to apostolic support. However, Paul distinguished himself as an apostle who depended both on missionary support and tentmaking as the means of raising support for his ministry. Paul made tents to support himself for several reasons.

---

15. Guthrie, *New Testament Introduction*, 432.
16. Barnett, "Tentmaking," 926.

- First of all, he wanted to contrast himself with the philosophers, teachers and lecturers of his time. He did not want his message and ministry to be associated with the lifeless messages of contemporary scholars (1 Thes 1:5, 2:3–6).

- Secondly, he worked to combat the attitude of idleness prevailing between both the Jewish and Greco-Roman societies. He therefore set an example of diligence and hard work by supporting himself—a responsibility required of all believers.[17]

- Thirdly, he worked so that he would not be a burden to anyone.[18] Due to his hard work, he was able to offer the Gospel free of charge and did not burden anyone financially (1 Cor 9:16–18).

- Finally, he distinguished himself as a peculiar apostle whose very life and ministry challenged his converts and offered a perfect example for other believers.

Labor of Distinction

In his letter to the Thessalonians, Paul stated in Chapters 2 and 3 the important things that they needed to note about his apostolic defense. He noted how missionaries and preachers were received in Thessalonica, their conduct while they were there, and the examples they left their converts (1 Thes 2:1–4, 9–12).

It is important in this study to consider how Paul raised financial support, how he conducted himself and the example he left. Insulted and having suffered seriously in Philippi, Paul indicated that his visit to Thessalonica to share the Gospel would be in the context of his many struggles. In the end, he noted that his visit had not been in vain because it did not lack purpose (1 Thes 2:1–2). Paul's presence positively impacted the behavior and faith of many Thessalonians and was never in vain.

In the midst of great confusion and accusations against him, he preached the Gospel to the Thessalonians using the word often rendered as "exhortation" or "persuasion" instead of "exposition" (1 Thes 2:3). Scottish theologian John Eadie elaborated on Paul's example as "earnest practical preaching. . .bringing every motive to bear upon his audience, plying them with every argument and working on them by every kind of appeal, in order

---

17. Ibid.
18. Ibid.

to win them over to the Gospel and to faith in Him who delivers from the wrath to come."[19]

The Thessalonians identified Paul as a religious wanderer—or one who was believed to be in error. Yet, Paul combated these accusations and cleared the minds of his audience with his practical preaching (1 Thes 2:3). He did this against accusations of immorality. His use of the word exhortation conveyed his heart's desire for his audience, and how he wished they would just follow his instructions to receive the benefits of salvation and a personal relationship with God. Moreover, his choice of practical instruction combated insinuations that he and his colleagues were religious wanderers, Sophists, imposters or propagandists of a religious sect.[20]

The apostle was likewise accused of trickery and guile (1 Thes 2:3). It is believed that the trickery charge was about Paul's perceived lack of integrity regarding the contribution to the Jerusalem relief fund levied on his converts without warning. This problem arose after he refused to live at their expense. "It was common that wandering Sophists and jugglers often resorted to all manner of devices to attract audiences, trick them and ultimately wrestle away their money."[21]

He differentiated himself from his opponents by indicating that he and his companions had been approved of God and divinely entrusted with the Gospel. His calling was not under the authority of any man, but superseded all by the authority of God (1 Thes 2:4). Therefore, he did not preach out of impure motives because God, and not a trickster, had approved him. The apostle's aim was to please God, not men.[22] Paul specified that God is the one who approves and tests the hearts of men. The idea of God as the tester and searcher of hearts is very common in the Old Testament (Ps 7:9; Prov 17:3; Jer 11:20; 12:3). The writer invoked God as the one conclusive witness to the integrity of his motives regarding the Thessalonians. He was not out to exploit them like others had done.

Paul dealt with his opponents by asserting in 1 Thessalonians 2:5 that he did not go to Thessalonica out of covetousness or greediness. The expression signifies a deep craving for what one does not have and the desire to have it, or simply a desire for material possession. On this note, Paul called the Thessalonians and God as his witnesses. He did not use flattery or covetousness, for his motives were pure in whatever he did in his ministry. On the other hand, Paul's opponents did not seek the interest of men in any

19. Eadie, *Thessalonians*, 58.

20. Frame, "Epistles of St. Paul to the Thessalonians," 94.

21. Bruce, *1 & 2 Thessalonians*, 26.

22. Morris, *Thessalonians*, 71.

place but pursued their own ends, and ironically appealed for the public's approval (1 Thes 2:6).

Furthermore, Paul contrasted himself with his opponents during his visit to Corinth where he made tents just as he had at Thessalonica. He stated in his letter to the Corinthians that he did not claim his right but refused it; although he worked the hardest among the Corinthians (1 Cor 9:12). As much as he deserved a reward, he refused to collect any because his opponents were behaving this way. On the contrary, Paul and his colleagues deprived themselves of all benefits so that they were not counted among their opponents (1 Cor 9:12). Rather, he did this so that the Gospel would not be hindered in any way. Although Paul received missionary support in other places, he refused missionary support in Thessalonica and Corinth because of the insinuations and accusations made by his opponents. He worked to support himself and likewise differentiate himself.

Luke's account supports Paul's description of his tentmaking career. Luke indicated that Paul worked hard and did not covet anyone's silver, gold or clothing (Acts 20:33–35). The principle is that work is good and enables one to help the weaker brethren in the fellowship. However, the addition of the Lord's saying mentioned in (v.35), "It is more blessed to give than to receive," cannot be found directly in the Gospels, although it is implied in Luke 6:38. Toussaint believes that this represents an oral tradition passed to the early church.[23] However, Paul made tents when it was necessary and this distinguished him from his opponents and enhanced the spread of the Gospel.

APOSTOLIC EXAMPLE AGAINST IDLENESS

Paul's tentmaking was not only a challenge to his opponents, but it was also an example to the idle believers among the brethren in Thessalonica. He wrote, "And we urge you, brothers, warn those who are idle, encourage the timid, help the weak, be patient with everyone" (1 Thes 5:14). From that context, he elaborated four responsibilities that believers have to one another. They are as follows:

- The idle should be warned and those who neglect their duties must be stirred to action.
- The timid need encouragement.
- The weak need help.

---

23. Toussaint, "Acts," 414.

- All need to be patient with one another.

Paul worked in Thessalonica to refute those who advocated idleness and neglected their duties. Although his appeal was to the brethren, some believed that he was speaking specifically to the leaders in Thessalonica. Eadie noted that the church itself must act as well as its officers or presbyters. Therefore, this is not limited only to the leaders.[24] The expression "admonish the idle" is used only once in the New Testament, but the adverb appears in 2 Thessalonians 3:6, 11 and the verb in 2 Thessalonians 3:7. The word idle literally means "out of rank," which is the opposite of a soldier in rank.

Men who are lawless in life or disorderly are useless. Eadie asserted, "[T]he 'disorderly' appears to be those whose minds and habits had become unhinged from their misapprehension of the nearness of the Lord's coming; those who were neglecting the duties of common life and had ceased to maintain themselves by such honest labor as characterized the apostle himself when he sojourned among them."[25] Ignoring the warning in 1 Thessalonians 4:11, the Thessalonians neglected their daily duties and lived in idleness at the expense of others. Paul admonished them to mind their own business and work with their own hands to provide for their needs. He had to tell them to mend their ways.

Although Paul worked among them and took the opportunity of the hours left to share his faith, the example did not go down well with his audience. Paul had to deal with the same issue he had confronted in his second letter to the Thessalonians. This time the command to the idlers was a little harsher than the previous admonishment in 1 Thessalonians 5:14.

In 2 Thessalonians 3:6–13, he used the phrase rendered as "that you draw back," instructing believers to avoid idleness. This means drawing away from brothers who want to be idle. Apart from their refusal to work and earn a living, which resulted in want and idleness, they also made demands on the church for support as mentioned in 1 Thessalonians 4:11–12.[26] The Thessalonians probably found such conduct more palatable in view of the Greek idea that labor was degrading. They believed that menial occupations such as tentmaking were fit only for slaves but not free men.[27] Evidently, such conduct would be highly detrimental to the Christian call of discipleship. Paul did not only teach as one lecturing, but taught by example so that the Thessalonians would have an object lesson from which to learn.

24. Eadie, *Thessalonians*, 201.

25. Ibid., 202.

26. Frame, *Thessalonians*, 299.

27. Morris, *Thessalonians*, 251.

Indeed, the Gospel that Paul preached could not have been effective if he had not supported it with his lifestyle. He therefore never allowed the preaching of the Gospel to prevent him from making tents as a practical witness to his ministry. Paul stated that he was not idle, but toiled night and day so that he would not be a burden to anyone. Instead, he would but leave a model for the Thessalonians, for his work was not without purpose or for mere showmanship but very purposeful.

Paul used the phrase, "if anyone does not wish to work neither let him eat" (2 Thes 3:10). The source of this precept has been a matter of speculation among theologians. Some claim the precept is from Jewish and early Christian literature. We see Paul as the one who made this precept part of the Christian view of labor with the emphasis on combating negative habits of laziness and sloth. The clause is not merely a statement of fact, but an imperative giving the idea that Christians have no choice but to work if they are to eat. The use of work here refers to any activity by which one can earn a living instead of being a financial burden on others.

He further narrowed the idea to an issue specific among the Thessalonians. There were some of them who did not want to work at all, but who instead became busybodies. The issue here was not simply brethren living in idleness. But worse than these idlers, was the group that did not mind its business. They rather meddled in the affairs of other brethren—trying to use funds from the common treasury of the group. It was evident that these idlers not only got their living from others, but they also persuaded them to share their point of view about the second coming of Christ, encouraging them to stop working.[28] These idlers claimed that Christ was coming soon, and there was no need for believers to work.

Considering the situation, Paul gave a strong directive "we charge and exhort," which is a combination of two verbs emphasizing an injunction. That is, in the name of the Lord Jesus Christ believers are to refrain from such idleness. The mention of Christ's name in this injunction makes Him a partner and witness urging them to comply with the directive. The point of the action is that the idlers should rather work quietly and eat their own bread. Paul's tentmaking in Thessalonica was very crucial if he was to communicate change and persuade the believers that idleness does not glorify God. Paul's work eventually became a strong and impressive example for the Thessalonians.

28. Ibid., 256.

Preaching Without Charge

The Apostle Paul convincingly established his apostolic right to financial support from the Corinthian church. Still, he refused the support to avoid being accused of fraudulent or exploitative behavior. His opponents generally had no qualms demanding such support despite questionable ministry practices. Paul consistently affirmed his integrity and commitment to ministry for which he was called without choice. His preaching was not a voluntary vocation. Rather, he was discharging a trust bestowed upon him. Due to this calling, therefore, Paul could boast of preaching the Gospel free of charge. He also had the opportunity to see the Gospel at work in the lives of those who received his ministry. The Corinthian church was the fruit and reward of his ministry.

Since he worked to support himself, Paul preached the Gospel free of charge. In the midst of great confusion and unavailability of proper identification due to the activities of the false apostles, Paul's tentmaking became necessary. In a corrupt and commercially minded generation such as the one we live in, this is an important distinction that every minister of the Gospel would do well to likewise consider.

Avoidance of Being a Burden

Paul was a full-time minister of the Gospel and an apostle of Christ. Despite his station in life, he did not deny the financial burden of his basic daily needs. At the same time, he did not make his need everyone's problem. Rather, he made tents to support himself. The tense and mood of the verbs in this phrase, "and being present with you and lacking," from 2 Corinthians 11:9 implies that his lack was not a hypothetical condition but an actual experience. However, his response to this lack was completely different from that of his contemporaries. Only partly did he depend on believers from Macedonia who sent him gifts to support his livelihood.

Although the apostle had a reputation of preaching the Gospel to audiences free of charge, there seemed to be a certain level of inconsistency in this. He refused maintenance from the Corinthians. But, he did not make a secret of receiving maintenance from the Macedonians.[29] Apart from being a burden to the Corinthians, Plummer noted that Paul wanted to be free to rebuke and exhort, without fear or desire of losing favor with them. Moreover, he did not want to be accused of seeking fame for the sake of material

---

29. Plummer, 2 Corinthians, 304.

gain.[30] So, he put himself in a position in which Corinthians did not have to support him—did not have to drain their resources. As he said, "I was not a burden to anyone, for the brothers who came from Macedonia supplied what I needed. I have kept myself from being a burden to you in any way, and will continue to do so." (2 Cor 11:9). That denotes a conscious exercise of discipline and self-control. For three years, Paul stayed in Corinth, but he never reprimanded the Corinthians for not meeting his needs as if the poorer Macedonians had by their gift put them to shame.[31]

Furthermore, Paul was constrained by the intent and purpose of his ministry stopover in Corinth. More than anything else, his aim was to win them for Christ. Hughes indicated, "[A]ny thought of winning material gain from them would have endangered the full and undivided intensity of that purpose; and so he resolutely set his face against expressing a privilege to which he had an indisputable title."[32] He did not want to burden them because they were his children. Out of his parental love for the Corinthians, Paul gave up his very self for them, requiring nothing but their response of changed hearts. Unlike his opponents who used craftiness and guile to burden them by exploiting their resources, Paul sacrificially gave himself to the Corinthians.

While in Thessalonica, Paul did not mention anything about the support he received from Philippi (Phil 4:15–16). It might be that the money sent from Philippi was not enough to remove the need for manual labor in Thessalonica. On the other hand, it may be possible that Paul did not want to embarrass the Thessalonian Christians by mentioning the gifts given by other Christians.[33]

Instead, he expressed his love to share the Gospel even to the extent of sacrificing his life. His heartfelt desire was not to impose any burden on the Thessalonians but to serve them. His kind of labor went way beyond that of a worker for wages; his was a whole life ministry that he described as being done "night and day" (1 Thes 2:9). As Eadie put it, "labor and toil" is a terse and familiar idiom with toil denoting weariness and labor indicating utter exhaustion out of manual work.[34] It is significant that at night when rest seems to begin, in Paul's life, work is just beginning. Apostle Paul often placed night before day (Acts 20:3; 1 Thes 3:10; 1 Tim 5:5; 2 Tim 1:3).

---

30. Ibid., 305.

31. Hughes, *Second Corinthians*, 388.

32. Ibid., 463.

33. Bruce, *Thessalonians*, 35.

34. Eadie, *Thessalonians*, 68.

Marshall noted that the phrase indicates Paul worked either at night or by the day, but not continuously throughout the twenty-four hour period.[35]

Consequently, Paul went on to challenge the Thessalonians to follow his example of hard work, whether it was manual in nature or not (2 Thes 3:7–8). They were not only to work hard, but if they ate anyone's food, they should be prepared to pay for it. The use of an adverbial-accusative phrase "freely or as a gift" (v. 8) was similar to Jesus' use of the phrase in Matthew 10:8, when he sent the twelve disciples out to preach.

Jesus taught that a workman or laborer is worthy of his meat (support), a message that Paul repeats in 1 Thessalonians 2:9. Frame concluded Paul's rationale for tentmaking by saying, "[He]. . . worked not because he had no right to demand, as an apostle of Christ, support from the church but worked, waiving his right to [offer instead] a visible and constant example of self-sacrificing industry for them to imitate."[36]

PROBLEMS CAUSED BY PAUL'S WORK

It was believed in Paul's time that work, especially manual labor, was good only for slaves and not for free citizens. Artisans and manual workers occupied the lowest social strata. Paul's work therefore might have offended members of churches he established, particularly in Corinth, since a workshop is no place for free citizens. It was therefore unthinkable that Paul—a Roman citizen, a former Pharisee, a person of high standing—should stoop to such a level.[37]

Barnett noted that Paul's work to support himself created three problems:

- First, it broke the conventional practice that the wealthy provide for their visiting lecturer.

- Second, it apparently made Paul guilty of refusing support, which the Corinthians found difficult to forgive.

- Finally, it helped him to live without support from the Corinthians, but he still had to accept and receive assistance from the Macedonians, drawing charges of hypocrisy, even bias (2 Cor 11:9).[38]

---

35. Marshall, 1 & 2 Thessalonians, 72.

36. Frame, Thessalonians, 303.

37. Barnett, "Tentmaking," 927.

38. Ibid.

Therefore, as much as Paul's work had many positive sides, it was not without problems. We shall look at how these problems affected his ministry.

Paul Misunderstood for Tentmaking

In 2 Corinthians 11:7–10 Paul mounts his defense against the misunderstanding regarding tentmaking. His attempt to respond to the problems started with rhetorical questions.

> Was it a sin for me to lower myself in order to elevate you by preaching the Gospel of God to you free of charge? I robbed other churches by receiving support from them so as to serve you. And when I was with you and needed something, I was not a burden to anyone, for the brothers who came from Macedonia supplied what I needed. I have kept myself from being a burden to you in any way, and will continue to do so. As surely as the truth of Christ is in me, nobody in the regions of Achaia will stop this boasting of mine. (2 Cor 11:7–10)

He began by asking, "Did I commit a sin?" In other words, was it a sin for him to lower himself in order to elevate believers by preaching the Gospel free of charge? Bernard noted that Paul disgraced himself by engaging in manual labor so that his followers might benefit by learning from his example.[39] Although Paul dealt with the question of why he decided to work, why he refused missionary support, and why he shelved his apostolic authority in 1 Corinthians 9:14–19, his explanation did not resolve the problem. His opponents took advantage of the situation to accuse him of falsehood.

However, by lowering himself, Paul exalted the Corinthians as children of the Most High. Was this genuine concern and love misunderstood by the Corinthians and thus created room for the false apostles? Barnett observed that the problem was that in reality, the Corinthians were not opening their hearts to him (2 Cor 6:11–13), but rather preferred the false apostles (2 Cor 11:1, 4, 19–20).[40]

Regarding the problem of his tentmaking and assistance from Macedonia, Paul indicated that it was for the benefit of the Corinthians. He expressed himself with hyperbole, saying he robbed other churches to take care of them. The phrase "I robbed" is also used in Acts 19:37 and Romans 2:22. It is an image denoting how a soldier strips armor from a slain enemy.

39. Bernard, 2 Corinthians, 101.

40. Barnett, The Message of 2 Corinthians, 167.

That is, he allowed other churches to do more than their share.[41] Accordingly, he was not a burden or an encumbrance. Often gifts from churches were sent to him after he had left those churches. Therefore, whatever Paul received from the Macedonians was not regular pay or wages but a gift for his sustenance.

The idea of an encumbrance illustrates a torpedo-fish, which paralyses its victims by contact and then preys upon them.[42] Paul indicated his avoidance of this practice of encumbrance, which on the contrary, is a typical description of his opponents. He kept himself from being a burden to the Corinthians and all the other churches—including the Macedonian churches—that supported him. He steered clear of any slander as far as the issue of preaching the Gospel for material support was concerned.

Paul's Apostolic Right at Stake

The essential sign of Christ-likeness on the part of him who preached the apostolic message was to convince them that he was indeed an apostle. "Nothing could be more openly contradictory of the claim to apostleship than for conduct to be incommensurate with profession."[43] Paul was therefore careful to add that his ministry done with patience and perseverance, essential qualities of an apostle for a Christian mission. These signs, which were wrought through his agency, were to characterize the ministry of an apostle but were not by themselves sufficient to justify any claim of apostleship. Therefore the phrase, "the things that mark an apostle" did not refer to any apostle who performs miracles, but to Paul's distinctive and unique calling as an apostle, of which these signs were visible proof.[44]

Paul treated neither the Corinthians as inferior nor, worse yet, any of the churches founded by the twelve apostles. The only thing Paul did not do in Corinth was to burden them with missionary support. As an apostle, the only sign he did not exhibit was to receive support from them. For this reason, Paul asked their pardon because of the negative feelings the Corinthians suffered due to his refusal to accept assistance from them.

41. Robertson, *Word Pictures*, 258.

42. Bernard, *2 Corinthians*, 101.

43. Ibid., 456.

44. Barnett, *The Message of 2 Corinthians*, 167.

Principles for Theological Institutions

According to Apostle Paul, tentmaking is not an inferior alternative to traditional missionary activity but a valid biblically authenticated option, an important evangelistic spearhead and effective means of reaching our world. The tentmaking strategy makes it possible to influence areas in society usually not touched by missionary endeavors. This strategy adds a whole new force to the Christian movement and has the potential to transform the financial landscape of theological education in Africa.[45] Tentmaking dislodges the notion of dependence on donations alone and helps believers to think of creative ways to raise support with the intention to advance the cause of developing Christian leaders.

When it comes to tentmaking we are often torn between applying biblical principles versus following denominational or an organization's policies. As good as these policies are, we have to subject them to biblical scrutiny, especially if they contradict basic biblical principles. The Scriptures make it emphatically clear that Christian ministries can depend on donations and tentmaking endeavors, when necessary to fulfill the mandate of the ministry. There are several principles that theological institutions can draw upon from Paul's tentmaking example to overcome challenges and achieve financial sustainability.

Paul wanted to contrast himself with the philosophers, teachers and lecturers of his time who minimized the Gospel to a commodity to be sold rather than freely shared. Such teachers distorted the Word of God, enslaving those to whom they peddled the message. Today, there is danger that theological institutions might too closely resemble those false teachers of long ago due to misunderstandings regarding fundraising activities. It is true that professional fundraising organizations have devised all kinds of ways to raise money and some of these strategies have been accepted in the mainstream. However, institutional leaders can become susceptible to these unethical schemes, whether intentionally or inadvertently.

Upon closer inspection some potential strategies could actually be schemes to peddle a distorted Gospel. For instance, past deceptive methods have ranged from auctioning biblical relics, to all kinds of raffles and finally offering special blessings for specific donation thresholds. Therefore, institutions need to be cautious about similar fundraising efforts. Otherwise, when scholar-administrators rise in rank to serve on governing boards of these institutions, they risk the danger of introducing questionable fundraising

---

45. Ibid., 10.

methods. Without cautious deliberation, leadership could easily fall into the trap that teachers and philosophers of Paul's era encountered.

Similarly, institutions must strive to refrain from any form of forced commitments that result in enslavement instead of liberal, joyful giving. It is imperative that institutions distinguish themselves from these practices, to instead apply skills and talents that generate income for the school. There are many income generating projects that could allow institutions to utilize their gifts toward the betterment of their ministry. An income generating project is important but more importantly is the manner in which the project is initiated and effectively managed. The process of generating this income is as critical as the income itself. Hence, there is no better way to demonstrate good business practices as a believer than through such an endeavor.

Actually, pursuing tentmaking options in addition to donations will distinguish theological institutions from other organizations. Christian institutions are in the world but not of the world as Jesus rightly declared and therefore must make every effort to avoid the perception of taking undue advantage of the body of Christ. Otherwise, the integration of fundraising with operations presents an opportunity for institutions to influence society. Through faith demonstrated on a daily basis, theological institutions can interact with donors as disciples learning stewardship. Tentmaking can even help institutions make significant contributions towards the building of their host countries. All in all, everything done for the Lord must be done in a manner consistent with biblical principles.

Apostle Paul worked to combat the attitude of idleness prevailing among the Jews and Gentiles in the context of their Greco-Roman society. Tentmaking depicted the importance of work versus idleness, a tendency prevalent in many parts of the body of Christ at the time. Idleness can come in many forms and shapes even within institutions. There are many ways theological institutions could be productive in the training of leaders. Yet, once they abandon opportunities to generate more funding through tentmaking, there is a chance the objective may embrace what needs to be done without adequate efforts to generate the necessary resources.

Paul distinguished himself as a peculiar apostle whose very life and ministry challenged his converts through his faithful example. He therefore set an example of diligence and hard work to be self-supportive, a virtue that is required of all believers today. By pursuing tentmaking activities, theological institutions set an example showing that roles outside of Sunday church service are legitimate efforts to serve the Lord.

Sometimes people give up what could be great tools and talents in order to pursue theological training. However, professionals and others with expert skills could more often effectively interact with unbelievers using those specific skills and knowledge than not. Students training to serve in the church, para-church organizations and society get opportunities to interact with people at the marketplace through effective projects because they are able to relate their work experience to ministry. Many have a wrong notion that serving in the church or other Christian circles is easier than serving in a competitive marketplace. Unfortunately such people are unable to effectively do their schoolwork when they become students in theological institutions.

Initiatives for generating income should not only focus on profit but also instill in students who work on such projects, a sound biblical work ethic. It must be impressed upon students that neglect of one's duties is not acceptable. Staff, faculty and students of theological institutions must be spurred to strive to accomplish good works. Indeed, there is room for the inexperienced and timid who need encouragement to change long-held values. Such an endeavor requires patience, but must nonetheless ensure that everyone who calls on the Lord departs from idleness to embrace hard work as demonstrated by Apostle Paul through his ministry example.

Institutions must learn to rely on other sources of income besides donations, if they are going to be financially sustainable. In this way, donations can maximize institutional capacity as tentmaking activities complement general fundraising. This ensures that institutions do not depend on one source for their income, and ill-advisedly resort to diverse kinds of manipulations to please the source. Sometimes going to the same sources year-in and year-out risks donor fatigue and opens the door for all kinds of tricks and games for both parties. Paul worked so that he would not be a burden in any way. Due to his hard work, he was able to share the Gospel free of charge. Tentmaking reduces pressure on donors to meet specific thresholds and improves the relationship between institutions and their sponsors. It is therefore not an either/or situation, but a collaboration.

Paul beautifully demonstrated the importance of cultivating other sources of revenue; although, his reason for working may have been slightly different from ours. On the other hand, what would Paul have done if he did not have the skills and competence for tentmaking? He probably would have practiced law to earn a living because he was an accomplished lawyer. God in his wisdom has endowed every institution with gifts and abilities that can be translated into tentmaking activities, and it does not matter whether abilities are in a profession like law, or a vocation, like an artisan working manually to build tents.

Tentmaking requires planners to have many skills to effectively respond to business culture, social landscapes, and political systems. The times and seasons call for different responses and individuals and institutions must discern the time and seasons so that they know how to apply their gifts, abilities and skills as they serve the Lord. Institutions must respond to various options God might reveal to generate revenue for his work. He cares about his work and does provide for it.

Often times we are entangled and blinded by organizational and denominational policies that cause us to fail to see opportunities God reveals to reduce financial stress and strain. Paul was sensitive to receiving support from the churches that supported him. Although he knew that by supporting him a ministry partnership was enhanced, he was careful not to be a burden. Theological institutions must develop the same sensitivity in their partnership with sponsors so donations can be secured when absolutely necessary. So, other means of funding such as tentmaking are explored to supplement donations.

This sensitivity translates into responsible interdependence that is healthy and praiseworthy. As sponsorship grows, respect and trust for partners can also strengthen. In a responsible interdependent relationship, donors are blessed as they give, and recipients are able to fulfill the divine mandate to train men and women for church and society. Lack of sensitivity can significantly hinder the work of God as sponsors might feel tempted to break relationships causing the work of a ministry to suffer. This Paul described as being a burden to the donors, which should not be.

It is normal that tentmaking will ruffle feathers among leaders on governing boards, in theological institutions, mission agencies or denominations who initiated the legacy of an institution. Paul encountered misunderstandings to the extent that his apostolic status was challenged because he was involved in tentmaking. His detractors failed to see how his life and actions advanced the Gospel of Jesus Christ. Instead, they were fixated on customs, traditions and personal expectations of the role of an apostle. Paul did not fit any of these preconceived definitions. Rather, he broke with conventional practices that wealthy patrons came to expect in their relationship with visiting lecturers. Consequently, Paul paid a high price for being a maverick in this regard.

Likewise, theological institutions must dare to move into new territories and step into untested waters in their efforts to be involved in tentmaking. Of course, as such efforts flourish, there is a great chance that institutions will break with tradition by setting off on new roads. Like Paul, schools must be resolute in their planning to ensure that their actions are supported by sound biblical and legal principles.

The perceived impact of guilt resulting from unconventional initiatives has paralyzed many institutions, as they were unable to take the bold steps needed for tentmaking activities. The Corinthians heaped guilt on Paul and found it difficult to forgive him for his tentmaking activities when he visited them. Yet, the prestige and honor they lauded on him did not influence the manner in which he ministered to them. However, the conflict arising from his independence influenced the ire of his audiences for which he apologized. They forgot that the very act they despised made Paul effective among them, because he was able to rebuke the evil ways of the Corinthians and correct their acts of shame. He showed no favor and had no fear that his rebuke would hurt ministry support from them. In the same way, as institutions pursue tentmaking, they will grow as they have the flexibility to refuse certain gifts that might distract them from the core mission.

Schools will become more judicious in their selection of projects and programs if their voice is strengthened in partnership with sponsors. Institutions will be challenged to live through the dynamic tension of fundraising for the ministry if tentmaking is emphasized at the same time. Paul still had to accept gifts from the Macedonian church while at Corinth but he worked at the same time, making this arrangement possible. Though he drew charges of inconsistency, Paul defended his right to ask for missionary support while also working toward a viable means to fulfill the Great Commission. African theological institutions should not aim for anything less.

It is the dynamic tension and supposed inconsistencies that generate growth and development, predisposing an institution to learn and depend upon God as the ultimate source of all provisions. God has divine grace to provide from the mouth of a fish or through the support of those who control the least resources in a society. The most critical lesson is that we understand the principles at play and are able to apply them to our situation. However, this is not enough, because we must be able to defend our actions based on the Scriptures, while seeking the grace and humility to listen to correction when required.

PART THREE

Toward Financial Sustainability
of Theological Institutions

Chapter 6

Church Ownership and Institutional Governance

HISTORICALLY, THE CHURCH IN Africa was established without any explicit plan to train leaders to shepherd the flock. Many African church leaders merely had apprenticeship training from missionary leaders affiliated with specific denominations. Formal theological education as we know it today happened several years after the establishment of the church.

The position of the church regarding theological institutions had been that the schools existed exclusively to train leaders to meet the needs of the church. Consequently, the role of the church in theological education would be limited to specifically sending pastors—not lay leadership, to seminaries or Bible colleges for training. This had been the situation for decades and not much has changed in recent years. Therefore, theological education became an appendage instead of an integral part of church life.

Ironically, if leaders wanted to return to school they found that they could not because basic entry requirements were too difficult. Instead of a supportive warm embrace from the church, the relationship became increasingly antagonistic. Institutions were not only considered special projects of missionaries, but the schools were also regarded as ivory towers for elitist young men who had lost touch with the realities of ministry. The role of theological reflection as a form of worship was distorted to mere intellectualizing, not worship. Many considered theological institutions to be a place where people developed doubts about God, about church traditions, and even about their own spirituality. Eventually, they feared losing faith in God and abandoning ministry entirely.

The involvement of missionaries in emerging education training programs was misunderstood, as well. Consequently, theological education was
perceived as the special project of missionaries who handed over leadership
of the church to their local counterparts and ultimately found institutions a
good place to continue serving the church by training leaders. The fact that
early leadership in local churches did not have the same educational opportunities that institutions were providing gave them little or no motivation to
appreciate theological education.

Although institutions were legally owned by denominations because
they were established by affiliated missionaries, local leaders did not share
the philosophy of training adopted by theological institutions. So, these
institutions often felt semi-detached from the central power seat of a denomination. As much as local leaders were proud to be associated with the
institutions, they did not in essence own the institutions. Hence, the operation of the schools was left to boards and sponsoring mission agencies.

The evolving circumstances among institutions started by non-
denominational mission agencies was not much better. This was because
non-denominational theological institutions in Africa began as independent organizations. Contrarily, denominational institutions are closed to
academicians and leaders outside the specific associated denominations,
which facilitates inbreeding through the representation of one theological
tradition.

On the other hand, non-denominational institutions were meant
to draw students from different doctrinal backgrounds, denominational
persuasions, and academic disciplines. Therefore, theological institutions
became attractive because of the dynamic collegial environments they provided for academics and ministry. Such non-denominational campuses also
host eclectic faculty who provide varying view points on theological arguments and church dogma.

Unfortunately, institutions started by non-denominational agencies
struggle for identity and often have great difficulty securing any form of
recognition from the church. The future of these theological institutions
after the departure of their founding missionary leaders, as we shall later
discuss, is always bleak in so many respects. Unfortunately, as the old adage
suggests, "Everybody's business is nobody's business." No particular church
or denomination actually owns these institutions.

Certainly, theologians are important stakeholders who work with
ideas and analytical tools that are exclusive to the discipline, like any other
professional field. Donald Luck noted, "As remote and comical as fussing
with ideas may seem, ideas are real and are very important. They change the
world. In other words, even by pragmatic standards, ideas are real because

they have practical consequences."[1] Theologians expect the church—more than any other constituency—to be most sympathetic with lofty ideas and social causes. Instead, the result has been alienation. This slow but gradual drift between the academics and church leadership over the years has seen every effort for church ownership dwindle.

Aloof theologians are often not the kind of people with whom society easily associates. Theologians seem to spend considerable amounts of time analyzing the past but seldom make recommendations for the present. Their preoccupation with the future is always in doubt except when discussing signs of the end times and God's divine judgment. They are perceived as scholars who take pride in challenging, questioning, and raising doubts about the activities of the church. They often come across as more arrogant than concerned about the simple biblical traditions of the past. This seeming arrogance and spiritual pride of theologians is an affront to church leadership, resulting in the church's withdrawal of interest in whatever goes on in theological institutions.

Regardless, the church is a major stakeholder in theological education. Therefore, ownership of the institution is worthy of consideration if these campuses are to experience sustainability—particularly financial sustainability. Yet, theological institutions desire independence from the church with regards to major decisions. This has further aggravated an already sour relationship. The OCI survey indicated that church leaders are not among the top three agents of change in theological education in Africa. On the contrary, they represent the top three obstacles to change in the institutions. The prevailing emphasis should be to explore various ways to work with, instead of against each other.

WHY CHURCH OWNERSHIP IS VITAL

Theological institutions exist not only to train leaders in ways to serve the church but to serve the whole of humanity. Institutions exist to reveal the saving and sustaining power of Jesus Christ to everyone in the community of faith and to society at large. This is also the primary responsibility of the Church and in Africa she works with numerous initiatives and programs to accomplish this goal. Theological institutions must exist with, within, and for the church in order to demonstrate ownership affiliation between the two parties.

Theological institutions can exist with the church as an extension of the work of the church to strengthen leadership capacity within its ranks and to

1. Luck, *Why Study Theology?*, 28.

deliver its core mandate to help people outside the church understand the church's mission. The institution should come alongside the church as an advisor to advance the cause of the church and equip the church's leadership to answer perplexing questions that emerge from the community of faith.

Currently, there are varying issues and debate in many African countries where the voice of the church is mute. When the debate on curbing the spread of HIV/AIDS started in Africa, the front stage was manned by foreign sponsored interest groups and other faiths. The Christian church and theological institutions were silent until the use of condoms was declared the best option to control the spread of the disease. Suddenly, the church awoke to take a stand and opposed condom use as a weak compromise among many viable alternatives.

The church then started preaching abstinence and condemning condom use among the unmarried, a position that was unfortunately late in the discussion and repugnant to the non-believing secular public. The church was accused of being the proverbial ostrich, burying its head in the sand when people were dying of HIV/AIDS, and that her position was not tenable. In such a situation, theological institutions could have quickly equipped the church with the strongest argument possible and facilitated the church's discussion to establish the way forward instead of coming to the party late and reacting to the resolutions and decisions that had already been made. Pushing theological education to the center grants the church a legitimate right to utilize the voice of the institutions in a language that is appropriate and in areas where such voices are readily impactful.

It is ironic that theologians go to church but are often found at the periphery of African church activities. Rather, the idea of theological institutions being within the church means that an institution must be at the center of the church's missional engagement. They must feel the heartbeat of the church, participate in its core activities and provide resources the church needs to function effectively. Leaders of institutions must also be leaders of the church, at least as associates, serving as pastors, elders, deacons, deaconesses, heads of church departments, on boards, committees, and in other positions the church may have. In this way, theological institutions can deliberately immerse themselves in daily ministry opportunities and challenges faced by the church. As insiders, institutions would be able to identify challenges to ministry that the church is not addressing. Institutional leaders could be available to make informed decisions on curriculum review that has direct implications on ministry activities in the church and consequently society.

Once in a while, theologians will lead an initiative in the church, teach or preach but overall, do not wield the kind of influence that should be expected of biblical scholars. Sometimes, speakers in the pulpit make reference to them when they are unsure about a particular area in theology; however, there is more to theological leadership from the academy than mere occasional points of reference. There are needs in the church that must be addressed through the design of creative Bible-based programs.

Leaders in theological institutions should be able to design informal programs with limited formal content to address immediate challenges on the ground without having to go through the red tape of official recognition and certification. This kind of initiative could enhance existing ministry activities, minimize the impediments and improve services to congregants. The interaction of the academy with the church as an insider reduces the academic power distance between church leadership and theologians that has existed for decades. Leaders are able to serve the Lord as brothers and sisters to achieve the overall goals of the church without any fear or intimidation. There is a greater acceptance of ideas, concepts, and guidance from church leaders when theological institutions play this important role as insiders.

The phrase "theological institutions for the church" refers to institutions existing to fulfill a mission and vision in partnership. Selfish pursuit of the vision and mission of theological institutions apart from the church is a dangerous road to irrelevance and eventual extinction. The mission of the church makes theological institutions relevant. Otherwise, what is the use of a theological institution if it is unable to meet the fundamental leadership needs of the church? The basic rationale for the existence of theological institutions is to facilitate the fulfillment of the great commission through various programs and activities, primarily sponsored by the church.

It is notable that the mandate of theological education is beyond the preparation of men and women to serve in the church. However, if the fundamental reason for the establishment of theological institutions is compromised, it throws the entire existence of the institution into question. Theological institutions for the church is a symbiotic relationship whereby the institutions are closely connected to the church in a manner that ensures the church can depend on institutions to help solve difficult questions. In return, institutions can enjoy encouragement and financial support from the church.

The church needs to engage theological institutions not only on how they train leaders, but with challenging questions to initiate dynamic debates and resolutions that the church can implement in her effort to disciple the world. This is a unique avenue for growth and influence that the church in Africa cannot afford to lose. The identity of theological institutions has to be inextricably tied to that of the church in such a way that the consciousness of the church is apparent in all of an institution's major decisions and direction. Hence, this is how the theological institution becomes a strategic partner of the church. Institutions are able to share their struggles and successes with the church in a manner that allows the church to respond strongly and yet appropriately. This healthy interdependence is necessary if theological institutions are to strengthen their ability to serve the church.

As for theological institutions being with, within, and for the church, such relationships from the institution's standpoint must shape and define dynamic engagement with the church. These relationships must keep an institution on its toes to ensure that its rightful place in the deliberations of the church is duly explored and optimally utilized. Theological institutions can function alongside church because they become the source of encouragement and a sounding board for innovation and development.

The institution functioning within a church can be the life-giving spring that provides insight into difficult doctrinal dilemmas that perpetually confront church and society. The institution strengthens the voice of the church during societal transformation and commands respect attributive to the elucidating power of the academy. The institution and the church can lock arms together to redefine purpose and procedures of the institution to best serve the church. We cannot over-emphasize the continual interaction theological institutions must have with theological institutions to inform revisions of curricula based on changing needs. Theological institutions must be involved in the community and must seek interaction in a manner that brings credibility to the process of education. This is not to neglect the clerical paradigm but rather to establish a wider engagement with society that is based on a much stronger and enduring framework of the church.

The church is a community and microcosm of society—and the stronger a voice it has through theological education, the greater the impact it will make. Church ownership is not an effort to disengage with society and the wider community but rather involvement that provides moral accountability and a platform for the institution. The need for ownership does not depend on what the institution can and should be doing for the church. Instead, it should be a mutually supportive partnership with the theological institution.

WHAT DOES CHURCH OWNERSHIP MEAN?

The discussion on ownership can take different forms and directions depending on the church and institutions involved. However, there are basic thresholds that must be reached for a mutually supportive relationship to be established. There are two important components that speak directly to this subject: accountability and responsiveness.

The impact of accountability as a virtue in society has been minimized due to the widespread emphasis on relativism and political correctness. This issue of accountability has polarized society and blurred social lines of responsibility. Yet, everyone is responsible for their actions. Unfortunately, what is considered to be wrong or right are not perceived as social absolutes per se. The church cannot afford to adopt this position in its relationship with theological institutions. Churches must establish theological institutions to train their leaders for the work of the ministry. At the same time, while treading with caution, I must say that this premise must not restrict institutions to exclusive functions.

The church should claim ownership of an institution in its entirety even from as far back as inception when missionaries provided leadership. The whole idea that an institution is a project of the missionary is not now tenable because the same can be said of the church. Therefore this is not a valid reason to continue the distance between church and institutions. Theological institutions are accountable to the churches that birthed them. This is most apparent when the church assumes its leadership role and demands accountability. It is very difficult to require accountability from others when one has failed to be accountable in matters regarding its own processes and procedures.

The church in Africa must first make herself accountable to structures and systems that she has put in place. Then require accountability from its strategic partners, including theological institutions. However, this will require time and personnel to understand what it really takes to operate a theological institution and the church's role in that process. Certainly, this kind of effort should involve the church's participation in creating standards and procedures for accountability. This leads to the governance structure and its relationship with the church's leadership. Institutional governance as a means of financial sustainability will be discussed later in this book. However, the church cannot claim ownership of theological institutions unless it is accountable for them. Accountability is fundamental and crucial to ownership of African theological institutions.

Responsiveness

The essence of responsiveness undergirds any responsible relationship. It is reciprocal, enhancing mutual benefits for all parties involved in a particular relationship. However, having discussed the responsibility of theological institutions to the church in the early part of this chapter, I will now focus on the responsiveness of the church.

The church in Africa has a responsive role to care for theological institutions in the same way it cares for its other programs. The church draws its leadership from theological institutions with the exception of some emerging independent churches. Among leadership from independent churches, many serve without theological education and are pastoring megachurches, which they have planted. The neglect of theological education by these churches demonstrates neglect of its own leadership and subsequently the organization's health. It is self-defeating to ignore the crucible that shapes the hearts and minds of leadership while still attempting to accomplish organizational goals. Tragically, such is the situation of theological institutions founded by the church in Africa.

Responsiveness also denotes the church's willingness to meet some of the needs of its institutions, especially financial needs. The church in any part of the world is the most sustainable institution—particularly in Africa where its growth rate outpaces that of the population. Financial support of theological institutions from the church has been minimal over the decades and this has partly contributed to the financial crises the institutions constantly face on the continent. For denominational institutions, lack of financial support from the church is an apparent neglect of its primary duties.

This is not to say the church must bear all the expenses of an institution. Rather, it must provide support that is significant enough to justify a clear indication of her responsiveness. With such responsiveness comes an accountability that undergirds the ownership of the institutions. True ownership is about responsibility and responsiveness to financial support of theological institutions. Mission agencies and missionaries have done their part and it is about time the church rose to a responsive position to financially support the operations of its institutions.

Furthermore, responsiveness that demonstrates financial commitment gives the church a legitimate voice when engaging institutions regarding problem solving. There are countless human resources within the church whose commitment to the church can be extended to the institutions to provide expertise necessary for solving myriad problems. This kind of responsiveness makes the church a powerful advocate and marketer of its institutions to attract more students to enroll in its programs. The church becomes one of the center pieces because it creates opportunities by identifying needs in the community for institutions to develop solutions.

STEPS TO STRENGTHENING CHURCH OWNERSHIP

The church in Africa cannot leave the institutions alone and expect them to provide quality leaders for the church. It is not a scenario in which to produce effective leaders who are adept and can respond to current challenges the church is facing. The following are some of the ways institutions can facilitate church ownership:

1. Institutional leaders (administrators and faculty) must participate in local church leadership positions to actively serve the church. This provides opportunity for the local church to experience the benefits of theological education.

2. Institutional leaders must explore ways to serve the larger body of Christ at the national and continental level through teaching, preaching, and facilitating conferences, workshops, and seminars. This provides a platform for an institution to market its programs and products.

3. Institutional leaders must provide training solutions for specific endemic challenges that local denominations as well as the national church and para-church organizations are grappling with. This posits the academy as a caring organization in tune with its constituencies and willing to serve in the trenches.

4. Institutional leaders must invite influential church leaders to serve on governing boards, as well as other special task forces (e.g., fundraising and building committees). This creates avenues for the church to speak directly to issues in the institution and fosters stronger ownership.

5. Institutional leaders should volunteer themselves to be the spokespersons of the local and national church on difficult theological matters in public forums. This demonstrates support for the church as the academy locks hands with church leaders on common theological matters. The church can then celebrate the institution as a strategic partner whose vision and mission must be perpetuated.

6. Institutional leaders must utilize the gifts and abilities among church leadership and the wider Church of Christ to enrich learning and development of students by inviting these resource persons into the academy to teach, preach, and train on various issues pertinent to the organization's mission. Then later send students to the local and national church to volunteer as academic interns. This ensures that the academy is not the preserve of a few theological elitists but a community of learners seeking to advance the kingdom of God.

7. Institutional leaders must boldly but humbly solicit financial and in-kind assistance from the local and wider church from time to time as a means of enforcing accountability and responsiveness to the institution. This will continually present the support of the institution as an important budgetary item in church operations.

Characteristically, this feedback provides the impetus for institutions to continuously review their programs and align them to the ever changing needs of church and society.

GOVERNANCE AND THEOLOGICAL INSTITUTIONS IN AFRICA

Governance is the art of collective stewardship exercised to achieve common goals of the institution. Collective stewardship denotes a vested trust that demands accountability from all parties involved in the governing process. Fundamentally, it manages internal and external threats and opportunities to the advantage of the institution. The vested trust in this case is the mission of the institution. Church ownership of theological institutions automatically demands involvement in the governance of institutions.

What is Governance in Institutions?

Successful delivery of the vested trust is the responsibility of parties involved. This group is often referred to as the governing board. Aleshire identifies governance as "the process by which a theological school makes the decisions that identify and renew the school's mission, implements the mission and assesses the degree to which and the way in which it is being attained."[2] Aleshire's emphasis on the mission from its identification, to the degree it is attained is critical because God is the originator of the mission and therefore a governing board must apply due diligence in understanding that commission. Consequently, the governing board is primarily accountable to God and then to the institution's stakeholders. As much as the strategies for implementation of the organization's mission are open to the governing board, the comprehensive attainment of the mission is non-negotiable.

Eurydice identified institutional governance as "the formal and informal exercise of authority under laws, policies and rules that articulate the rights and responsibilities of various actors, including the rules by which

2. Aleshire, *Earthen Vessels*, 96.

they interact."[3] This defines the terms of reference under which a governing board functions and outlines not only the collective responsibility but
also the guidelines by which parties in the governing board should interact.
Aleshire's outline of authority, structure, and process of governance in a
theological school does not only emphasize the governing board's functions
but also the purpose for which it exists. A governing board has formal authority to make decisions that impact the policies of the institution. It wields
the collective stewardship of courage and foresight to engage in activities
that advance both an institutional mission and vision.

The ownership of theological institutions and governance are identical
functions that ensure the perpetual fulfilment of the institution's mission.
Unfortunately, over the years, church involvement in the governance of
theological institutions has dwindled as institutions have grown and their
operations have become more complex. Similarly, there is an apparent drift
by theological institutions away from involvement with church governance.
Hence, the institutions are often governed by well-meaning leaders with
little insight into how the church functions. Or, there is very little input if
any from church leadership.

Governance is crucial to the financial sustainability of theological institutions in Africa. Yet, many theological institutions do not have the kind
of governing boards that represent the main actors of its mission or who
have the ability to steer the institutions from crisis. This, to a great extent
speaks to how governing boards are often constituted, with little knowledge
of ways to empower other members or management toward effective and
efficient operation of the institution.

THE CONSTITUTION OF INSTITUTIONAL BOARDS

The constitution of boards in theological institutions in Africa follows various patterns. Some were clearly planned and systematic, while others were
haphazard and misaligned with the needs of their institutions. John Carver
identified various forms of boards such as governing, advisory, line, and
workgroup boards. He also distinguished between "for-profit, nonprofit,
and governmental boards" in his discussion of the economic nature of a
board.[4] Aleshire narrowed down the discussion to four typical practices
among North American theological schools:

3. Figel, ed., *Higher Education Governance*, 12.
4. Carver, *Boards That Make a Difference*, 2–5.

1. Governing boards of a free-standing school that have full power and authority to make decisions related to the school. Board members are elected by sponsoring denominations by the board itself or by some combination of both and once elected they have full authority to govern the school.

2. A bishop or religious order that legally owns the school but appoints a board. This board is advisory and has decision-making power in designated areas.

3. An integrated theological school in a college or university as a department governed through the administrative structures of the larger institution's board. In this case, the board of the school has little power regarding the finances, program, legal issues, or human resources.

4. Dual system in which one outside consulting group exercises full authority to manage fiscal, property, and corporate business issues. While another body (usually faculty) has full responsibility to administer curriculum and academic programs.[5]

Although these models are gleaned from North American institutions, they are not very different from structures in many theological institutions in Africa. Different nomenclature may describe the African schools but the organizations are inherently the same since many of these institutions were established by mission agencies and denominations from North America and Europe. Many theological institutions in Africa fall within the first three models, although a majority tends to operate as governing boards of free-standing schools.

Whatever model a theological institution adopts, the role of the church in that governing board needs to be evident to ensure responsible ownership by the church. Unlike other college boards, an institutional board needs members who are alumni and have experience in ministry positions. Those who are not ministers are able to provide significant insight optimally guiding institutions to accomplish goals under a strong sense of ownership.

In general, board membership should include pastors, theological educators, accountants, business people, lawyers, civil servants, and professionals from other disciplines. Of course, this requirement can make finding governing board members much more difficult as one balances those who must have internal working knowledge of the institution against those who have no such specific knowledge. There is also the balance of connectedness between alumni members who care deeply about the institution contrasting with those who have no history with the institution. As Jim Collins indicates

---

5. Aleshire, *Earthen Vessels*, 105.

in his book *Good to Great*, to have the right people on the bus and in the right seats is half the battle.[6] In reality, this is critical to the successful delivery of an institution's goals.

There is no fixed formula for institutions as to the best process for recruiting and vetting members to serve on a governing board. Rather, every institution has the responsibility to identify its current challenges and future needs in order to recruit the caliber of people who will facilitate the achievement of those goals.

John Leith outlined four basic minimum qualifications that members of a theological governing board should meet to serve effectively. Although these are not exhaustive, they provide a starting point from which institutions can expand their requirements for board recruitment. The basic qualifications include the following:

1. Personal faith and commitment to Jesus Christ as Lord and Savior plus a commitment to the task of the seminary to educate pastors to preach the Gospel;

2. Documented resume or curriculum vitae offering examples of effective work in a local congregation as a member or as a minister;

3. Maturity of judgment and lifestyle;

4. Verified documented administrative experience making the kinds of serious judgments that seminary boards are required to make and an ability to anticipate the consequences of these decisions.[7]

5. Most of the time, leaders are chosen to serve on governing boards without prior verification of their faith, ministry experience, or ability to function as high capacity decision-makers. Leaders join a board and are hastily saddled with responsibilities and a level of decision-making that they have never encountered in their previous leadership positions. This is very dangerous to a theological institution because of the high risk of fiscal and operational mismanagement.

The due diligence required to ensure that the right people occupy the right seats is important to the mission of an institution. It therefore behooves primary sponsors of the institution, whether a church or mission agency, to work together with institutional leadership to recruit a governing board. On many occasions churches and mission agencies selected board members who neither had the skills nor a commitment to advance the goals of an institution.

6. Collins, *Good to Great*, 41.
7. Leith, *Crisis in the Church*, 94.

Such a style of recruitment by the church or a mission agency is retrogressive and holds captive the efforts of other well-meaning and skilled personnel on the board. Many professionals who commit to serving on these boards often feel frustrated and confused about their role after time. Their ability to critically examine issues and offer creative suggestions that can facilitate the achievement of an organization's mission is reduced to rubber stamping the whims of a few representatives from church or a mission agency.

It is understandable that theological institutions are not businesses and their organizational operation could differ from those of a business organization. However, after many abortive attempts to lead change, professionals may lose the motivation to serve on an assigned board. The effect is often lackadaisical appearances at board meetings or a pattern of excessive absences. A lot of effort is needed to educate professionals on the mission of an institution. The patience, grace, and perseverance required from professionals to serve on a theological governing board is a gradual adjustment to the nature of the organization's business. Like a friend of mine once said, "Theological education is a messy business."

Theological schools are primarily church institutions, and for many churches and mission agencies, ownership only means having more representation on the board, or having the sole prerogative of deciding who serves on the board with or without any collaboration from the institution's management. Such displays of power are a sure catalyst for the drift of theological institutions from their parent organizations. There is an urgent need to strengthen the trust relations between management of a school and the primary sponsoring agency. This is so collaboration prioritizes the interests of the institution far above other secondary considerations.

The process of selecting a governing board must involve input from primary sponsors, management, and current board members so that those who are selected receive a warm reception and smooth integration into the operation of the board. Similarly, composing an exit plan for board members is equally important so that members do not stay longer than necessary. Many governing boards limit terms to three or four years of continuous service, with an option for renewal for another term. After terms expire, old members exit and new members must be recruited. This ensures that the skills and ability of members are utilized to the fullest and at the same time room is created for the injection of new ideas and insight.

Sometimes, board chairs serve one particular institution longer than necessary either because they are very good leaders or have not trained anyone to succeed them. Likewise, there are situations where remaining board members do not want to assume the added responsibility of the chair because of the enormity of time commitments and responsibilities. Therefore, members of governing boards should not only be recruited to serve but must also be trained during their tenure as board members. Training through workshops, seminars, conferences, and retreats can also build strong relationships among members and facilitate greater understanding and appreciation for the core function of their theological institution.

Leaders must be trained to embrace succession as a function of their role, so that at any given time there is a pool of candidates ready to take the reins of board leadership. Sometimes, institutions are tempted to keep good board members beyond their tenure because they have demonstrated wisdom and deep insights in their leadership, or have been generous in financially supporting the institution. Instead, members should honorably exit a board at the end of their tenure, while also being given other responsibilities to extend continuity of their participation in areas where they are most gifted. Service on a board committee, as an adviser or coach to leadership or on special task forces, even as alumni hall of famers, and lifelong members of an institution can accomplish continuity.[8]

There are many resources available to develop boards in fulfilling basic functions. However, every board must have a board policy manual (BPM) outlining the specific functions of its operations. A BPM should outline how members should interact with each other, as noted by Eurydice. These guidelines will forestall any possibilities of having rogue members take advantage of an institution for personal gain or social aggrandizement. Frank Laughlin's book, *Good Governance for Nonprofits* (2007) provides a fine template for BPM documents and can save an institution many hours of work.

Governing boards depend on management to make informed decisions on operations. However, if the information is skewed, then the effectiveness of the board can be greatly undermined. Management must take the trust vested in them seriously to provide a true and honest picture of the institution so that the governing board can make appropriate policy decisions to ensure success. There is always a fine line between how far a governing board should go to verify information received versus interfering with management's areas of responsibility. The two parties must operate in trust. Specifically, board chairs must develop a good relationship with institutional leaders so that confidential organizational issues are not inappropriately aired publically, but instead shared informally. In that way, the board gets details of the condition of the institution outside the board room, which allows the chair to wisely take appropriate action.

---

8. Andringa, "Governance and Board Relations," 1.

There is nothing as frustrating for leaders of theological institutions as an apathetic board that lacks the initiative and commitment to provide leadership and support for management. Whether a governing board remains apathetic, active or dormant can all be traced to the recruitment process, the board manual, functions, structures and deliverables. Sponsors of theological institutions will achieve more through the institution if they are willing to balance listening with imposing their views on stakeholders—including recruits and assistants—even if they feel uneasy or threatened by critiques and suggestions.

Church ownership and institutional governance are fundamental to the financial sustainability of a theological institution. When churches demonstrate a true sense of ownership, they hold theological institutions accountable to their mission and vision, and ensure that the primary needs of the church for effective leadership are met through graduates of the institution. Ownership and accountability keep the church abreast of internal needs and the needs of its theological institution—holding the two in tandem.

Church accountability requires active participation in the governing board to continuously educate board members on the relationship between institutional mandates and the needs of the church. Ownership through responsiveness requires that the church explores various ways of supporting a theological institution including regularly collected donations. Similarly, theological institutions must be diligent in responding to calls from the church for expert biblical and theological responses in establishing the church's stand on contemporary matters. Institutions must be willing to see themselves as the think tank and voice of the church on controversial issues confronting society.

Reciprocal engagement enhances an institution's status, and makes it attractive to potential donors in the church to finally commit to financially support the institution. This support is necessary in contributing to the institution's overall drive for financial sustainability as enrollment increases and local commitment to giving grows steadily. The task of the governing board is to ensure that an institution remains financially sustainable through whatever means it deems reasonable without compromising faith and institutional core values. The collective stewardship of the board for financial sustainability can reinforce the concept of ownership in a far reaching manner.

TOWARD EFFECTIVE GOVERNANCE

The ability of governing boards to ensure financial sustainability is dependent upon how effective they have been in their primary functions. Often, much time and energy is expended on the constitution and duties of the governing board without much consideration for effectiveness in performing functions. Aside from the fact that very few governing boards in theological institutions are properly constituted, very few receive adequate orientation at the inception of the terms of service. Often continuing education opportunities are not provided during a board member's tenure. Currently, I do not know of any organized activities geared toward the training of non-profit boards nor those of theological institutions.

Overseas Council International is the only agency that has made strides to train board members through their annual conferences. However, due to the numerous concerns they have to address regarding theological education, the focus on boards does not occur as frequently as they would like. Inasmuch as institutional leaders have a responsibility to ensure that their boards receive the training they need, daily challenges often relegate training to a lower set of organizational priorities. Some are contending with repeated inquiries for the very governing boards selected to support them but are pushed to answer the "whys" of their financial problems.

There is little or no effort from governing boards to pursue the kind of training that would make them more effective in discharging their duties. Jason Ferenczi noted that true governance must go broader and deeper to draw from multiple voices to accomplish the vision and mission of an institution. Ferenczi indicated, "[A] board itself is clearly the critical final authority in governance processes. Yet, the overall work of governance stretches beyond the boardroom and into the fabric of the institution as a whole, drawing on insights, talents, and abilities of the CEO, management, staff, faculty, as well as the board."[9]

The governing board, therefore has a primary responsibility to harness all the resources available to accomplish its tasks, if it is going to be effective. This is an approach Ferenczi theorized as the "concert of governance." Although this approach has been utilized by several boards on the continent, it is limited to special projects and task forces. Moreover, this limited application is sporadic and uncoordinated; therefore, institutions have not derived the full benefits from a concert of governance approach. The strong sense of community and consensus approach to problem solving regarding life in Africa could provide fertile ground for a concert of governance approach

9. Ferenczi, *Serving Communities*, 167.

to thrive. However, this must be captured on the continent and integrated into organized training programs that will empower governing boards in theological institutions to draw from their existing communal values for leadership.

Although Ferenczi's research focused on governance in theological institutions in Asia, South America, Eurasia, and the Caribbean, the principles for governing board effectiveness transcend the geographical areas from which the data was collected. Indeed, the challenges faced by governing boards in these areas were not at all different from those experienced in Africa. It is therefore expedient to explore how some of the principles might apply to the African context, and critically examine the five important characteristics that contribute to governance effectiveness. These include community of trust, strong alignment, shared commitment to responsiveness, the presence of a strong CEO, and adequate preparation for transition.[10]

The Community of Trust

The community of trust refers to a mutual respect for positional and authoritative power of the board, CEO, management team, faculty and staff. It is driven by a fabric of trust that transcends power or authority at any position. Respect for position and authority of various governance organs within the institution provides checks and balances, and ensures professionalism. Governing boards should be careful not to strip authority from the institutional leader reducing that person to a puppet of the board. Neither should the institutional leader want to utilize the governing board as a rubber stamp for personal gain.

Instead, this level of respect for roles between the board and the leader is very important in ensuring that the relationship contributes to a community of trust. The same respect for position and authority applies to the leader's relationship with the management team, and their subsequent dealings with staff and faculty. Mutual respect for various arms of the institution is critical for building a community of trust.

The position and authority of the governing divisions in this relationship provides some boundaries for respect. However, achieving a fabric of trust that transcends power or authority of position moves the bar several notches higher among community relationships. Ferenczi noted the frustration among his respondents in their attempt to achieve a fabric of trust across the institution by initiating conversations and conflicts necessary for growth and development. Contrarily, the inability to handle these

10. Ibid., 158.

frustrations in a positive manner could degenerate into strained relationships eroding boundaries of respect for power and authority. It takes time and effort to build trust. Unfortunately, the same can be easily lost or destroyed by a few missteps.

Often, governing boards do not vigorously engage in trust building activities to transcend power and authority struggles. Activity is more consistently centered on leaders, management team, staff, and faculty. Therefore, if a management team has little faith in a leader's ability, decisions might breed mistrust and undermine the effectiveness of the leader. Similarly, a leader's doubts about the ability of management team members to deliver on certain tasks could erode confidence and render activities ineffective. In return, a management team's response to faculty and staff needs can significantly breed disrespect, negatively impacting the community of trust.

A community of trust fosters unity within an institution, which is essential for resolving financial sustainability problems. Therefore, this is not a one-time goal but a dynamic relationship that requires continuous nurturing to address any trace of conflict and frustration likely to circumvent positive efforts directed at sustaining the community. The center that holds all the pieces together is the governing board modeling respect for position and authority. Conveying this respect to other levels of an institution enhances a community of trust. The result is an environment conducive to empowering a governing board to implement sound policies and achieve the goals of the institution through its vital divisions.

Presence of Alignment

Alignment is the congruity of administrative actions of the various units of the educational institution. Ferenczi noted that this is anchored on values and shared commitment of the various divisions to the vision and mission of the institution. He further discussed that alignment draws on the strengths and skills of the governing board, institutional leader, staff, faculty, and even students to achieve an overall coherence of life in the institution. Alignment is truly desired by every governing board and institutional leader but difficult to achieve. An institutional leader once compared his leadership experience to the proverbial "herding of cats." The different understandings of the vision and mission of the institution and how they should function can lead to various divisions of the school pulling and pushing in different directions.

The frustrations associated with this kind of disharmony are often evidenced in the creation of factions, either along disciplines or interest.

It is not uncommon for faculty, administrative staff, or students to band together for a cause that is unrelated to either mission or vision. This creates misalignment in the institution. In many African institutions, misalignment can arise along tribal lines, missionary groupings, or denominational affiliations. Overcoming the challenges to alignment is the true test of institutional leadership. Because in reality, the institutional leader is faced with perhaps one of the most difficult tasks of ensuring that every member of the constituency espouses the explicit and implicit values of the institution.

Institutional values can be equated with the desirable experiences that consistently shape, motivate and guide our choices, actions, and lifestyles in specific environments through specific interactions.[11] Characteristically, they are both the obvious and imperceptible forces that influence and determine how institutions use limited resources when faced with extreme constraints and not superficial inferences made occasionally to disguise or impress others. Consequently, the impact of values on the healthy function of an institution to achieve alignment cannot be overemphasized.

Usually out of embedded institutional values flow a shared commitment to an organization's vision and mission. Shared commitment for overall activities and programs created by an institution often dissipate in the wake of crisis if troubleshooting is not based on values. Commitment to concerted engagement that draws on the strengths, skills, and competences must be undergirded by institutional values. No great task such as attaining financial sustainability can be achieved by a governing board without a thorough process of ensuring that the entire constituency subscribes to an institution's values. Ideas for financial sustainability can be better generated and individual abilities more effectively deployed to successfully resolve existing problems and to attract funding needed for the operation of the institution when decision-making is aligned with organizational values.

When all concerned are pulling in the same direction, burdens become lighter and goals are achievable in the least possible time. If governing board effectiveness is measured by the presence of alignment, then boards must proactively model institutional values and find ways to perpetuate the same across every strata of the institution. Governing boards can achieve this by working with institutional leadership through various programs and activities to receive, respond to, cherish, internalize and practice specific values as a way of life.[12] Understandably, many governing boards need to be equipped in order to create a presence of alignment. Already, 61 percent of African institutions surveyed perceived governing boards as the second

11. Bellon, *Transforming Leadership*, 53.

12. Ibid., 130

leading agent of change in an institution. This goodwill, coupled with the respect and authority accorded to governing boards should translate into a kind of influence that aligns skills, gifts, and competencies into a harmonious working environment.

Responsive Interaction

Institutions do not operate in a vacuum and therefore responsiveness to context is vital for healthy survival. Responsive interaction is the ability of an institution to see, interpret, make sense of, and proactively relate to a changing environment in which it operates. Just as the institutions in Ferenczi's study were actively responsive to their environments, so should institutions in Africa be with all diligence relevant to church and society. This internal and external awareness and engagement with the environment allows an institution to acquaint itself with the needs and opportunities informing its activities. The contexts in which theological institutions operate are more dynamic than one would like to expect, but so are the needs of the environment.

Perhaps, one would like to believe that the academic institution will be at the cutting edge, staying ahead of everyone else. Unfortunately this is not the case. Often, the academy is behind on many environmental changes that it experiences and this makes responsive interaction very difficult. The ultimate duty of the governing board is to ensure that the institution fulfills its mission, which is primarily to train leaders for church and society. It therefore behooves a governing board to continuously assess the extent to which an institution is meeting social needs.

The level of responsible interaction desired can only be achieved through governing boards asking the right questions and bringing their contextual experiences to bear on the core mandate of the institutions. This keeps institutional leaders on their toes and triggers overall institutional evaluation of performance. Accountability from the governing board does not require technical theological knowledge but a simple analysis of what is happening to leadership in the churches where they serve and the quality of training received. An institution's response to social challenges where graduates of an institution can make a difference is highlighted so needs and challenges can be aligned through training materials. The information derived from such learning should not be kept on the back burner.

Lessons learned from social contexts must be processed and incorporated into curriculum and pedagogy. If the governing board is selected well, this approach to training and learning will take priority. For instance, it would be quite effective to have one or two theologians available who can speak specifically to the areas of change that need to occur for responsive interaction to be achieved. Of course, the governing board must assume responsibility to ensure that the institution is responsive to its immediate and distant environment without compromising management duties. It is this responsive interaction that can unleash other financial resources in the environment to support operations. Therefore, to achieve financial sustainability requires leadership from the governing board and management, but also responsiveness.

Presence of an Enabling CEO

The presence of a strong and enabling CEO of a theological institution is a rare commodity. Instead, strength is often misunderstood as arrogance and stubbornness. Yet, to a greater extent that is what is expected for one to keep a difficult institution afloat. It takes strong, wise leadership to move a theological institution forward, and implement the necessary changes desired to achieve the mission of the organization. Often such enabling CEOs can achieve a lot for the institution if supported by management, the governing board, and mission agencies.

The governing board must be willing to select a leader with such characteristics and provide the necessary protection for him or her to succeed. Ample room is then created for the leader to provide insight into board activities from the knowledge of the goings-on of the institution. A strong, enabling CEO must also be visionary and come up with creative solutions that are supported by management, if an institution is to overcome challenges to financial sustainability. Creative solutions should draw on the experience and expertise of governing board members and their individual networks to undertake projects that will address challenges faced by the institution. However, if the governing board does not select or has no part in selecting the CEO, then they have to work with whomever the church or mission agency selects to lead the institution.

The effectiveness of the governing board will depend on its ability to enable and equip the institutional leader to function effectively. Many governing boards have been frustrated by leaders they had no part in selecting and as a result lose the participation of otherwise resourceful individuals. The situation is compounded when the leader is not enabled and the governing board is poorly constituted to effectively address any financial issues encountered by the institution. Governing boards need to be equipped to enable institutional leaders to maximize output from the board. This two-pronged approach and collaboration from management and other stakeholders should be sufficient enough to establish a means of achieving financial sustainability.

Succession Planning

Sometimes, a governing board extends the term of a leader because neither the leader nor the board actively prepare others for the position. There are times when denominational leaders may insist that a particular person stay in office as long as the denomination deems reasonable. A painstaking effort to ensure proper succession planning of leadership is foundational to the strength of an institution over the long-term. Consequently, a strong and enabling leader does not necessarily ensure a proper succession, especially if other stakeholders are involved.

Leadership transition poses a greater threat to financial sustainability than many factors in the operation of the institution. There are situations when a leader stays for a protracted length of time in office, because no potential leader has been trained to take over. There was a situation in an African institution where the leader led an institution for 18 years, but shortly after his departure, the institution was plunged into financial crisis because the entire leadership structure was built around that one individual. The governing board had not facilitated the development of other leaders for the future.

Mission agencies are not very different from denominations in keeping leaders in positions too long. The politics of who gets to lead an institution and for how long can differ from one institution to another. The details can be messy. When there is a bigger hand overshadowing the board in their decision-making, then the board is rendered handicapped and unable to play its strategic role. A governing board must find a balance between fulfilling the wishes of the sponsoring organization, whether it be a church or mission agency, and asserting its influence to deliver performance. There is always a fine line, but so thin it can easily be broken creating displeasure among owners of the institution.

A strong and enabling leader may begin a project working closely with the governing board that is likely to address the long-term financial challenges of the school. If a new leader takes over but does not share the vision of the predecessor, then an entire project could be jeopardized and resources wasted because of something as basic as an incongruent new philosophy of leadership. If the circumstances were not pleasant under which a former leader vacates office, the new leader might want to distance himself or herself as much as possible from everything the previous leader started. Therefore, it takes a focused and dedicated board to ensure that time and other resources poured into a project are sustained for the betterment of the institution regardless of who leads.

The strength of an institution must mature through the years. However, when there is poor transitional planning and every departure is painful and traumatic, an institution losses the opportunity to grow, drawing from the wisdom and insights of predecessors. An endless cycle of starting anew every time there is a transition erodes gains made and weakens the ability of an institution to build a solid financially sustainable infrastructure. The governing board owes it to the institution not only to avoid an overdependence on a strong and enabling CEO, but also must ensure that there are other leaders in training to lead, should the need arise.

Certainly, the board itself must facilitate smooth transitions within its ranks, so that members do not stay on the board longer than is advisable. In this regard, a procedural board manual that stipulates the terms of office and effective recruitment of new members with new ideas is essential for the effectiveness of the board. A well-managed and planned transition of board leadership and members, as well as the CEO is vital for the growth of an enduring institution. A good governance transition plan builds capacity that transcends even the achievement of financial sustainability in an institution.

Effective governance of theological institutions can be achieved if there is a community of trust, presence of alignment, responsive interaction, a strong enabling CEO, and succession planning. It is the confluence of all these factors that makes a difference. The governance process is like a concert in which "a fluid function centered on the board but [draws] expertise, skills, and time of the rest of the organization as well."[13]

Although Ferenczi's study did not include African institutions, all the institutions in his study were part of the OCI survey on financial viability. As he noted, perhaps the most important implication for institutions in Africa is the "affirmation that theological schools must remain in close touch with their dynamic environments and contexts to find ways in which they can adjust while at the same time guarding their founding values and principles."[14] Every factor mentioned above has direct application and implication for effective governance in an African institution if such an institution is to realize financial sustainability for now and into the future.

---

13. Ferenczi, *Serving Communities*, 182.

14. Ibid., 178.

GOVERNING BOARD IN FINANCIAL MANAGEMENT

A governing board has an important responsibility to ensure that the financial outlook of an institution is well-managed and that it has enough resources to carry out its duties. A governing board that lacks the ability to facilitate this function exposes the institution to all manner of unwarranted financial risks. The board must therefore have within its membership, people who are knowledgeable in financial management. Similarly, the board needs to support management by hiring qualified finance and management personnel at different levels to lead the operation of the institution.

There have been times when faculty members who have no background in finance and management have been given responsibilities such as deputy vice chancellor, vice principal or even deputy director of finance and administration. These faculty members who are otherwise great teachers are plucked from the classroom to fill administrative positions for which they neither have the training nor the experience. African institutions do this because of the high cost of hiring qualified personnel. The sad result is that their inability to creatively lead their divisions to financial sustainability eventually costs an institution more than it would have cost to simply hire qualified people to do the job.

Unfortunately, even as we speak, there are many faculty members in finance and administrative positions without requisite experience or training. An institutional leader shared in confidence that the deputy for finance and administration on one particular campus was struggling to perform, but could not do anything about it because that person has become too deeply entrenched in the position. Another institutional leader shared that a faculty member serving in a position is an ally of top leaders in a mission agency and therefore changing roles might jeopardize the smooth operation of the institution.

The effective financial management of an institution is one of the primary responsibilities of the board. Moreover, a governing board does not only have to exemplify knowledge and skills in matters of finance and administration, but must facilitate the alignment of skills, competencies, and abilities to specific functions. For instance, the role of prudent financial management must be inextricably tied to strategies that ensure financial sustainability of the institution.

One way to accomplish this is the development of a strategic plan that draws from the mission and vision of an institution to spell out ministry priorities through time. Strategic objectives, implementation processes, and mobilization of human and other resources are identified as strategic targets to achieve an overall plan. The expertise of the governing board in making this process a worthwhile exercise adds significant value to the institution.

Many leaders of theological institutions in Africa are not exposed to the mechanics of strategic planning because of their training and background. Although operating an institution requires a wide range of skills and knowledge, there are not many opportunities to acquire this knowledge in a contextualized way. Leaders must often labor to fit new knowledge into a context and find ways to secure support from other members of the leadership team. The governing board needs to work closely with institutional leadership teams to develop periodic strategic plans that explore avenues to achieve financial sustainability and fulfill the institutional mandate in the long term.

The process of strategic planning is an undertaking to explore creative solutions to financial challenges and various ways of implementing these solutions without jeopardizing the core mandate. The board must assume the responsibility of driving this important process not just for the development of a document but to guarantee the careful implementation of the strategy. This careful implementation must be coupled with the willingness of a board to engage external expertise to support the strategic direction of an institution. Oftentimes, the expertise required to achieve a particular strategic objective may not be present among board members. Therefore an openness to co-opt expertise is critical. A board needs to lead this engagement.

In many institutions in Africa, there are no comprehensive financial policies and those that exist were established with the commencement of the institution and therefore are currently archaic and retrogressive. However, institutional policies are meant to advance proprietary causes and fulfill goals. Financial policies are often perceived in the light of controls and checks that enhance transparency and accountability to all concerned. However, if financial policies stifle growth and limit ability to engage emerging opportunities critical for the well-being of an institution, then the board needs to proactively change those policies.

For years, the emphasis on control has been the focus of financial policies and very little has been explored in terms of policies to create room for institutions to change as their contextual needs change. Governing boards have a responsibility to continually review an institution's policies, especially financial policies so that they provide a financial framework that supports management to pursue opportunities to facilitate financial sustainability. Well-crafted financial policies will free members of a board to selflessly and generously give to the institution as a form of legacy.

The board needs to regularly evaluate itself on its performance in line with accomplishing an institution's mission and vision. Whether it is managing financial risk, aligning staff to specific functions, increasing expertise, developing strategic planning or progressive financial policies, a board needs to achieve the overall mandate by training leadership for church and society in a financially sustainable manner.

Chapter 7

The Role of Third Stream

SINCE THE ESTABLISHMENT OF theological education in Africa, institutions have used tuition to generate revenue; although in some countries, theological education was offered tuition-free for many years. It was only after this charitable period that tuition was gradually introduced. When compared to theological institutions in other parts of the world with similar socio-political histories and economic growth, the difference becomes startling. Consequently, the addition of donations as yet another revenue stream has played a significant role in sustaining theological education over the years.

Unfortunately, given weak institutional infrastructures in Africa, growing donations under persistent global economic crises has been formidable. Donations to theological institutions, consequently, have been plummeting steadily in recent years. Therefore, despite the reality that donations and tuition are two important revenue streams, they are still well below financial levels needed by most African theological institutions to remain viable. Consequently, a third stream of revenue is needed. In other words, a third stream refers to any revenue generated by theological institutions apart from tuition and donations. It is a revenue stream that exists for the sole purpose of fulfilling the core mandate of theological education at an African institution. However, generating third stream revenue requires creativity and expertise that are not necessarily available to many theological institutions. Third stream revenue strategies to sustain theological institutions over the long haul are promising options.

William Carey stated, "My business is to witness for Christ," while he mended shoes to raise financial support as a missionary in India. He learned the Bengali language and together with two other tentmakers translated the entire Bible into multiple languages.[1] These pioneering missionaries effectively utilized a third stream concept through the enterprise of mending shoes. However, such a strategy to advance the Gospel has yet to be replicated in Africa in similarly successful fashion.

In the 19th century, three Swiss farmers who were members of the Swiss Basel Mission first introduced the cocoa plant to Ghana, West Africa from the plant's native South American environment. The missionary farmers greatly encouraged their workers to be self-supporting and established a trading company in the coastal African country. The trading company eventually sent the first-ever shipment of cocoa from Africa to Europe in 1891 and twenty years after that initial shipment, Ghana became the world-leading producer of cocoa. During that period, her per capita income became the highest in black Africa.[2] In areas where they were not able to open mission stations, the company opened trading posts where its business staff could also share the Gospel. Wilson noted that the Swiss Basel Mission always sought to do everything to show that "godliness is profitable unto all things, having promise of life that now is and of that which is to come" (1 Tm 4:8). William Carey in India and the Swiss Basel missionaries in Africa both followed what Apostle Paul taught and practiced.

The individual entrepreneurial ventures of these early missionaries still attest to the viability of biblically inspired third stream strategies. Their efforts helped them to be self-supporting while fulfilling the Great Commission. Therefore, if these strategies worked in the mission field, then third stream sustainability ventures can and should be applied to supporting theological education, as well. In this chapter, we will look at how donations and tuition are used as a means to generate revenue for African theological institutions before delving into third stream projects as a creative way to support financial sustainability.

DONATIONS

Requesting donations is often the first revenue-generating strategy for many theological institutions in Africa. Actually, many institutions got their start because of successful donation campaigns coordinated through a church or mission agency. In typical fashion, campaigns were usually funded by friends and supporters of Western missionaries planting churches in Africa. The financial support would be used to fund a church building but also over time, a small theological college. If the funded institution were meant

1. Neill, *A History of Christian Missions*, 263.
2. Wilson Jr., *Today's Tentmakers*, 35.

to train leaders to serve a particular denomination, that institution would adhere to the tenets of that particular denomination. Otherwise, non-denominational institutions identified themselves as independent campuses sponsored by a particular mission agency. However, many more African theological institutions began with the support of a denomination, rather than that of mission agencies.

Certainly, without donations to open and maintain these institutions, many of them would not be in existence today. Although donors may not always be on the ground where training is taking place, their financial support does influence the growth and direction of their theological institutions. As most donations are designated for specific needs such as student scholarships, faculty development, library resources, development of new academic programs, and so on, thankfully, these donations have continued to support specific initiatives in many schools.

Despite an OCI survey conducted in 2011 showing that designated donations recently average thirty percent of overall institutional budgets, donations to theological institutions in Africa have been declining. Consequently, an institution's capacity to leverage donations for greater impact has remained weak. The reality is that despite the many ways capacity and management infrastructure affect the financial outlook of these schools, donors also strongly determine the operational health of an institution.

Often, institutions tailor their requests to the interests of donors instead of addressing operational needs. Consequently, donations may not always focus on strengthening or developing institutional capacity, since donors could designate funds for popular projects and programs. In such cases, the effect of donations would be to strengthen programs and activities but not the operations of an institution.

However, wise and effective management of donor funds means that institutions must identify and address real problems instead of tailoring proposals to solely satisfy the demands of donors. In this regard, short-term capital projects often make a more compelling case for support than long-term capacity building projects. Donor financial support must be strategically assigned in order to avoid bigger problems from arising.

On the other hand, it is very difficult to raise funds without considering the interests of the donor. Although many donors consider institutional capacity building important, very few consider it a priority or prioritize funding for it. Affected institutions end up struggling under financial pressures because institutional capacity building is not a priority. The challenges institutions face are complex and do undermine the worthy efforts of funding organizations. Ultimately, these challenges undermine capacity building goals, too.

The diverse requirements of foundations, trusts, businesses, and individuals to engage in nonprofit funding make fundraising a sophisticated function that demands expertise and well-equipped offices to manage this area specifically. This is a capacity need that many theological institutions on the continent are unable to meet. Due to regular funding shortfalls, almost no funding is available to strengthen the institutional structures that facilitate effective fundraising. Dedicated departments focusing on fundraising can contribute to good donor relations through effective communication. The intended outcome of these strategic efforts is increased funding. Conversely, weak fundraising development results in lost opportunities to generate local and foreign resources, and even a loss of donors.

Fundamental to fundraising development is the use of a public relations team with the assigned task to tell the institution's story. Otherwise, the inability to share what is happening in an institution in a manner that can be understood and appreciated globally, will negatively affect an institution's opportunities to build a strong donor network. For instance, donors may anticipate a familiar level of professionalism. Unfortunately, the specific tone of professionalism a donor group may expect will be lacking in an institution without experts working on its behalf with donors. The expertise to establish where or when or how a campus will prioritize donations contributes to professionalism.

Although some institutions have been in existence for decades, many lack the ability to create and manage on-going fundraising campaigns. Institutions that focus on fundraising development and public relations using communication officers are not currently available in Africa. Therefore, theological institutions, especially the ones I have closely interacted with do not have qualified personnel to lead and manage effective, strategic fundraising campaigns. Communications systems, robust databases, alumni tracking systems, networking, rigorous strategic resources planning and grant proposal writing are all essential tools of which theological institutions in Africa can only dream about, but have no resources to secure. There are many local philanthropists who could support the mission of theological education in Africa if approached appropriately and with an air of professionalism. Even an inability to utilize existing technologies for money transfers (e.g., M-Pesa, Zap and similar platforms) to enhance the convenience of fundraising campaigns can limit an institution's ability to draw from local resources for its programs.

Many theological institutions limit themselves to using traditional fundraising events such as dinners, which often yield no more revenue than what it took to organize them—a breakeven return on investment. I remember the effort my leadership team exerted year after year organizing fundraising dinners in cost prohibitive hotel facilities. It just turned out that each time we held such a dinner the weather would not cooperate. It would rain heavily and people would not attend. This is because in many African cities when it rains, traffic comes to a standstill and people just want to stay home.

You can imagine a fundraising dinner on such a day. Somehow, it did not matter the season in which we held the dinner because, it still never failed to rain. This was my consistent experience over a three-year span. Although we always managed to raise some money during those dinners, the amounts were far short of what we anticipated. In reality, there were so many more effective alternate, creative ways available via technology to have enlisted during our fundraising efforts. However, we did not have the experience, personnel or resources to take advantage of those alternatives. Today, many institutions are still stuck in a similar dilemma insofar as local fundraising development is concerned. From the time African theological institutions were introduced to the West, relationship building has continued. Yet, we have not been able to enhance those relationships by building the ability to leverage resources available through those relationships.

Obviously, people inside of organizations have the ability to support a vision if they choose to do so. Therefore, one needs to cast a vision clearly and passionately. The relationship with the West has been very important because it has created opportunities for the global body of Christ to participate in God's work across the African continent. Over the years, I have come to clearly observe that people give to people, and then to whatever vision inspires. Every gift to a mission's vision has a face behind it. It is either the face of the leader, the institution, or particular individuals connected to the institution. More often than not, donors intentionally support people who represent an organization's vision.

When individuals depart from an institution, it can mean the potential loss of a donor, as well. This is why having a well-established fundraising department is important because a broader group of people can be equipped to conduct effective fundraising campaigns and strengthen social links between institutions and donors. Many local leaders and missionaries who have left leadership positions in the past, also inadvertently left with their donors. This is because regardless of the overt support of specific institutions, the reality is that people give to people. Therefore, it is critical—for the sake of financial sustainability—that donors are directed to social links within an institution but beyond individual personalities. This is so that donors can support institutions through strong social networks built into sophisticated fundraising programs for long-term institutional sustainability.

Policies and Procedures for Gift Acceptance and Utilization

Many theological institutions in Africa do not have written guidelines to determine which gifts to accept or how to utilize specific gifts. When one is always short on finances, the last thing to discuss is whether one has a gift acceptance and utilization policy. The reality is such that institutions are eager to accept every gift and use it as prescribed by the donor regardless of the purpose or condition of the gift.

Institutional capacity and policies help organizations determine whether a donation meets certain criteria before it is accepted in order to help strengthen specific areas of the institution to grow and develop. There are times when institutions are perceived to be doing well. Then, they are approached with funds to develop academic programs that do not fit any existing department. Multiple problems arise in these cases due to a lack of staff to teach in that field. The inevitable result is more costs incurred to develop something that never existed and was never intended to exist on a campus until an ill-advised donation was accepted. Programs that are purely driven by donors can be irrelevant to the success of an institution's mission if donations address issues outside of the context or strategy of a school.

Sometimes institutions will pursue a particular agenda because of established relationships and support received from a donor for previous projects. The short- and long-term costs associated with such programs (i.e., hiring faculty, accreditation of the program, physical facilities, administrative support, marketing, library resources, student scholarships, and other concerns) may not be factored into the donation. A donor may assume that existing resources will house the program and the same faculty will teach these courses. Yet, the reality may be that the program is costing the institution significantly more than the one-time donation. This is equally true regarding donations of used office equipment and library resources from North America or Europe. Sometimes, it can cost institutions more money to clear customs, or to make repairs, or even to provide essential accessories, and maintenance than simply purchasing new equipment and resources locally. Gift acceptance and utilization policies can alleviate the challenges institutions face in dealing with these situations.

Do institutions have the right to allocate donations to more urgent needs? The absence of gift acceptance and utilization policies often affects the allocation of a particular donation. Using designated funds for other purposes is considered an unpardonable sin. Institutional leaders are frightened to death when it comes to this issue; however, they do not always have a policy in place to guide their communication with donors. That a particular gift was accepted is no longer as important as the designated allocation.

In a true spirit of partnership, and in the interest of institutions, choosing how to allocate donated resources should be possible if an institution already has a gift acceptance and utilization policy in place and it informs donors. Institutional leaders are often trapped in this situation and either continue with a project as earlier discussed, even as irrelevant as it may become over time. Or administrators may cave to the pressure to divert funds towards another project without prior approval from funders, a situation that is totally unacceptable and truly avoidable.

Donations to build institutional fund development infrastructures are critical for growth in every institution. There are times, when a project receives fewer funds than needed. Especially, when the donation is a matching grant, the difficulty arises when no one else comes forward to fill the gap. Consequently, institutions get stuck with the funds because they are unable to raise the additional amount needed to complete projects for which they have written proposals. For this reason, it is critical that governing boards and administration work together to formulate gift acceptance and utilization policies to create a transparent procedure for acceptance, management, and utilization of gifts. This type of policy document can be shared with donors to educate them on the institution's stance regarding gifts before any donation is made. Such a policy document will free leaders and protect institutions from perceived unethical behavior and corresponding mistrust. However, Governing boards and administration have the onus to proactively formulate policies that strengthen institutional capacity and thereby promote financial sustainability.

TUITION AS INCOME

Although tuition is one of the two main streams of revenue for theological institutions, the impact of tuition on financial sustainability in many institutions has not been felt. According to an OCI survey, tuition covers 25% to 30% of total operating expenses of most institutions. Consequently, student enrollment has been viewed as a way to increase revenue and reach a breaking-even point. Although, it is wrong to assume that all other costs will remain fixed while tuition increases. Evidently, there is a big difference between teaching a class of 30 students and a class of 12 students. The preparation time and other resources deployed by the faculty for each class will almost be the same.

Obviously, faculty will have more papers to grade and the level of interaction in class will be different, but the institution will have tuition income for 18 students that will be unavailable if the total number of students in the class is only 12. However, the additional 6 students in the class does increase the overall cost of organizing the class and if the 12 students are not paying the full cost of education in fees, the tuition gap created by the additional 18 will be larger. Student enrollment drives many projects to increase tuition revenue; however, there are also hidden costs that institutions incur with additional students. Therefore, discerning financial equilibrium can be difficult. This is because increasing student enrollment to increase tuition revenue may trigger other institutional overhead costs.

Institutional leaders still argue that there is a cut-off point from which the institution begins to make a profit. Of course, every institution must determine its own cut-off point based on their overall operating costs and margins given the level of revenue generated for the institution. Considering that current tuition income for many theological institutions in Africa is around 30 percent of their operating cost, it would take a long time, increased fees, and many students for an institution to reach a break-even point and enjoy a surplus of revenue.

It is highly unusual to find a theological institution in Africa that has for example 30 students or more enrolled in a class, considering that the average total enrollment in most theological institutions in Africa is 200 according to the OCI data. Those schools with more than 300 matriculating students offer lower-level courses, short courses, or online studies. Theological programs in Africa are not as naturally attractive as other social science courses for reasons discussed in Chapter 3. Therefore, it is difficult to increase enrollment to levels that could achieve financial equilibrium or pass the famous break-even point. This has been an elusive dream for many institutional leaders and it is about time we accepted the reality that revenue in the form of tuition to finance theological education is a limited solution to consistent financial solvency.

The costs associated with student recruitment such as travel, salaries, equipment, printed materials, and other marketing expenses are often higher than amounts budgeted. So, institutions wrestle to justify such expenses knowing that at best, tuition will only cover thirty percent of their operating costs. The situation is worsened when big universities with strong religious studies departments splash expensive advertisements in daily newspapers. Competition for students takes more energy than anticipated. Theological institutions hounded by financial problems will usually find themselves at a disadvantage in the scramble for more students in highly competitive countries like Kenya, Ghana, Ethiopia and Nigeria, among others.

Many institutions do not have the financial resources or internal systems to support effective recruitment campaigns. In attempt to advance institutional ethos, sometimes schools insist that potential students seeking to apply must have a calling from God and a certain number of years in the ministry, negating the fact that the calling can be received while pursuing the education. In familiar environments like the church, marketing academic programs in such a manner may have some value but it does not yield much for non-denominational institutions that do not enjoy strong church ownership and platform to market their programs. Even for denominational institutions, much effort is needed through church leadership to create awareness and interest in the institution's programs to recruit students.

Scholarships have been used to recruit students. Unfortunately, their inherent high cost contributes to financial instability due to unhealthy policies that offer no stable funding commitments. Often scholarship policies are based on donations from partners, which are bound to change from year to year. Reduction in donations affects the awarding of student scholarships, increases student financial responsibilities, and triggers higher student dropout rates and lower enrollment. The situation is even more complicated when a multi-year scholarship is awarded from an African institution. The school is forced to bear the remaining cost of the award. The final decision made by many potential students considering theological education hinges on the degree to which scholarships offset the burden of tuition, and the likelihood of winning one. This is a very different situation from what happens with students in other university social science programs.

As discussed in Chapter 3, the marketability and demand for theological education compared with other social sciences in Africa is very low. As great as student scholarships are, theological institutions must rise above the allure of scholarships to increase enrollment which market the benefits of theological education over and above serving in a local church. Leadership equipped with theological education is valuable to church and society. Every aspect of society needs leaders with theological education serving in various life disciplines such as the army, police, hospitals, politics, businesses, and others. Therefore, programs need to be marketed well to represent the true value of such education provided by institutions.

The mountain of debt generated by students responsible for paying tuition for theological education leaves much to be desired and raises ethical questions for graduates serving the church and other Christian organizations in Africa. Debt is generated from not only tuition, but housing and utilities, as well. Recovering from debt and preventing it from growing bigger is an area of financial sustainability that requires further research.

Total student debt for an institution I know was once enough to cover institutional operating costs for several months. From a leadership standpoint, many students enroll in theological institutions based on the mere promise of financial support from their churches and other Christian leaders. Sometimes churches go to the length of sending commitment letters without any intention of fulfilling their promise to financially support the student or the institution. The whole process is flawed with miscommunication and deception in the name of ministry and a call to serve the Lord. I have observed international students stranded on their first day of school because the funds a church, Christian organization or an individual promised did not materialize.

Sometimes it is difficult to tell whether a student is telling the truth or not, but even more difficult to believe that a student will travel to a far off country to study without the funds needed to pay the first semester tuition. Some students even travel with families, yet do not have resources to provide housing or food for them. Churches and organizational failure to remit funds promised to students, acts in the name of faith, and sometimes student lies about their true situation undermine the entire process of training Godly leaders to shepherd the church and transform society.

Students attending theological institutions are faced with high debt-to-payment ratios. Unfortunately, the schools have the frustrating task of kicking students out of classrooms for non-payment, which steals the joy out of teaching. I remember a student who was kicked out of class several times in one semester and other student sympathizers went around convincing the faculty to let the student continue.

However, student sympathizers and others forget the difficulties institutions have in paying faculty to continue teaching. Somehow, there is this notion that training in other social sciences should be paid for, but theological education should be free. Student debt collection angers alumni and deters them from supporting the institution financially. However, there are so many bishops and senior pastors of mega-churches and big Christian organizations who have yet to settle their student debts. They are influential leaders in Christian circles and society but the institutions that trained them are not proud of them because of their failure to settle a debt they duly owe their alma mater. While alumni in other parts of the world are donating to their alma mater, alumni from theological institutions in Africa are taking financial resources away from the institutions and ultimately impoverishing the training of those coming after them.

Institutions sometime resort to the "list of shame" to morally force students to honor their obligations. The "list of shame" is a poster of students owing the institution and often posted on notice boards before exams, warning students of potentially being barred from taking exams if they do not pay. Measures such as withholding transcripts and certificates to ensure that the last cent is paid do not always work because sometimes churches employ these leaders without having to see their final transcripts or original certificates. When pressure is exerted on students to pay outstanding fees or suffer the threat of not graduating, these same students will go to great lengths to provide guarantees to ensure the payment of the debt.

These guarantees may include land titles, vehicle certificates, bank guarantees, promissory notes, and others. Yet, the problem with such guarantees is that institutions will have to go through complicated legal processes to reclaim the funds not to mention incurring associated legal fees. For institutions struggling to stand on their feet, this is an additional unwanted expensive task. Student graduation banquets are full of stories of how they started school without any money and how God provided through student scholarships and favors from the institution. After listening to some of these horror stories over the years, one could assume that graduates privileged in this way would give generously to their alma mater and support the institution in as many ways as possible. Unfortunately, that has not been so.

Revenue from tuition contributes to overall operating costs. For this reason, theological institutions are sometimes forced to increase tuition in a situation where students are already struggling to pay current fees while already saddled with extraordinary debt generated from school expenses. Although tuition in theological institutions in Africa is much lower than many comparable social science programs, perception and marketability of graduates keep tuition low.

Tuition is necessary and contributes to financial sustainability therefore institutions must do whatever it takes to get the most out of this stream because of the numerous challenges associated with it. If tuition amounts to thirty percent of total revenue, then we are sure that this amount will not cover expenses such as facility maintenance, staff salaries, supplies and other general services. One of the driving motivations pushing theological institutions to become Christian universities is the need to increase tuition. It is believed that with more diversified programs, an institution can attract more students, increase its tuition to arrive at a break-even.

Although the argument makes sense and the wind of change in this direction is blowing across the continent, efforts made so far toward this end have been elusive and no more than hope deferred. Since these programs did not attract the number of people as quickly as hoped, the results have been disappointing. Among the many people in theological institutions that have become universities, there is still a perception that these theological universities do not have the same attraction as other institutions, which started as secular universities. Although programs are being diversified in many theological institutions so that these campuses can become Christian universities, it will take a long time to see tuition increase naturally through rising enrollment if at all possible. However, if institutions lack capacity to operate as theological entities, how will they manage as universities, which demand more resources and sophisticated leadership skills?

THIRD STREAM PROJECTS

As we established at the beginning of this chapter, the third stream is a biblically based creative fundraising strategy to generate funds, beyond tuition or donations, to support ministries. However, the concept has not been fully developed to the extent that assures institutional leaders of the viability a third stream mindset. Moreover, institutional leaders not only lack the basic experience and exposure required to administer third stream projects, but consider the idea an uncomfortable one, if not all together secular. I remember chairing a senate meeting where this concept was raised in a heated discussion. Emotions flew all over the place.

Some strongly believed that this was a clear departure from what God called us to do. Others considered it a clear demonstration of a lack of trust in God. This latter group even quoted biblical passages to persuasively support their stance on why we should trust God to provide for all our financial needs. One group emphatically declared that we should continue with tuition and donations (the two streams) as we had always done and find ways to increase revenue with those familiar strategies. Another group strongly supported the idea of a third stream simply to avoid school closures. Still others were clueless about what we should really do at all. That committee was pulled in all directions because we were entering uncomfortable, uncharted waters as winds of change drove our fears and anxieties to the surface.

I could identify with all the groups in the meeting because I had worked through my fears on all the different ideas represented at the senate. The confidence to even table the idea of a third stream for discussion emanated from protracted hours of reflection and prayer about the perpetual financial challenges the institution would continue to face otherwise. Although the committee eventually agreed to go ahead with third stream projects after many emotional deliberations, it took the governing board about two years to warm up to the idea and give the green light.

This was a big change for the governing board because now they would have to be engaged more than they had been previously. It would be crucial to bring their professional skills to bear in this regard. It would no longer be business as usual: approving tuition increases or sharing dispassionate comments regarding fundraising activities curated by management. The concept of the third stream started pushing the governing board beyond questions such as "Why are students not paying fees?" or "Why are they allowed to attend classes if they have not paid?" or "Why is management not recruiting more students to increase tuition?" or "Why didn't the president of the institution raise more money on his/her fundraising trips?" or "Why is management not challenging donors to give more?" or "Why have staff and faculty salaries been delayed?" and so on.

Suddenly, instead of asking why, the governing board had to start wrestling with formulating effective policies about third stream projects and assist management with expertise to successfully implement them. The third stream idea forced leadership onto a new path of responsibility and accountability by requiring their full engagement. Governing board members who could successfully remain passive during their tenure under the two-stream model suddenly had to serve on task forces because of new responsibilities arising with the third stream. The new model for generating revenue required members to exercise their leadership skills to reach purposeful outcomes.

Unlike the former era in which members merely had to show up two or three times a year to tacitly participate in meetings, third stream projects require full active participation through collective creative problem-solving to theological education. This new activism might explain why sponsoring organizations such as churches and mission agencies are as scared about third stream projects as governing boards. Ironically, theological institutions sponsored by Western mission agencies have the greatest difficulties working with third stream projects, especially if they are self-proclaimed faith-based organizations.

A central problem is the perception that third stream projects reflect a lack of faith in God. Yet, comparatively speaking, churches tend to be more agreeable to third stream projects more so than mission agencies because of their experience in raising funds locally for church-related projects. Therefore, few churches may have difficulties allowing their institutions to embrace the third stream. Nevertheless, change is always uncomfortable for most people because we are creatures of routine when change is introduced.

It is encouraging to reflect on the Apostle Paul's tentmaking activities as well as consider strategies from early missionary fathers like William Carey (Chapters 4 and 5). Even so, the third stream concept applied to projects in support of missionary endeavors conducted by these early missionaries was initially misunderstood until practical applications proved successful. If Apostle Paul's tentmaking activities were misunderstood and challenged, we should not expect an easy path following the introduction of third stream projects at African theological institutions. In similar fashion, as among the work of the early missionaries, several battles will need to be fought and roadblocks removed before theological institutions in Africa realize the potential of implementing third stream projects.

The God-Given Seed

The God-given seed is the talent or resource divinely placed within the reach of every theological institution to develop third stream projects successfully. The seed supports an institution's mission to generate financial resources for continued development of leaders and like the biblical talent in Matthew 25:14–28, God has provided every theological institution a seed to guide the success of a third stream project. Of course, seeds will differ with every institution, as some institutions are better endowed than others. Nevertheless, all institutions have been gifted with a seed. Consequently, theological institutions must trust God to open their eyes to identify and explore their unique seed for the benefit of the institution.

God-given seeds come in all forms and shapes, such as land, buildings, expertise, the student body, faculty, administrators, churches, affiliations, and the like. Although these things are often obvious by most standards, institutions often overlook God-given seeds in areas critical for the success of third stream projects. Discovery of God-given seed is often hindered by policies, customs, traditions, and the culture of an institution. Sometimes these hindrances are wrapped around the policies of primary sponsors such as churches and mission agencies.

The role of the governing board is not only to formulate policies but to change existing polices and cultural practices that hinder discovery of God-given seed in order to liberate management's problem-solving ability to address financial challenges. Governing boards have three important responsibilities in getting third stream projects off the ground. They must remove barriers negating God-given seed and facilitate the process of strategic planning. Boards should establish task forces to work with administration in identifying, planning, implementing, managing and accounting to ensure transparency across all facets of a third stream project.

As we saw earlier under church ownership and governance, governing boards are directly responsible for the financial sustainability of theological institutions. They must be diligent in first changing internal prejudices and removing substantive barriers poised to strangle such initiatives. The governing board must work tirelessly to win the approval of sponsoring churches and/or mission agencies if their school is to stand a chance of overcoming frustrating challenges to any initiative. A victory in this area could remove major barrier to seed identification and establishment of third stream projects.

A governing board must spearhead the preparation of a strategic plan for the institution that provides a framework for third stream projects. The envisioned strategic plan must promote the establishment of third stream projects as mandatory goals with objectives spread across given time periods. Such a plan once approved, empowers both a governing board and administration to take action. An effective strategic plan will force a governing board to engage the seed discovery process so that whatever is outlined in the plan as possible third stream projects can progress through necessary feasibility and viability tests for further action.

In advance, a governing board should outline feasibility criteria for a project. Administration of the institution must ensure that those standards are met in the discovery, identification and presentation of third stream projects to the board. Otherwise, leaders of theological institutions are bound to become frustrated and burnt out if their governing board is not an active participant in strategic plan development and implementation.

Depending upon the nature of the God-given seed, governing boards must set up task forces to scrutinize a variety of third stream projects to further ascertain viability and appropriate implementation. A task force must have the liberty to contract Christian experts who may not otherwise qualify to serve on the governing board but have skills critical to the success of a project. I have witnessed occasions when creative ideas for third stream projects have been generated through such task forces. It is advisable to employ professionals both inside and outside a governing board because a wider array of talent could likely collaborate more resourcefully in the development of a third stream project, than, say, task force members from a limited pool of candidates.

One of the main responsibilities of a task force is to ensure that third stream projects do not interfere with the delivery of an institution's core mandate. It is the governing board's major responsibility to formulate policies that specifically mitigate mission drift. Otherwise, mission drift would be unavoidable if necessary precautions have not been taken from the outset to protect the mission. For some institutions, this may require a registration of a separate entity with a different management board that would report directly to the governing board of the institution. Such an arrangement would free the leadership and administration of an institution to continue to administer daily operations. All the business decisions and activities that go into the operation of a third stream project could be assigned to specific task force members.

The philosophy of managing a theological institution is quite different from managing a third stream project. Therefore, delegating responsibilities to dedicated members for the overall health of a theological institution would be an expedient decision. Everything must be done within the power of the governing board to ensure that the interests of the theological institution and its mission are safeguarded.

The task force's responsibilities are not simply limited to identification, establishment and management of projects, but also should include enforcing accountability of administration and financial practices. Without accountability, success of any third stream project would be questionable. Such task forces can also review the financial health of an institution in terms of its risk management portfolio, decision processes and administration. They can assist a theological institution to increase efficiency and reduce overhead.

Until bad institutional practices are adequately addressed by governance systems, no amount of third stream project revenue can salvage theological institutions from foreseeable financial crises. The house cleaning exercises, introduction of efficient and effective systems, reduction of overhead, debt management, and successful delivery of the core mandate are all critical to successful outcomes of third stream projects.

EXAMPLES OF THIRD STREAM PROJECTS

The reason to discuss third stream projects is to understand their role in facilitating an institution's financial sustainability. Of course, a discussion of third stream projects without practical examples is a discussion without substance. There are many examples of third stream projects; they include collaborative research projects, consulting services, agricultural projects, rental facilities, and similar services. These examples are not exhaustive in themselves but provide a conceptual reference to the variety of projects that may qualify as third stream, depending on one's country, relevant products and services, and available institutional capacity and resources.

Collaborative Research Projects

There are opportunities for faculty and students to pursue collaborative research projects with other universities and research institutes. Although faculty members at theological institutions are equipped for all manner of research, they are not always able to attract research funding. However, a growing interest in multi-disciplinary research across the social sciences provides unique opportunities for faculty to pursue joint-research projects.

Theological institutions bring a special perspective to research issues related to behavior and socio-political changes in African societies. This is because there is a spiritual dimension to every behavioral intervention on the continent. Theological faculty members in modern Africa conduct minimal research; yet, this is a viable means of generating operational income toward the fulfillment of an institution's mission.

There is a need to build research capacity to enhance joint research and research proposal development among theological leaders. This as well as, can be a third stream category. In the past, the continent enjoyed the leadership of gifted theological scholars who made big strides individually and were likewise recognized globally for their influence. Although, as notable scholars cement their legacies, intentional collaborative research among younger scholars should be part of future planning. Theological institutions must seriously consider research as one of its main activities.

Consulting Services

Third stream projects can include consulting services provided by theological institutions at reasonable costs. For instance, the development of Sunday school curriculum or printed materials such as discipleship manuals, are examples of ways theological institutions can use intellectual resources to both generate revenue and help constituents. Additionally, short-term training for lay leaders, or social development projects that integrate faith and basic life skills are but a few examples of areas in which theological institutions could assist the church and para-church organizations and at the same time generate revenue by charging a reasonable fee. Students of theological institutions could also assist with special outreach projects such as providing counseling services for communities affected by natural disasters or socio-political conflicts that the church or para-church organizations cannot provide for lack of human resources.

Otherwise, an institution could outsource its administrative support staff to provide services to other organizations if such activity would not overburden them. Administrative services such as accounting, logistical planning, procurement, property management and similar tasks could also generate third stream revenue for an institution. However, campus administration would need to evaluate the extent to which it is utilizing the time of current staff to the fullest. Based on the results of an assessment for this purpose, an institution could then explore different ways to deploy additional staffing hours to provide paid services to other organizations. In each case, these are examples of additional ways internal talents on staff at an institution could be deployed as paid consulting services to generate revenue.

Agricultural Projects

This is an area that many theological institutions have difficulty considering because of the dichotomy of the sacred and the secular. Yet, every work done within the prescribed law of the land to the benefit of humankind is ordained by God. The controversy surrounding the idea of full-time or bi-vocational ministers, sacred or secular work is not necessarily right or wrong. Therefore, whatever we do whether in word or deed, we should do all to the glory of God (Colossians 3:17).

Farming is one of the most common means of generating income since many theological institutions in Africa have uncultivated land that could be utilized for such purposes. Institutions must begin by considering production of enough food and other products first for internal consumption and then balance that with extending the same services to the general public. This would significantly reduce internal costs for food and other products. A successful agricultural project could serve the public while also generating revenue for the school. Cultivating profitable crops, or raising poultry, livestock, or fish could be a major source of revenue.

Food production is a high-demand project throughout Africa. Therefore, in this regard, a governing board could help theological institutions by setting-up profit-making projects and managing them so that they do not distract institutional leadership from fulfilling a school's core mandate. There are a number of examples of African institutions that have shown signs of increased revenue through agricultural projects. Hence, it is a feasible enough third stream alternative to explore as a way to maximize a needed revenue stream.

The reason agricultural projects have been attractive to many institutions is because the principal capital in such endeavors is land, which institutions own. The prospects for such projects to be profitable are very high and institutions that do not want to invest in these projects can still lease the land to commercial farmers who would, for instance, lease the land annually from an institution. Otherwise, allowing institutional land to remain under-utilized while facing financial crisis is totally unacceptable and poor stewardship of God's resources.

Leasing Facilities

Leasing fully equipped facilities that are well developed could possibly generate a fair amount of revenue for an institution depending on local market trends. However, leasing an institution's facilities is a major undertaking that requires careful study and involvement by the governing board. There is a high level of investment required. Whether an institution intends to develop a rental facility for office space, conferencing, lodging (i.e., guesthouse services), residential housing, or shopping area, such a deployment of the school's facilities would require a significant investment, and would be feasible only if there were a more than average potential to generate revenue for the institution. Therefore, a thorough feasibility and risk analysis assessment should be conducted before such plans are undertaken. This is in order to ensure that the development of the facility would not sink the institution deeper into debt and financial crisis and the most prudent course of action is always taken

The meticulous process required to undertake such projects should not deter institutional leaders from working with board members to determine ways to proceed—especially if such there is potential for a strong return on investment. Many theological institutions teach and preach faith but are ironically highly risk-adverse because of a comforting dependence on tuition and donations to generate revenue. Yet, there has to be a balance in how these projects and the needs of an institution are safeguarded. The governing board must provide leadership in this regard.

Other Services

There are many other services that theological institutions could provide to the public as a means of generating income to defray operational costs. But these options depend on the needs of the community and available resources from an institution to meet the need. Among the many theological institutions that have many under-utilized school buses, different ways to lease them to the community could be planned. Likewise, library facilities could be improved so that the public could utilize this resource for a fee. This would be a way for the campus to reach out and serve the needs of the community. Photocopying, printing and Internet services could also be offered to the community for a fee, depending on the demand and availability of resources. Or, creating staffing services could provide students an opportunity to earn income and generate revenue for an institution. Such partnerships between the school, the student body and the community are among many creative ways through which institutions can generate third stream revenue.

PITFALLS OF THIRD STREAM PROJECTS

For all the benefits, there are also dangers associated with third stream projects, which institutions must address, if they are to fully realize financial health. Pitfalls can include mission drift, challenges to management oversight, financial loss, and change in an institution's legal status (i.e., loss of not-for-profit privileges), among others. Failure to address these challenges at the initial stages of third stream project development could result in partial or even complete failure of a project. All the potential opportunities mentioned above require a careful feasibility study and a robust business plan to ensure delineate profitability before any investment is made. Since the goal is to achieve financial sustainability, all necessary efforts must be made to both ensure that losses are not incurred and that financial challenges are fixed during the run of a project.

Mission Drift

Third stream activities are a way to generate additional revenue in order to fulfill the core mission of an institution. Conversely, a gradual departure from the core mission of an institution into peripheral activities is a drain on already strained resources. Therefore, it is important that all third stream activities contribute fundamentally to the mission of an institution. Third stream projects often take more time and energy than envisaged, and this can be stressful to the institutional leadership if an initiative does not have effective, skilled managerial oversight.

The cumulative time and energy spent on a third stream project is time and energy taken away from core organizational operations. Sometimes, these projects can be very successful and may outgrow the theological institution that initiated them. Budgets, staff, profitability, and other resources can change and subsequently change the viability of a project. Although a theological institution might continue to depend on a project for additional revenue, steps need to be taken to ensure that projects do not replace the core mandate of an institution. An optimal way to manage and fulfill projects should be superintended by a separate legal entity that is accountable to the governing board of an institution.

There is need for a governing board to carefully evaluate the extent to which time, energy, and other resources are allocated to fulfill core mandates so that third stream projects do not inadvertently suffer, as well. The quality of leadership provided by a governing board is critical in this matter and must ensure at all costs that an institution focuses its energy on fulfilling both mission and vision. This presupposes that the institution has a strong and able board endowed with the expertise and skills needed for such endeavors. Many theological institutions in Africa are still grappling with the decision whether to accept third stream projects or not and have not fully embraced the philosophy of pursuing them owing to a founders' ministry model, as discussed earlier. Therefore, theological institutions are very far from experiencing mission drift at this time but warnings need to be sounded early so that institutions tread with trepidation and diligence as they engage third stream activities to forestall mission drift.

Management Challenges

Management of third stream projects can be difficult especially if mis-handled by an institution's leadership team. Evidently, many theological institutions in Africa already suffer managerial challenges either because staff members are not qualified or the system lacks policies and procedures to ensure a management team's success. For this reason, the burden of ad-ditional managerial responsibilities created by third stream projects may pose significant challenges to leadership. The stresses of managing revenue generating projects are very different from managing the daily operations of a theological institution.

Daily operations are concerned with income and expenditure, whereas successful third stream projects are driven by sales and overall profitability. Therefore, these projects should not be managed by the institutions con-tracting such projects but by legal entities run by professional management teams expert in the areas essential to the success of a third stream project. Experts can ensure that projects are ethically managed for efficiency and profitability. Governing boards and institutional leadership must be fully aware that the current paradigm of administrating theological institutions is nearly the antithesis of the entrepreneurial spirit of initiating and growing third stream projects. This alertness must be properly managed to avoid the pitfall of jeopardizing current ministry activities or stifling creative ideas that have the potential to generate wealth for the institution.

Financial Loss

The risk of financial loss is the fear of every governing board and institutional administration. It is the reason institutions hesitate to start third stream projects. Of course, third stream projects like any other business venture carry a certain level of risk. However, risk must be calculated and managed within the overall scope of the project. Although the level of risk varies with projects, nonetheless there is risk of loss if there is any potential for profitability.

The fear of financial loss can be so strong that it can paralyze an institution's ability to adopt any creative ideas for third stream projects. In response, the governing board must endeavor to sift through ideas and opportunities, so they can help institutional leadership overcome the paralysis of risk-aversion by directly approving third stream opportunities supported by accurate research to determine risks. This is what feasibility study and business plans accomplish—they are a means to ascertain profitability and identify potential risks. Information can empower leadership with the tools to decide feasibility of potential third stream projects and in turn, encourage institutional leaders to fully support those plans that prove to be appropriate for an institution to pursue.

Financial loss does happen with business ventures and depending on the magnitude, it could either strengthen leadership's resolve to pursue more feasible options or destroy any motivation to further explore third stream projects. Overall, very few businesses start with profits. Usually, businesses identify marginal losses or break-even financial targets with a detailed business plan. The business plan is basically a map plotting where thresholds of profitability and growth are achievable over time.

A fully detailed plan helps decision-makers effectively delay tendencies toward instant gratification or quick-result mentalities often characterized by the decisions made among institutions lacking good business sense. The need to achieve financial sustainability as fast as possible may drive a quick-result mentality, but this is a danger, which must be avoided if third stream ventures are to have any chance to succeed. Financial losses are not necessarily bad if they do not cripple the ability to invest in and refine a venture until it proves profitable—if in fact, that is an option. Success and failure provide tangible lessons that can lead to profitability if managed well.

Administrators and managers should be greatly concerned if there is no watertight business plan, because the effort and discipline to break-even or achieve profitability is impossible without a compass to direct appropriate decision-making. A situation where financial loss is incurred year after year is totally unacceptable and must not be condoned since it drains leaders' energy and causes stress within the entire institution. This is why the governing board must be actively involved in third stream projects, to ascertain the potential for profitability by scrutinizing feasibility studies, business plans, and institutional capacity for suggested projects. This will reduce repeated financial losses and safeguard the interest of the institution.

In reality, this is a primary responsibility of the governing board in the first place. Theological institutions must apply all diligence to pursue successful projects when taking the risk to invest in third stream projects. Diligence means, ensuring that financial losses from a project do not increase institutional debt or stifle the fulfillment of any core mandate. Third stream projects are necessary for financial sustainability of every theological institution in Africa and must be pursued, but pursued wisely.

Nonprofit Privileges

Many theological institutions in Africa are registered under various national not-for-profit acts. Or some institutions can be legally categorized as a non-governmental organization (NGO). Still others operate within the legislative authority of higher education boards, ministries or commissions in their respective countries. Some campuses are registered under various religious education acts and therefore considered synonymous with a religious denomination. As a result of these registrations, certain privileges are extended to theological institutions that other business organizations cannot enjoy, such as tax exemptions and waivers of certain fees and tariffs associated with securing and providing goods and services. The implications of third stream projects potentially compromising those privileges must be carefully weighed.

Some governments are flexible with the plans from theological institutions to create third stream projects to generate revenue. There are many countries that require such ventures to be managed under a different legal entity so that profit from these projects can be taxed accordingly. Therefore, understanding the legal provisions within one's respective country about such ventures is critical before any third stream project is launched. The saddest thing that can happen to an institution is to lose its not-for-profit status because of a third stream project. Therefore, every effort must be made to avoid such an error. The kind of legal registration an institution possesses in a country should be kept in perspective, with regards to all activities and governing boards. This is to ensure that institutional leaders comply with all legal stipulations of a respective country.

The role of third stream projects in achieving financial sustainability in theological institutions in Africa is so crucial that leaders must give these projects priority and focus to keep institutions financially afloat. Donations will continue to impact the way institutions are managed and grow. However, this will be budgeted to specific areas and for institutional development and advancement. Organizations that care more about the future of theological education will continue to support institutions in Africa. At the same time, they should not gravitate toward the usual piecemeal grants that provoke an appetite but do not satisfy hunger. Funding organizations and theological institutions in Africa need to develop strong relationships that allow open and honest discussions on the best ways to achieve financial sustainability. In such a safe environment, there is no patronage. Instead, partners work together to achieve a common a goal.

For instance, donations can be used to primarily focus on addressing the weak state of institutional structures that threaten the future of theological education in Africa. Leadership will change from time to time, but strong institutional structures will facilitate continuity of vision, mission, and funding; thereby, providing a framework for all manner of leaders to grow and flourish. Likewise, donations could also be used to address capital projects that provide opportunities for institutions to leverage revenue to grow their sustainability muscles. These then become seed grants to kick-start third stream projects, under requisite professional guidance and support. This strategy is to ensure profitability. Although donations can fluctuate along local and foreign economic trends, they are an essential part of advancing theological education across the globe.

Revenue from tuition will continue to grow as efforts to increase student enrollment are intensified; however, tuition will always grow proportionately with operational costs. Therefore, tuition can only contribute marginally to operating revenue. Despite tuition in Africa being far lower than comparable institutions abroad, students will continue to struggle to pay fees. Tuition income therefore should not motivate the rollout of diverse academic programs or change of institutional status to university. Although increases in student enrollment can have significant impact on operating revenue, such increases are unlikely to happen given that market demand is low for theological graduates from theological institutions. Yet, the growing involvement of laity is changing the classic face of theological education. The result is increased enrollment of part-time students. Therefore, tuition revenue will undoubtedly at best cover nearly a third of overall operational costs, meaning the other seventy percent will need to be secured from other sources. The advent of third stream projects has been serendipitous for many theological institutions. Well-researched third stream projects that are meticulously planned have great potential to create significant revenue to fill budgetary shortfalls.

God has graciously lavished on every institution a seed of opportunity through gifts and abilities that can be translated into revenue-generating third stream projects. These gifts need not be despised, but must be utilized to the fullest as financial sustainability is explored. Governing board involvement in choosing the third stream projects, identifying the appropriate management structures to operate them, and working to reduce risk cannot be overemphasized. Unfortunately, many leaders of theological institutions in Africa do not have what it takes to effectively and efficiently operate third stream projects. Hence, the involvement of the governing board is necessary, not to operate the projects themselves but to ensure that requisite structures are instituted to facilitate smooth operations. Ultimately, a strong institutional capacity to manage tuition, strengthen donor base, and grow profitability through third stream projects will set theological institutions on the path to financial sustainability.

Chapter 8

Strategic Collaboration and Modes of Delivery

STRATEGIC COLLABORATION OFFERS THEOLOGICAL institutions a way to leverage their strengths for cost effective and sustainable outcomes, while minimizing the potential impact of organizational vulnerabilities. Collaborative problem solving is a contemporary global trend that no institution dares oppose. Instead, many institutions are adjusting their strategies to align with this inevitable push. The future belongs to learning institutions that are able to discern new trends and act upon them appropriately. This is the needed strategy to thrive in an ever-changing environment.

Strategic collaborations are perceived as a great way to harness resources and achieve more for the kingdom. Unfortunately, collaborations can tend to be more competitive than mutually supportive. All manner of meetings have been held in the past to foster collaboration. Yet, in reality very few theological institutions partner to share program activities. Very few leaders actually go beyond long speeches and consultations to really collaborate. It has often taken the guarantee of funding and help from organizations to bring African theological leaders together to collaborate. Given this reluctance to collaborate, a lot of work needs to be done to gradually encourage cooperation between organizations. The goal is to unite the best minds in order to better solve sustainability challenges.

There are different areas of concern that could greatly benefit from collaboration. Among these areas are academic programming, accreditation processes, financial and administrative services, faculty recruitment, and acquisition of library resources, physical facilities, and many similar essential services. Deliberate efforts to collaborate in these areas could significantly reduce the cost of operations and improve outcomes. Indeed, strategic collaboration is one viable way to address sustainability measures.

ACADEMIC PROGRAMS

Academic programs across Africa are very similar because many institutions have patterned their curriculum after Western seminaries such as Fuller Theological Seminary, Trinity Evangelical Divinity School, Dallas Theological Seminary, Calvin Theological Seminary, Biola University, Asbury Theological Seminary, University of Aberdeen, Durham University and The Reformed Theological Seminary, among others. The content and philosophy shaping programs and courses are also similar, with only a few minor changes relevant to African realities. Therefore, collaboration is very possible if institutions and mission agencies were willing to overcome their political and idiosyncratic denominational differences.

One compelling reason for collaboration across institutions is the decline of enrollment in certain programs. One way graduate theological institutions across the same city could address dwindling enrollment is for example offer a Master of Divinity degree in such a way that students from one institution could register for a similar class at a neighboring institution. The principal benefit would be budgetary: only one lecturer would be needed to teach a combined class rather than two or three in duplicate programs at different institutions. In some cases, faculty in these institutions are already doing this—teaching two or three smaller classes, instead of a combined larger class.

Many lecturers move from one institution to another teaching the same classes with the same notes that are seldom revised. Nonetheless, if collaboration were the rule of thumb across academic programs, management would be able to maximize faculty instructional engagement with students by reducing duplication as well as excessive commuting between campuses.

Since the design and philosophy of many of the graduate courses often replicate Western institutions, collaboration across African academic programs could be a pragmatic option. Yet, collaboration across academic programs aimed at developing doctoral-level African faculty is almost nonexistent. There are few graduate institutions offering doctoral programs in theological studies and there is little effort being made to train high-caliber students to consider teaching as a post-graduate career.

Although institutions tend to focus on distinctive aspects of their programs to better distinguish themselves from competing programs, actual practice is different from what is marketed to the public. The argument for institutional branding and marketing of academic programs breaks down when efforts to recruit faculty to these highly visible campuses fail. The critical shortage of faculty in many respects is what drives faculty recruitment, not the marketed and branded face of a particular institution. Therefore, institutions need to realistically understand the challenges among targeted demographics in order to strategically collaborate for greater and higher impact instruction for these constituents. Strictly focusing on branding for marketing purposes widens relational gaps and too often discourages partnerships.

However, the critical shortage of effective faculty could be reversed if graduate program enrollment increased to extend positive tuition margins, and world-class doctoral mentoring became widely available. The resulting impact of high-caliber graduates could be felt if institutions collaborated to offer graduate programs. Strategically focused doctoral programs are not only cost effective compared to Western programs but are also contextually relevant to the prevailing challenges facing Africa. Students would be empowered to wrestle with contemporary issues and creatively develop solutions to best respond to the needs.

Collaborative efforts to design academic programs that not only train leaders to serve both church and society, but also increase the number of theological institutions are worthwhile endeavors. Developing a new generation of faculty members equipped to be instructors in theological institutions through collaborative academic programs would afford institutions the luxury of engaging church practitioners who may also qualify to serve as faculty. The teaching load for each faculty member could be reduced considerably, creating time for research and publishing—two pursuits, which are currently at their lowest ebb in many theological institutions on the continent. This new focus could further reduce the financial strain on institutions in terms of payroll since faculty could generate another revenue stream through research and development projects.

If there is anything we have learned in Africa regarding the computer technology industry, it is that when knowledge and potential are released through collaborations, local experts can develop technology that addresses global challenges. Money transfer systems through African mobile phone technology are an example of this. These technologies have been combined to revolutionize money transfer systems. Likewise, efforts to increase the number of effective instructors could revolutionize the manner in which faculty are used as a critical resource. If institutions are able to design collaborative processes across advanced academic programs then faculty development can be prioritized.

FACULTY

Although institutions would like to hire more faculty than are currently available, the reality is that the struggle to meet staffing needs is a perfect opportunity for creative solutions through strategic collaboration, if institutions decide to work together. This could be considered a temporary measure, but if we consider the number of years it takes to train one faculty member and the cost involved, adequately meeting staffing needs is an ongoing challenge. Since faculty members are already lecturing at multiple institutions to make extra income, collaboration in this case would be for institutions to recognize the staffing overlap and actually schedule personnel in an effective manner so as to assist staff not to spread themselves too thin, and thereby compromise the quality of teaching.

Another problem that has plagued African faculty development over the years, especially among those who train in Western countries is the high rate of attrition. High rates of attrition in general do not offer much hope that current staffing needs can be sufficiently met at many theological institutions in Africa. Many well-meaning leaders who enrolled in Western theological institutions to seek advanced training with the aim of returning to teach in Africa are now teaching and working in Western institutions, churches, and organizations. There are several factors that account for such high attrition rates.

The same potential faculty members are given many attractive competing offers from abroad. Yet, at the same time, the very fact that African institutions are struggling financially reduces the chances to attract high-caliber faculty-in-training. This is because candidates for African faculty positions face insufficient financial resources, the burden of paying for quality education for their children, lack of job placement programs, and inadequate re-entry plans, along with a lack of opportunities for family members to fully pursue their dreams. Therefore, as long as there are no collaborative academic programs for faculty development, faculty shortages will continue to be the norm.

Through collaboration, institutions can identify staff strengths and weaknesses by working with other institutions to best utilize faculty in specific assignments. For example, staff with strong academic backgrounds in church history might coordinate history class instruction. Likewise, the best biblical language scholars could be assigned to coordinate language classes, and so on. Under this kind of system, it is conceivable that collaborating institutions would likely coordinate the best outcomes as they draw upon each other's strengths. Moreover, this practice would not only address faculty shortages, but also strengthen the quality of theological education and produce well-equipped graduates armed with the wisdom to tackle issues on the continent.

Just as iron sharpens iron, it would be a benefit to create forums within such collaborations to showcase academic and professional talents, on the one hand, but also to create in-service training opportunities for higher productivity can be achieved. Inspiring collegiality among members of such forums could enhance opportunities for joint research and publication in similar areas of interest. In addition, creatively fertile working environments also prove to attract faculty from other continents to participate in on-going academic discourse. Strategic collaboration among faculty in theological institutions across Africa is long overdue, and therefore the clarion call is for institutional leaders to step out of their comfort zones and start the dialogue for collaboration, on behalf of scholars, church and society, and the future of theological education in Africa.

LIBRARY RESOURCES

In general, the current quality and quantity of library resources available at many theological institutions across Africa leaves much to be desired. Library resources are often donated from Western countries and are resources that those institutions no longer need. Consequently, the materials are often outdated long before arrival. Dependence on outdated resources always keeps African students and faculty way behind current trends and deliberations, and hence robs them of the opportunity to contribute to global scholarly debates. In addition, many institutions in Francophone Africa have even less opportunity to acquire quality resources since donated resources are often written in English.

Many library resources in theological institutions were gathered when schools first opened their doors. Since then, institutions have not always had the resources to update neither instructional or library materials for decades. This is mainly because the financial investment needed to update library resources is huge. Consequently, given on-going difficulties to pay faculty and staff salaries, updating library resources ranks very low among operational priorities. Few new books are added from year to year unless there are significant donations from Christian book drives, for instance. Even with such a boost, new resources which are acquired are also almost always outdated. Consequently, the status quo remains. Since teaching takes precedence over faculty research and publication, library resources will likely continue to be collections of outdated Western materials.

One way institutions are trying to upgrade current library resources is through subscriptions to online databases. These kinds of subscriptions require Internet connectivity and payment of annual fees. Internet connectivity is available in almost every theological institution in Africa; therefore, online databases seem to be a reasonable strategy and deserves allocation of financial resources to address the need. It is true that sometimes the bandwidth is small and speed is slow. Nevertheless, connectivity is always available at a reasonable fee. The greater challenge is the payment of annual subscription fees to access the databases.

Institutions are able to submit initial payment to apply for subscription services, but in the long run are too often unable to sustain the continuous payment for the resources. Many institutions have lost access to various databases for non-payment of fees, while others are saddled with huge outstanding balances. Purchasing printed library resources is totally out of reach for many because of the cost not only of the materials, but also of shipping. Therefore, opportunities for campus libraries to provide access to quality instructional resources are limited when an institution faces significant financial challenges and must stretch scant resources to sustain basic operations.

Collaboration would also allow libraries to share best practices to curtail theft of books and materials, since theft is a common problem in libraries with poor security systems. Securing a collection often includes barcoding every book and printed resource for barcode readers, scanners, and detectors. In some cases, closed-circuit television (CCTV) security systems are needed to provide visual monitoring. Institutions do not only have to strive to secure library resources, they must also secure the safety of patrons and workers. All of these considerations do significantly impact the cost of operating quality libraries.

Theological institutions should strategically collaborate to share library resources, because collaboration will enable schools to secure joint database subscription services and access to a wider variety of library resources and services across different campuses. In this way, each institutional library can specialize in parts of collections and holdings to benefit the greater community of institutions in a particular country.

Institutions would be able to generate additional income through these arrangements to offset their operating expenses without jeopardizing the fulfillment of their core mandate of training leaders for church and society. Several theological institutions could also collaborate in the development and publishing of learning materials similar to those available through TEE but geared toward learning in a classroom.

ACCREDITATION

Institutional and program accreditation is a major factor in educational activity on the continent, because of the emphasis people put on certification—sometimes even over skills and competencies. Accreditation allows institutions to join networks of similar institutions where best practices are learned and shared. Many training programs do not require rigorous academic accreditation or any particular kind of physical facility. Therefore, such programs could be hosted in rented or donated spaces.

However, more importantly, certification is often the one most persuasive factor influencing a prospective student's choice of campus, because an institution's academic programs may be validated by accreditation. The prospects for continued education in accredited post-secondary institutions are guaranteed when such certification is in place, and thereby provides students with a sense of certainty of future advancement. Accreditation also attracts certain kinds of faculty and staff who may want to associate with a particular status or class level within the institutions they serve.

Accreditation comes with many demands and conditions that can compromise the very mission an institution was established to achieve. National and regional accreditations in particular have the tendency to push such an agenda, driving institutions to a path of change that is completely different from the mission an institution originally intended to achieve. Such missional drift can be avoided through strategic collaboration to earn accreditation.

Institutional accreditation is very different from program accreditation, because the requirements are broad in terms of staff, faculty, strategic planning, library facilities, classrooms, equipment, student enrollment, and funding, among others. Institutional accreditation attracts annual or biannual inspections of a particular institution as a requirement to retain accreditation. The rigorous process of meeting these demands and the ever-changing requirements from the accrediting bodies can weigh heavily on an institution and divert attention from the main goal of training leaders for church and society.

Program accreditation on the other hand has different requirements and does not have to be secured directly from an accrediting agency. Although many accrediting bodies on the continent require institutional accreditation before validating an institution's programs, there are situations where a school can secure accreditation for one or two academic programs through another accredited institution. In that way, an institution has the freedom to offer many other courses and programs that do not need accreditation. There is flexibility in this strategy because overall course content will not be subjected to the same scrutiny as accredited programs. It is therefore expedient for a theological institution to consider national and regional institutional accreditation, but strategically.

This is especially true if an institute's mandate is to train leaders at lower and non-academic levels via short in-service courses and continuing education programs leading to non-examinable certificates. Academic short-term and non-examinable training courses have been acceptable offerings within the social and physical sciences for decades. Theological education in Africa should consider the value of such courses as relevant training paths, despite their exception to accreditation. Some institutions in Africa should resist the temptation to pursue institutional accreditation if strategic collaboration will accomplish the same objectives.

For years, the Association for Christian Theological Education in Africa (ACTEA) has been providing accreditation for many theological institutions in Africa to maintain their core mission while offering examinable programs at higher levels. The agency also provides enough latitude for institutions to offer non-examinable programs to advance the mission of the church within internationally acceptable standards. Consequently, there is no continental accrediting agency in Africa for theological education that can match this feat. ACTEA, like other regional and continental accrediting bodies has distinguished itself by promoting not only institutional accreditation but also program accreditation through its systems. Strategic collaboration through accreditation allows institutions to avoid mission drift but meet the needs of ministry at the grassroots.

The mission of theological institutions is not necessarily to churn out more graduates or to raise profits, but rather to raise men and women who will help fulfill the Great Commission, which is a time sensitive mission. There is no room for delays or feet-dragging when it comes to pursuing the Master's business. Jesus rightly noted that we must therefore work while it is day, for night quickly approaches when no man can work (John 9:4). These are ministry needs accredited institutions alone are unable to meet.

FINANCIAL AND ADMINISTRATIVE SERVICES

Due to size and financial position, many theological institutions in Africa are unable to afford highly qualified financial and administrative staff. The cost of providing financial and administrative services can weigh heavily on an institution's budget and drain its limited resources. Unless we have missionary staff, often institutions must choose between two options: either hiring qualified staff at high costs or settling for an average staff at much lower costs. Therefore, many hire staff with the barest minimum skills at a lower cost, often resulting in poor performance or less than effective management of resources. Consequently, certain important financial and administrative decisions fall through the cracks for lack of competency. Theological institutions in Africa must seriously consider ways collaboration can fundamentally safeguard an organization's values while still advancing the overall goal of developing leaders for church and society.

Organizations that desire high quality financial and administrative staff services but are unable to utilize the services of their qualified staff to the maximum often subcontract the services of their staff to other organizations at a fee. This enables institutions to utilize qualified staff optimally. Alternately, some organizations outsource their financial and administrative paperwork during the year such as during annual audits. This results in much lower costs than hiring full-time staff. Every institution must have efficient and effective financial systems to manage its resources.

Institutions in a particular country can strategically collaborate to form a not-for-profit financial and administrative organization to provide essential services at a much cheaper cost than what they are using now. If setting up such a group may create certain legal complications, then institutions can collaborate to share services of qualified staff still at a much cheaper cost. The ideal situation is having the qualified staff one needs and having the resources to pay them at market rate.

The next option is for institutions to form an independent body to provide these services for a more economical rate across a network of institutions. In other words, they can share the most qualified and expensive staff by allowing that staff to provide services for two or three institutions at a shared cost. Strategic collaboration is possible, especially if business organizations are willing and able to strategically collaborate for such services. If business organizations use such methods, why should it be difficult for a network of colleges to do the same?

The biggest hindrance to collaboration is the entrenched exclusivity adopted over the years by various church and mission agencies. Perhaps the idea of our-way-is-the-only-way approach to operations developed out of doctrinal and philosophical ministry differences. Yet, institutions must unite rather than remain divided into separate denominational camps, because our common faith must motivate us to do so.

We are so polarized across denominations that even when it makes good sense to strategically collaborate, we do not do it lest we be misunderstood and sacrifice precious reputations. Even when strategic collaboration provides a clear benefit far outweighing precious reputations, we still insist on doing our little things in our little cocoons depriving the Lord the opportunity to do greater things through our unity. Sometimes the most common excuse is to maintain confidentiality.

However, the tendency to avoid transparency is often more a case of organizations covering up ineffective financial and administrative practices, than protecting privacy. I am always amazed at the level of hypocrisy we practice when leaders of different theological institutions meet at common forums. These displays of collegiality often fall short of real action that can translate into results that will advance the cause of Jesus Christ, the one we claim to represent.

Institutions can collaborate by sharing staff to fulfill financial and administrative services, which can surprisingly comprise one-third of overall operational costs. In certain countries where there is diversity among theological institutions such as in South Africa, Kenya, Nigeria, Cameroon, Ghana, and Uganda, collaboration of financial and administrative services should be the norm and not the exception. Such collaboration can be encouraged by all stakeholders including churches, mission agencies, and funders.

Even business organizations and non-governmental organizations with wildly divergent values and principles are more willing to strategically collaborate than theological institutions in Africa who share core values. Jesus Christ our Lord foresaw this tragic situation and prayed in John 17 that we should be one body, just as he and the Father are one. He emphasized that the harvest is ripe and the laborers are few. Therefore, we should pray to the Lord of the harvest to send more laborers into the fields. Theological education is not just about education.

Rather, it is the equipping of men and women with the leadership skills to disciple church and society. It is the raising up of a generation fully committed to the cause of Christ to transform our church and society. This cannot be achieved with the splintered-theological mindset we currently have in education. Instead, it requires a level of selflessness and sacrifice to achieve the goal of raising more laborers for the kingdom. It requires a clear departure from hypocritical innuendos and lip service in order to deliberately work together regardless of our evangelical differences. If individual mission organizations or parent churches focus all their energy solely on promoting themselves, African institutions will collectively squander opportunities to collaborate now and in the future. Every opportunity must be utilized to create a common front for growth and development of theological education in Africa.

PHYSICAL FACILITIES

Apart from academic programs, faculty and library resources, accrediting agencies have specific standards that must be met. Physical facilities in particular, are important because they are the learning environment. Physical facilities consist of classrooms, offices, library spaces, fittings and fixtures, as well as common spaces devoted for student, faculty, and staff interactions. Research confirms the importance of physical facilities to the learning process; however, in a generation of blended learning, there are several creative ways to address challenges inherent in building and maintaining physical facilities. Strategic collaborations for the use of physical facilities could help institutions avoid rising costs of building new structures in many cities across Africa.

Institutions through strategic collaboration with mega-churches, para-church organizations, and other schools can secure space in geographic locations perfect for leadership training events. No real estate needs to be purchased. No physical structures need to be built. A collaborative arrangement with strategic partners such as a church or other organization could provide a quick and convenient solution for a training session's site requirements. Spaces that could serve as temporary classrooms through these collaborations are often affordable and could provide an environment conducive to learning.

Institutions that have gone in this direction have managed to increase their enrollment through these distributed learning approaches, reaching more leaders than they would have, had they planned for participants to travel to their campuses. The collaborative model allows students to stay in their ministry setting, continue with whatever they are doing to earn a livelihood while pursuing theological education. It allows them opportunities to apply what they are learning immediately in their ministries while they continue with their studies. At the same time, institutions are saved from the headaches of providing housing and finding the funds to create scholarships. Moreover, coordinating staff to conduct in-service training for leaders is easier when a larger pool of people is available to choose from.

Teachers for these programs can be deployed to readily accessible areas where a greater percentage of them already serve as local church pastors. Staff at theological institutions can train pastors and teachers who in turn will be responsible to run the in-service sessions. This will make reaching large groups of people efficient as a core of theology staff train and deploy a larger contingent of instructors into local neighborhoods.

Of course, there will always be the challenge of providing library and training resources for in-service participants. Yet, institutions can collaborate with other theological institutions and schools across a city to provide limited access to campus libraries. Program supervisors can secure designated materials at campus libraries or neighborhood public libraries in coordination with subject areas being studied. Similar arrangements could be made with mega-churches, which often have their own library collections and could add more materials specifically for these training programs.

There are always logistical challenges for the care, security, and management of these limited library resources. This may be the risk that institutions should be willing to face and perhaps as a program grows in a particular location, better services can be secured to reduce the risk and make library resources secure. Today, in every African town there is an Internet café where students can access the World Wide Web and look for free study resources online for their classes. Although some of these Internet cafés have slow connectivity, they are affordable and can be used to access other library resources from the institution's main library or from other sites online for training.

There are countless opportunities for institutions to collaboratively share physical facilities for undergraduate and graduate programs. When schools are on vacation, large sections of their classrooms and student housing are not used. Other institutions can use the facilities for classes, workshops, conferences, and conventions. Local churches and organizations can rent institutional facilities for meetings and training events. Through such collaborations a denominational institution with too many students to accommodate in a limited facility can utilize some of the under-utilized facilities of a non-denominational institution for classrooms, offices and student services.

African theological institutions do not necessarily need a traditional school campus to train leaders for church and society. There are opportunities to train leaders in locations far from campuses where institutions are currently situated. In the case of theological training at lower academic levels (e.g., one or two year programs for high schools graduates) this is particularly true. Many of these graduates may not qualify for admission into undergraduate or graduate educational programs, but are already in church leadership and require training. In any given African country, there may be thousands of leaders residing in scattered cities needing quality training at the grassroots. Yet, the unavailability of accessible physical facilities has always been a hindrance to providing training for these leaders.

ESSENTIAL SERVICES

The cost of doing business in many African countries is rising steadily because of heavy investment from Asia, Europe, and North America. Consequently, the cost of providing essential financial services from health insurance to retirement options can be overwhelming for one institution to take on alone. These services are often less expensive when organizations purchase them as a group. This is the idea behind investment accounts like revenue authority or health insurance products in other countries.

For the next few decades as African economies across the continent grow exponentially, overall costs to run campuses will inflate for all institutions. Currently, the hottest frontier for new investments in Africa is property, as many cities on the continent are experiencing unprecedented growth in new developments. Consequently, theological institutions must re-think strategies to circumvent the cost of operations, since the current rate of enrollment is becoming an inadequate source of funding for operations. A proven strategy to address rising costs is to create cooperatives. A cooperative is a business venture that is owned and run jointly by members. Cooperatives lower the cost of services, can generate revenue, and offer affordable financial services (i.e., retirement investments and health insurance) for members, which in the case of member campuses would include staff and faculty.

The full spectrum of insurance products for staff, as well as for facilities and property is more affordable through cooperatives than through individual organizations. This is a tremendous benefit today for many faculty and staff because affordable retirement options were not always available to former generations of campus staff and faculty. Since salaries have been historically low, contributions to individual school retirement plans were meager resulting in sparse but expensive retirement benefits. However, this situation could improve with well-organized options to provide higher yields for a larger pool of employees across member institutions.

This is how a large fund can be leveraged from a large membership pool to be invested in capital ventures for highly profitable returns and guaranteed dividends for investing members. As an example, theological institutions in Eastern Africa could form one big organization across that region to create a pension fund ensuring that member institutions receive the best benefit options.

Security services are a necessary expenditure on any campus and this is a cost that is continually rising as the need to create safe environments ensures a productive learning environment on campus. Because of the threat of terrorism, security has become a multi-million dollar industry with a

large workforce. It is not unimaginable that in the near future security organizations and ministries will be established solely to cater to Christian
institutions and organizations.

Safety is now a top priority for institutions enrolling international students and faculty, because no institution can afford a breach that in any way
endangers the welfare of students, faculty or staff. Therefore, every institution is enlisting campus security services to protect its students and staff. Of
course, the demand for these services pushes the cost upward annually as
the world becomes more dangerous.

An array of services, including financial investments and security systems, will become increasingly expensive fixtures in the operating budgets
of theological institutions in years to come. Addressing these budgetary expenses is part of the ministry mandate for many Christian organizations so
that the work of the kingdom can continue unhindered. The availability of
these services whether insurance or retirement plans, or even campus security will depend on the ability of theological institutions to strategically collaborate in ways to ensure the highest quality of service at affordable prices
for employees and students. The cooperatives have proven to be at least one
of the most feasible ways to provide these services because, the bargaining
power of cooperatives ensures that members enjoy the best services at the
least cost at any given time.

In any given African country there might be so many theological institutions at different levels of certification, institutions will seldom form
cooperatives to secure services. Nevertheless, in an increasingly global
economy, the importance of strategic collaboration to provide essential services cannot be overemphasized. Theological institutions must strive to find
what unites them and work to create cooperatives that can secure services
at the best possible prices.

As stewards of God's resources, we must explore the best ways to
advance the kingdom agenda by procuring resources and services in the
most efficient ways possible. As the future quickly approaches, and African
economies become more sophisticated, the establishment of national and
regional organizations to efficiently provide essential services for theological institutions will be a necessity.

Western and African Christian business leaders who are deeply committed to theological education and its spiritual impact, must seek God in
prayer and explore pathways that ensure the development of Christian leaders for church and society. These strategies must not diminish the message
but rather support its growth in strength and power. Just as the ministry of
many Christian funding agencies in the West were established by business
people to advance the cause of Christ, so too is the future of theological

education in Africa dependent upon strategic collaboration of institutions spearheaded by the same caliber of people. Strategic decisions and practices must go beyond the niceties of seminars and conferences to engage grassroots leaders, and empower them to achieve the miraculous for the extension of God's kingdom.

Strategic collaboration can have huge financial implications for theological institutions in Africa, if schools are to achieve financial sustainability. However, collaboration can also inform the most efficient modes of delivery. That is because cost effective learning approaches can be prioritized in course development. Collaborations through academic programs, faculty engagement, library resource sharing, accreditation, facilities allocation, and similar offerings are but a few ways to ensure that theological institutions comprehensively fulfill their mission mandate. More importantly, strategic collaboration is but one way that theological institutions can achieve financial sustainability as they train leaders for church and society.

MODES OF DELIVERY

There are a couple of consistent trends with regards to the operations controlling African theological institutions: first, the cost of running these schools has been steadily rising over the years, and second, theological education has not changed much in Africa since the beginning—especially when compared to other disciplines being studied across the continent. Lectures in classroom settings and schools offering boarding to accommodate learners traveling from a distance are both still the primary way instruction is delivered across Africa. One reason is because fewer missionaries are involved in teaching at African theological institutions, anymore.

If institutions are to achieve financial sustainability, then the residential model must evolve into something that is equally effective but less expensive to operate. One particular strategy is Theological Education by Extension (TEE) as discussed in Chapter 2. The main purpose of TEE is to provide an alternative mode of delivery. Of course, as with any significant change in the culture of an organization, there has to be a willingness to embrace new ways of achieving the same goal. In this context, cultural changes across organizations must be driven by the administration of each school.

Yet, for as much as TEE was effective for a period of time, the problems currently plaguing theological institutions in general, have been associated with TEE, as well. The TEE model has not been able to make its way into mainstream theological education in such a way as to be a credible alternative. However, a review of existing literature does outline a number of modes that theological institutions should consider. As institutions seek to embrace financially sustainable ways to deliver first-rate instruction, viable alternatives to consider include open and distance learning modes, church-based instruction, and integrated learning, among others.

Open and Distance Learning

The advent of open and distance learning has revolutionized learning across the world. These alternatives make it possible for those who cannot enroll in a classroom-based academic course to nevertheless still have accessible quality alternatives for ministry training. For one, distance (or open) learning courses can be accessible online, via mobile phones and computers. There can also be printed materials offered as correspondence courses; or even a blending of these instructional opportunities. Ultimately, technological advancements in this century have created various platforms through which to offer a variety of choices to learners—more than we have ever previously experienced.

Correspondence Courses

It all started several years ago when a number of programs adopted correspondence courses as a means of providing training for those who could not access classes conducted on distant campuses. Carefully prepared materials for self-study were mailed to students, who learned the materials and later took assessments to determine levels of comprehension of the materials studied. Students had to complete all materials from a course and satisfactorily pass an exam before proceeding to the next lesson.

Unfortunately, it often takes students longer to complete a correspondence course than the same course offered in a classroom. It is likely because students work at their own pace with correspondence courses. The many responsibilities of students including employment and other related engagements often compete with correspondence studies and delay completion. Some students who are self-driven perform very well. Others procrastinate, while others get discouraged for lack of necessary support to focus on and competently complete the work. Yet, correspondence courses are still viable today for those who have the discipline, self-drive and focus to do so successfully. However, the cost of printing materials and mailing is making correspondence courses more expensive now than they used to be. Although populations in many African countries have continued to increase over the years, the mailing systems in those same countries have not improved to match growing need. In some cases, the services are poorer than ever before as alternative technological forms of communication replace reliance upon national postal services.

The development of materials and production of the same is a cost that many theological institutions are finding very difficult to bear. This includes the cost of revising published materials every three to five years and re-printing them. Several years ago, I led an initiative to reach pastors in African rural areas through correspondence courses. The pastors loved the idea and wholeheartedly embrace the gesture. We invested in the program by employing instruction and content experts to design the materials for the courses. Initially, we had over 500 pastors sign-up for the courses. However, three-fourths of them were unable to pay the program's minimum fees. We approached an international non-governmental organization (NGO) working with pastors to provide them with scholarships to continue with their studies. Unfortunately, after the first three courses, the organization dropped the ball, leaving students with debt that the institution had to recover. Consequently, the program struggled for a while and was later discontinued. These courses definitely need to be subsidized because of the income levels of those who need them. This is where additional income from third stream projects can subsidize the delivery of correspondence courses in many parts of the continent.

So, the need for correspondence courses is relevant today for church workers ministering in the remotest parts of many African countries. However, such instructional programs must be done in a manner that is affordable to students who depend on meager incomes for their livelihood. Currently, very few theological institutions have correspondence courses for church workers in remote parts of Africa.

Online Courses

Online courses represent an instructional approach utilizing the Internet as a platform for learning. In reality, improved Internet connectivity across Africa has made online courses a preferred mode of learning among the educated urban middle class.

Courses are designed in a computer application and uploaded online for students to access across different geographical locations. The basic requirement is for students to have access to the Internet. Such courses initially begin with a tutorial showing users how the software application works. Tutorials will show students how to navigate the various sections, how to post papers, interact with other learners, and download reading materials. The institutions using this mode of instruction help to students overcome the challenge of commuting to a classroom. As a result, schools offering online instruction can enroll thousands of students hailing from different countries around the world to participate in online sessions. It is these campuses which have empowered students to study at their own pace, but still finish a course within a stipulated period.

To create online instructional programs, an institution needs all the technical elements to host and maintain a digital platform, all the production elements (including the talent and the equipment) to produce the instructional sessions, and the bandwidth to broadcast each session across the Internet. The main operating costs will arise from these elements, in addition to various licenses needed to legally share copyrighted materials.

Theological institutions that offer (face-to-face) classroom instruction can experience difficulties transitioning into online courses for a number of reasons. For one, faculty members are often reluctant to create time in their schedules to learn how to manage online courses; while others may harbor a fear that online courses will make them irrelevant. Secondly, among faculty members nearly all may be aware that online learning will reach many more students than they are currently teaching; however, they may be more concerned with protecting their life's work. Faculty members seeking to protect their intellectual property can be unwilling to release research or other original materials for production and sharing with a large audience of students, if they are not paid specifically for that material.

I remember spending months in meetings to discuss intellectual property policies and the changes needed to accommodate faculty misgivings about releasing those learning resources without being paid for such. Deliberate efforts had to be made to persuade and motivate faculty to embrace the concept for an institution to proceed with offering online courses. Otherwise, an online learning program will stall if faculty members fail to support the program. Faculty collectively constitutes an essential component of an online learning program. Consequently, they must be drivers of a program if it is to succeed.

Administration must find ways to pay faculty to train for this new venture Of course, there is the cost of training faculty to utilize software and the added time to schedule student group discussions and respond to questions online. This is a huge investment of time, since many faculty members are already overloaded with teaching responsibilities. At the same time, providing salaries for the cost of in-service training should be figured into the cost of training participants. Unfortunately, many theological institutions in Africa find it difficult to secure the financial resources needed to get over these fundamental hurdles. Still, some faculty members will be asked to add administrative duties to their teaching load. Therefore, working out a mutually beneficial agreement could take months, if not years and added financial resources to achieve.

Likewise, design and launch costs can be prohibitive for online courses. Institutions must invest in the platform, which need to be customized with specific program features to fit instructional needs. Additionally, schools should enlist the services of curriculum design experts who can create course templates and offer advice on the direction content should take in development. Consequently, the cost of customizing online applications with the help of instructional designers will certainly be an on-going expense for schools using digitals platforms.

Despite the benefits, there are challenges associated with online courses, both for institutions seeking to offer them and for students who enroll in such programs. Online courses require extensive digital library resources to support learning in a manner that does not compromise the quality of education offered. Yet, many theological institutions find themselves unable to pay for online database licenses. Under those circumstances, subscriptions are discontinued as some institutions become heavily indebted with overdue payments. On the other hand, students enrolled in online courses may live in areas where Internet connectivity may be very slow or fluctuate, resulting in several hours or even days without access to the virtual classroom. This is a significant problem for students living in remote areas trying to keep pace with virtual classmates.

Once the process begins, maintenance will continue for the duration of the online program. Unfortunately, this is a cost often overlooked in the planning stages. The reality is that the cost of maintaining and securing the entire learning system can be very expensive. So, even though an institution may be successful in obtaining a one-time grant to rollout an online program, the entire process can stall or even fail if the institution is not financially stable. This is why financial sustainability is so crucial for the efficient operation of an African theological institution.

There must be a demonstrated financial ability to sustain current programs before an institution launches new ones. Yet, given that tuition from student enrollment in online courses will grow revenue faster than enrollment in traditional classroom-based courses, campuses must resist the temptation to storm forward without careful planning. Hence, a significant portion of needed funding could be raised through tuition to meet operating costs. Still, institutions will have to reinvest in online programs for several years after launch to ensure growth and seamless operation. This must happen as enrollment and tuition grow to a point of profitability.

As mentioned before, many theological institutions are struggling to meet basic operational expenses and do not have the institutional capacity to pursue new instructional platforms. As viable as online courses can be, the expense of introducing and maintaining them make this venture potentially too expensive. However, if an institution is able to achieve financial stability through cooperatives and third stream projects, introducing online courses with all their complexity could be achievable. Otherwise, as already discussed, the expense of online courses would likely overburden an already sagging bottom line under existing overloaded budgets. In general, institutions must consider the operational demands of a program, costs, and duration of instruction to make the best strategic choice for instructional design.

Mobile Phone Courses

Instructional courses centered on mobile phone technology, including handheld devices like tablets and PDAs, are often referred to as m-learning courses (or mobile learning). This is a recent phenomenon and has gained considerable traction in Africa. I remember pioneering this mode of instruction with other software experts when I was the head of a theological institution. It was an exciting engagement with software experts from the Allogy Company. Allogy created the first mobile learning platforms, which was recognized globally for its innovation. My institution was involved in developing content for a pastors' training session in Africa. Basically, the course design used video to share content, and pop-up quizzes between lessons to assess understanding of the material. Students were able to ask questions for supplemental instructional support through text messaging. The texts were answered by staff in the learning center. The system allowed the learning center to monitor the progress of student output via the rate of lessons downloaded and assignments completed. The most ingenious feature of this platform was the fact that it bypassed the constraints of Internet connectivity with lessons loaded on micro SIM cards.

It is believed that over seventy percent of Africans have access to cell phones making this technology the most commonly utilized on the entire continent. The widespread use of this technology therefore makes it a platform most suited for hosting learning and training opportunities. The only limitation to the m-learning application is whether it is compatible with specific smart phone—android or IOS operating systems, for instance. Consequently, this can limit the number of phones that can be utilized for m-learning. Otherwise, m-learning is a great tool for training pastors in different parts of the continent. Unfortunately, very few institutions have access to the learning platform and many institutions are unable to invest in this technology because of the cost of creating digital applications and capturing instructional content.

Blended Courses

A blended course is a combination of two or more modes of instruction. It is often designed in such a way that students receive a certain percentage of their learning through traditional classroom-based instruction and the remaining percentage through correspondence or online courses. This mode of delivery is convenient if there are strategic collaborations to cover the cost of the online or alternative instructional modes. In this way, institutions do not need to develop an elaborate infrastructure to host online courses. This hybrid approach reduces traditional classroom time and the need for physical classrooms.

Theological institutions on the continent must find a way to pursue blended course offerings through collaboration as a primary strategy of instructional delivery. An added benefit from this strategy is the opportunity for institutions to test the waters before fully committing to online or mobile phone courses. They can gauge their capacity to sustain such endeavors if initiated and determine what further investments must be made. Blended courses should be encouraged as the preferred first step so that the transition to online or mobile courses becomes a gradual successful process. The traditional model of classroom instruction with students and teachers and textbooks is increasingly falling out of favor as many students opt for the more convenient blended-course models.

Church-Based Instruction

A church-based delivery of instruction focuses theological education on what is needed the most. This mode of delivery utilizes church facilities and provides on-site learning resources tailored to the needs of the learners and their environment. Instead of offering academic degrees, the focus is on training pastors and professionals to knowledgeably serve to the church. Instead of waiting for students to enroll in academic programs, an institution might develop modular courses for in-service session.

These are offered over time to those currently in ministry. The training is in specific areas to enhance leadership effectiveness in the church and the marketplace. Leaders will still have access to theological education, but in their ministry context so as not to compromise the quality and rigor associated with learning. Program requirements will focus on standards for matriculation and place entering students at different levels depending on their academic backgrounds. Churches can provide scholarships for pastors and advancement for leaders enrolling in these programs to serve at higher-levels of responsibility in the church.

Professionals in the church who do have resources to pay for training (i.e., department heads, deacons, elders, and so on) can enroll to sharpen their biblical and theological knowledge. They would have opportunities to sharpen their ministry skills as they study and apply new skills to their ministries. Institutions could also work with church leadership to ensure continuity between training programs.

There are many mega-churches in Africa with significant resources to fund theological education. Yet, they do not do so, because they perceive education as a separate endeavor from church ministry. In reality, church-based instruction could shape program ownership in ways that drive enroll-ment through the roof at a much lower cost of operation than many similar program offerings at institutional campuses. For instance, while mega-churches have physical facilities and resources to support their programs, small and mid-level churches could select a central location shared by a group of churches offering training courses. This would foster unity among church leaders and promote sharing of God-given resources for the growth and enhancement of the body of Christ.

Similarly, a group of churches could host specific training programs and rotate venues among the group, as a way to share instructional oppor-tunities to host a course for a period of time as church leaders may deem. Theological education is then moved from the ivory tower of academia to the real everyday life of ministry. Instructional resources for such training are made available on site and students are free to visit the institutions' li-braries for research as they complete assignments. Arrangements can also be made for students to access corresponding online resources to supple-ment learning and other instructional activities such as writing.

There are many people who would like to pursue theological educa-tion via their local churches as a form of life-long development but not necessarily for certification. Otherwise, if these extension-type course were not made available, such individuals might be unable to access theological education in general, because of barriers to academic study at a theological institutions (e.g., entrance exams, tuition, distance and so on). However, church-based instruction will provide thousands of Christians with an op-portunity to fulfill their desire to pursue theological education as a form of life-long learning and training to better serve the church.

This category of learners will not increase the number of graduates either over a window of time but will definitely contribute to ministry effectiveness. Effectiveness is the practical bottom line for theological institutions and therefore should not be shunned. Continuous interactions with church leaders and marketplace professionals will enlighten various church leaders regarding the relevance of theological education today.

Church-based instruction is conducted across a few scattered areas, but is not quite as systematic or well-organized as programs offered at formal institutions. Yet, should church-based instruction out-pace traditional classroom courses, there will be no more need for residential housing or a steady inventory of classrooms. Hence, reducing overhead and particularly staff payroll among theological institutions would be one direct benefit of church-based instruction. On the contrary, churches involved in educational programming would likely be more supportive of on-going capital campaigns sponsored by theological institutions. This could conceivably be because churches would feel the direct impact of theological institutions on their daily ministry; and therefore, would consider an institution as a supportive extension of church ministry.

Integrated Learning

Integrated learning is a manner of instruction conducted in institutions where academic disciplines other than theological education are offered. Integrated learning introduces theological education to every course offered in order to help students conceptualize the relevance of theology respective to individual courses of study and disciplines. Of course, at the same time, the winds of change are turning theological institutions into Christian universities. This transformation has become a recent phenomenon on the continent, and as much as this presents serious concerns about the future of African theological education there are situations for which this change appears timely.

It is therefore critical that we utilize every situation to promote theological education both through existing theological institutions and those transitioning into Christian universities. This is so that no opportunity is ever wasted. Fundamentally, theological institutions and Christian universities differ in the availability of non-theological programs aimed at preparing leaders for vocations other than Christian ministry. So, although theological departments in these institutions may be struggling just as theological institutions do, we must seek to utilize even the slightest opportunities that exist to support ministry preparation.

Efforts to strengthen the allure of theological departments in Christian universities must become an aggressive pursuit, with no stone unturned. However, in such institutions this must be done strategically using integrated learning. A deliberate effort to make theological coursework part of the core curriculum would help students gain practical insight the relevance of faith in various professional careers. Therefore, this more than simply adding a few Bible and theology courses to general education requirements in a disjointed and haphazard manner.

The task of melding theology across academic fields will require a meticulous and logical crafting of courses in such a way that speak to everyday life across every social discipline. These courses must raise the most pertinent biblical and theological questions that society is grappling with, while charting the way students can live influential godly lives in a fallen world. Integrated learning presents the kingdom of God as the legitimate integral feature of every discipline by delineating God's divine eternal intentions through every social discipline. Consequently, many students could encounter the risen Savior in their pursuit of secular careers in such universities as we create that environment. Therefore, integrated learning is not just about biblical and theological coursework or content, but includes the cultivation of consciousness.

Across every academic discipline, the influence of faculty is critical to embedding biblical truths about the presence of God in students. And this is not limited to those who teach Bible and theology, but also calls upon faculty across disciplines to weave their faith into the fabric of whatever they teach. For instance, a microeconomics professor teaching an undergraduate business class had so much impact on my faith that I still remember most of the things he taught me.

This is especially true because he integrated kingdom principles into the course. Professor Vince LaFrance at Messiah College at Grantham, Pennsylvania not only taught an economics class, but modeled kingdom simplicity and its applications in microeconomics. Needless to say, we have been friends ever since I left his class. The point being, faculty must integrate the divine into a material world, if instruction is to have a divine God-focused impact on all aspects of life.

Faculty members are the flesh and blood of an integrated learning program that transforms lives and careers, and subsequently society. We must hire such capable individuals onto our faculties. If the popular adage is true that "the faculty is the university," then every effort must be made to ensure that those who teach in Christian universities truly exemplify the ideals of an integrated learning program. Therefore, besides a well-crafted curriculum, there must be a fully-integrated faculty capable of communicating content in a manner that transforms lives and society.

Integrated learning is a delivery mode that theological institutions need to wholeheartedly embrace; but, more importantly it is an approach that emerging Christian universities in Africa must adopt if they are to maintain a dynamic Christian witness. It is expedient that theological institutions transitioning into Christian universities be encouraged to maintain their theological collegiality and institutional affinities so that resources from these partnerships can be harnessed. Likewise, funding organizations need to perceive this situation as a new frontier to engage a changing continent that needs support and guidance.

Theological institutions must find ways to provide short non-academic (i.e., in-service) courses for leaders serving in important roles for kingdom work. There are so many church leaders who do excellent work for the kingdom but still need to be equipped to increase their effectiveness exponentially. Most of these leaders may not qualify to be admitted into theological institutions because of their educational background, but are faithfully serving the Lord nonetheless in various parts of the continent.

Such courses would have to cover the essential areas of knowledge necessary for effective ministry and espouse creative communication strategies to promote interactive learning. These courses should not mirror the classical theological education that institutions have adopted from the West. Instead, creative communication strategies such as storytelling, drama, discussions, music, as well as didactic approaches should be the preferred instructional tools used to introduce biblical and theological truths in a contextually relevant way. A two-to-three day training session with a minimum charge would go a long way to equip leaders for the kingdom of God.

Strategic collaboration and the mode of delivery have huge financial implications for theological institutions in Africa. With these strategies schools can potentially achieve financial sustainability. The decision to enlist a particular mode of delivery whether it be open or distance learning or church-based instruction is very important in determining the overall cost of education. Approaches to open and distance courses (e.g., online, mobile phone, blended, church-based and integrated learning) will require investment. Therefore, institutions need to select the most effective approach for leadership training based on available human and financial resources.

Strategic collaborations must inform the mode of delivery because cost effective learning approaches must be a priority in course development. Collaborations through academic programs, faculty engagement, library resource sharing, accreditation, physical facilities allocation, and the provision of essential services are but a few ways to ensure that theological institutions comprehensively fulfill their mission mandate. More importantly, delivery modes and strategic collaboration are but a few ways that theological institutions can achieve financial sustainability as they train leaders for church and society.

Chapter 9

Leadership Development

CENTRAL TO FINANCIAL SUSTAINABILITY of theological institutions is effective leadership. The development of emerging leaders will ensure that future institutions and other organizations will have a bright future with knowledgeable and well-trained managers, supervisors and administrators graduating from African institutions. In particular, leadership development requires a style of mentoring that helps trainees learn ways to conceptualize, plan and implement relevant strategies and projects to benefit the health of an organization. In particular, leadership development for theological institutions is a critical component that holds all the other factors supporting financial sustainability together. Unfortunately, quality leadership development has been sporadic up to this point given the assumption that leaders will always emerge as a natural course of nature.

Equipping emerging leaders with the skills needed to address our modern daunting challenges requires development that nurtures God-given capacity in a manner that ensures efficient and effective stewardship. The focus here is on leadership development rather than molding individuals to fit specific positions. In other words, mimicking specific leaders is not the key to leadership development anymore. Instead, new forward-thinking mentoring is a clear departure from the former charismatic change-leader syndrome that characterized so much of leadership development in the past.

THE RATIONALE FOR LEADERSHIP DEVELOPMENT

Leadership is commonly understood as a process of influence toward the achievement of certain desired goals. However, Stogdill observes that leadership has as many definitions as the people who define it.[1] It is therefore necessary that the definition be narrowed to generally reflect the main idea of the term. The following definition offered by best-selling author Dr. J. Robert Clinton provides a succinct summary of a complex topic: "A dynamic process over an extended period of time in which a leader (utilizing the leadership resources and by specific leadership behaviors) influences the thoughts and activities of followers, toward accomplishment of aims— usually mutually beneficial to leaders, followers, and the macro-context of which they are a part."[2]

The idea of the follower wanting to be part of the interaction process denotes an inner motivation incited by a leader. Elliston also defines leadership as a "complex influence process in which leaders and followers interact in a context or a series of contexts over time. Within this context leaders exercise influence . . . toward a mutually desired goal."[3] The context in this case is an important one, which enhances the smooth interaction between the leader and followers. Kouzes and Posner describe it as "the art of mobilizing others to want to struggle for shared aspirations."[4] Certain factors are prominent in the definitions of Clinton, Elliston, and Kouzes and Posner, which draw on the conclusion that leadership is a complex mix of the following: influence, process, interactions, goal setting and context. Notably, leadership is not only the influence exercised by leaders, but it is also the willingness of people to be led.

Developing leaders to navigate groups toward desired results is an enormous task that requires an intentional and well-coordinated effort. In the case of fundraising, for instance, leadership must balance the various fundraising activities. Part of that balance can include conceptualizing and planning third stream projects. The ultimate goal for the group must be set and could be defined as making theological education affordable for more people.

The stages to pursue revenue-generating initiatives require leadership to conscientiously adopt cost effective delivery modes before forming strategic collaborations. In order to achieve organizational goals, leaders need

1. Stogdill, *Handbook of Leadership*.
2. Clinton, *Leadership Training Models*, 40.
3. Elliston, *Home Grown Leaders*, 7.
4. Kouzes and Posner, *Leadership Challenge*, 30–31.

to be carefully selected, trained, and deployed with an intentional plan for smooth succession. The fact that leaders will emerge with time and circumstances only exposes institutions to the dangers of appointing unprepared leaders who lack basic skills needed to excel in a position for the benefit of the organization.

Many leaders in theological institutions were promoted to their positions because they performed excellently in their field of expertise, mostly as faculty members. They often rise through the ranks as department head, academic dean, and eventually head of an institution. It is assumed that by being a good academic and having served in academic leadership positions, these individuals would be capable of leading an institution whose core business is academic.

Little attention is given to the fact that being a leader has more to do with leadership and management than academic expertise. As head of an academic institution, one is expected to demonstrate certain pedantic acumen, however, the bulk of what the position demands is competency in management. Moreover, developing leaders is not just about the leader but demands "the expression of a person's capacity to be effective in leadership development roles and processes."[5]

Leadership development is very important because in a typical situation it takes a leader two to three years to settle into a new institutional headship position. This means that during this period many things slow down, or are discontinued; while other initiatives are introduced. Institutions with frequent change of leaders lose so much with every change hence cumulative effect can be enormous over a period. Considering the high rate of leadership turnover in Africa institutions, the absence of deliberate leadership development exposes schools to continuous reinvention of the wheel. In this chapter, we will examine leadership selection, training, succession planning, and the dark-side of institutional leadership.

LEADERSHIP SELECTION

The three main factors apart from being an influential academic are social capital, political alignment, and professional achievements. Selecting leaders for theological institutions is often done by church body, mission agency or the board of an institution depending on how the organization's governance is structured. There is no expressed program in place to train those expected to lead in the future and neither are they trained after the selection. Selection only becomes a priority when a leader is leaving a position for one

5. McCauley, Moxley, and Van Velsor, eds., *The Center for Creative Leadership*, 4

reason or another. The church, mission agency, or a board then frantically sorts out candidates looking for a suitable individual to take over the reins of the institution.

Social capital influences the selection of leaders when the final decision lies within the confines of the board although other partners may play a role. Various boards of theological institutions are often not well connected with the goings on within the institution hence depend on the goodwill of the staff, faculty, and students in making decisions. Sometimes this social capital is built on ethnic or tribal affiliations depending on the predominant ethnic group represented among staff and faculty. It is not unusual that sometimes the predominant sponsoring ethnic group of a denomination create social capital for leaders.

The board establishes the fact that candidates up for consideration meet the minimum qualification for a leadership position, which is normally a doctoral degree. Following this requirement, the decisions then focus on who has the highest social capital. Who has built the social capital and networks within the community to the extent that they will be well received and supported if selected by the board? The board is often swayed by this goodwill in the academic community and selects the person who meets the academic requirement but more importantly enjoys the highest social capital among his or her peers. The board may score a very high mark across the academic community for such a selection, but the reality may sometime prove counterproductive for an institution's operations. If a leader possesses strategic leadership abilities in addition to the social capital, then he or she will likely to do well, despite the selection process overlooking this ability.

Oftentimes, leaders build social capital by making popular decisions that resonate well with the community. However, to lead well, one must make some unpopular decisions from time to time to move the institution forward. Yet, if all one has is social capital then that cache will diminish quickly with every unpopular decision and within short time the most popular leader will become the most disliked leader. Social capital is important in leadership but selection of leaders for theological institutions must be driven by factors beyond social capital after the minimum requirements have been met. Boards therefore must connect with the academic community in ways that lead them to good leaders with some social capital but not at the expense of effective leadership skills.

Political alignment with sponsors of an institution can influence who is selected to lead. Mission agencies and churches are always looking for leaders within their sponsored institution who align with a specific theology and ministry philosophy. Actually, such leaders are used as conduits to solicit insider information on how the institution is really doing in terms of staying true to the ideals of the founders or at least with the direction the current sponsors want the institution to take. These leaders enjoy significant support and protection because of the mission agency or church and their names are often paraded in forums for these mission organizations and church meetings. Although these leaders may be close to current leadership and even supportive of the direction, the unusual support they enjoy as a result of their political alignment seem to undermine positive efforts made by current leadership.

Political partisanship through alignment creates mistrust and division in so many different ways. Mission agencies and churches nurture partisanship when they do whatever it takes to ensure that their players end up in leadership positions and focus on the interests of the mission or the church. Many good leaders have been overlooked because they are not politically aligned to the main sponsors of an institution. This unfortunately has been the norm over the years rather than the exception for theological institutions in Africa.

Partisanship is a messy process that results in many casualties and rivalries that can continue long after a leader's term is completed. The residual toxic environment can create a substantial obstacle for future leadership preventing them from thriving and making changes to best serve the organization. So much effort is wasted in fighting unnecessary interpersonal battles and smoothing out differences in social and political cliques within the institution. Efforts that must be directed at solving the myriad of academic and financial challenges facing the institution are spent on issues instigated by this kind of selection.

Immediately the much heralded new leader starts making unpopular decisions contrary to what he or she has previously supported, and which benefitted his or her selection, then there is a fall out with the mission agency and the church and the support previously enjoyed slowly begins to wane. Regardless of the importance of the decisions to improve the effectiveness of the institution, so long as they are contrary to the position of the sponsors, they will not be accepted.

The gradual withdrawal of support and protection from a non-partisan leader committed to leading change will result in the spotlight being cast on another leader who is more sympathetic to the cause of sponsors and willing to play that role. The cycle will only end when sponsors finally understand that they must not select puppets but must work with all leaders in the institution's best interests. Unfortunately, many theological institutions on the continent are possessed with this curse to chase power through partisanship. Again, partisan leadership falls short of what should be expected in institutions seeking to train individuals to transform church and society—two arenas battling the same vices.

Professional achievements also can qualify a specific leadership selection. For instance, after long years of service, sacrifice, and dedication to scholarship in one's discipline, a leader distinguishes himself or herself as an expert and demonstrates influence that academic field. Selection of such an individual is easy for a board, church or mission agency even if the leader does not have the currency of high social capital or political alignment with the well-heeled. Despite churches and mission agencies being hesitant initially, this person will eventually be appointed to the leadership role because of their strong reputation. Subsequently, the board may tread cautiously in the wake of their selection hoping that the newly appointed leader will acquire social capital over time to also develop influence in the community.

In this case, no one is absolutely sure of what to expect from this leader. Will this individual be able to muster community support to create goodwill? Will the new leader change the core ministry of the founding sponsors? Will this individual be a good political ally for the church or mission agency? Will the new leader influence changes that revolutionize every legacy system and structure built over the years? Or, will this leader prove to be a lone ranger ignoring the board on important decisions? Support from the nominating parties to help such a leader succeed may be equally tentative, since everyone will be uncertain regarding the organizational direction such a leader will take.

Many leaders who ascended to the highest leadership role based on their professional achievements have certainly succeeded but many others have also failed. Professional achievement in one's field of discipline does not necessarily guarantee leadership success, because the two roles often require talents cultivated from different skillsets.

Hard work, sacrifice, commitment, and devotion to one's goals can surely translate to professional success and these virtues if properly applied can drive very good results for an institutional leader. However, many times institutions operate in not so obvious ways. Some organizations can be mired in minimal to significant dysfunction: power struggles, partisanship, heavy workloads and long hours expected, among other issues. These challenging situations can blindside unsuspecting leaders new to this type of high profile role.

For many, the primary motivation for professional achievement is the stream of accolades that follow. The effort and finally the recognition flow from processes within the control of the award-winning scholar. He or she determines how fast or slow to move and what investments to make to achieve the goals. On the other hand, effective institutional leadership is a role that should seek to promote the welfare of all the stakeholders, not just individual benefits. In reality, leadership processes are complex, because the bureaucracy normally does not facilitate swift decision making, and the people are usually unsatisfied, if not ungrateful.

The leader must hold up his or her head under all these circumstances and lead as if nothing is neither wrong with the institution nor the members who comprise the organization. Moreover, due to the tentative support a leader in this situation enjoys, much effort and energy is usually required to achieve basic goals or address even minor organizational challenges.

Leaders selected on the basis of professional achievements need tenacity and unique leadership training to survive the roles. These can be enhanced through mentoring and other forms of leadership discussed in this chapter. Rookie leaders can be good people who may need exposure, skillset refinement, and competencies critical to leading institutions. Then, if they survive organizational challenges for the first few years of their leadership term, they may also stabilize themselves in the whirlwind of duties to do well.

However, many such leaders do not survive the first few years in institutional leadership because their professional lives suffer, as they stagnate in their growth and the very achievements that took them to the top. They work tirelessly but cannot continue pursuing the subjects that had up to this point defined their professional lives. To escape or continue are their obvious choices: persevere as leader doing their best for the sake of the institution or resign and return to pursuits that will generate satisfying professional recognition.

Leaders who make a difference in the life of an institution especially in moving it toward financial sustainability, must cultivate a number of favorable factors. There are a myriad of extenuating factors that we have not addressed in this discussion. And, it is difficult to tell which factors are most needed, as every situation is different depending on the individual leader involved and the context of leadership. One needs to perceive this process more as an art rather than a clear cut formula for selecting leaders. However, the basic characteristics we should be look for in a good candidate for leadership, are still important to define.

In Freedman's book *The Art and Discipline of Strategic Leadership,* he outlined six basic characteristics that all institutions must consider when choosing leadership candidates. These characteristics areas are as follows: an ability to conceptualize solution, lead from a holistic perspective, be creative, expressive, tolerant of ambiguity, and embrace stewardship.[6] Other

6. Freedman, *Strategic Leadership,* 24–25.

characteristics include good judgment, passion and courage, a willingness to collaborate, and an ability to think strategically.

Leadership candidates must demonstrate a talent to conceptualize solutions in order to address organizational goals and challenges in creative but effective ways. This ability is most obvious among candidates who can envision long-term plans in the current context and deploy resources to support an accepted trajectory toward future growth.

Leaders with this talent inspire support and compliance within an organization to respond to needs and challenges in a collective way. On the other hand, the lack of such conceptual strength reduces a leader to a supervisory role that merely oversees the status quo. A supervisory role limits a leader to familiar solutions to a limited cadre of challenges that are constantly repeated. Fortunately, the ability to conceptualize can be taught and developed under the mentoring of experts who have grown their muscles in this area of leadership.

The style of theological education capable of transforming church and society is holistic in essence. Leaders of such institutions must also perform holistically to lead effectively. The leader must see all of God's creation as good—being fixed to serve God's purposes. In the same way, the training of men and women should be undergirded by that same philosophy.

Therefore, their understanding of holistic ministry is very important to the entire training process of the institution. This style embraces the philosophy that there is no difference between the sacred and the secular, spiritual and material, for each was created by the same God, the maker and sustainer of all things. Leaders trained to use a holistic perspective will seek ways to lead God's people in utilizing all his creation for his purposes.

Creativity allows a leader to move beyond existing contexts to generate radical solutions to existing challenges. In this sense, creativity does not refer to the artisan vocation, but to the way solutions are devised for grave challenges in institutions. The leader inspires committee members to approach circumstances in a manner contrary to conventional approaches. Of course, sometimes ideas may be successful but others may fail. The leader is therefore able to quickly learn from various problem-solving initiatives to improve collaborative decision making in an organization. Although theological education is generally traditional in form and function, creative leadership can transform how the organization operates across multiple departments. Consequently, creative thinking can significantly improve strategic planning and implementation. A leader can be strategic in thinking, planning, and implementation with creativity.

Fourth, the ability to communicate clearly to followers so that they follow instructions and directions is fundamental to effective leadership.

Expressiveness helps a leader to translate abstract thinking about the institution into clear words and pictures that are understood by others. Expressiveness does not denote eloquence or innate gifts of oratory, although that could always be an advantage in today's world. Theological institutions depend heavily on financial support from donors and inability to articulate what the institution represents and why one must support the core mandate can be a great loss.

Leaders must be able to express themselves to their strategic partners whose stake in fulfilling the core mandate is crucial. It allows both the internal and external public an opportunity to participate in the institution's projects and processes. The institution's leader therefore has a task to continuously work toward improving the articulation of various expressions of the set-up. If expressiveness is maximized in the day-to-day operation of the institution, it will build confidence in the leader, the immediate followers, and others affiliated to the institution.

One of the important characteristics and yet difficult to handle is the leader's ability to tolerate ambiguities in communication and decision making. The level of tolerance a leader is capable of exhibiting determines to a large extent his or her ability stay focused in the midst of intense criticism. It is often noted that tolerance for ambiguity indicates holding in dynamic tension conflicting information and deriving the best output from it.

However, institutional leadership requires more, one must deal with ambiguities within themselves, that of the institution, and the context within which the institution operates. Without it, one may easily throw in the towel in desperation over confusion and the stress it generates. The complexities of the factors undergirding these ambiguities require tolerance embedded in strong faith and confidence in God. It is the kind that transcends human ability and draws significantly from divine inspiration rooted in intimate relationship with God. Tolerance for ambiguities is not a onetime endeavor but a continuous way of life associated with many higher education leadership.

Stewardship is at the core of leadership, because every leader is a steward entrusted with the responsibility for which he or she must give an account. It encourages selflessness and sacrifice to meet the overall good of the institution. More importantly, a steward must do everything within his or her power to ensure the most efficient and effective management and utilization of the institution's resources.

A leader with a low sense of stewardship is dangerous to the survival of the institution and may destroy in a short time, what has taken years to build. One must be willing to sacrifice short-term victories for long term sustenance of the institution, securing its future for generations to come.

The leadership selection process must identify ways of establishing one's prior stewardship track record before entrusting the person with an institution as important theological education.

The track record of one's stewardship is a demonstration of one's ability to make good judgments under various circumstances. It is the ability to make the best decisions sometimes with only limited information but for the benefit of an institution. Leadership is about making decisions and decisions are based on our judgments at any particular time. Good judgments are developed through practice and one needs to have opportunities in various situations to practice.

This is where mentoring as a form of leadership development becomes very important in helping one to acquire decision-making skills. It is always difficult to know one's ability to make good judgments apart from opportunities to do so. The ability to make good judgments is always in doubt until an opportune time for such demonstrations. However, if a leader has a tendency to rely on the wisdom of God to make decisions then chances are that that leader is likely to make good judgments in the future. Theological institutions have limited resources and contend with various challenges both physically and spiritually. So, reliance on God's wisdom is a necessity if one is to be adept at discernment.

Equally important, institutional leadership must mix passion and courage to move an agenda forward. Passion without courage disappears quickly when adversities arise. Passion is the fuel that keeps the leader motivated and inspired to give more than expected. Passion is also the magnet that can be used to draw people to an organization's vision and mission. Passion gives people a reason to commit to a particular cause and to willingly make necessary sacrifices to achieve it. Of course, leadership is more than passion.

A leader must be able to face challenges arising in the wake of unpopular decisions. This is when courage enables one to stay passionate—even when circumstances look discouraging and disappointing. Courage enables one to persevere when things are not going according to plan and there is rising opposition from within the leader's own ranks. Like King David, the leader must be able to encourage self and others in the Lord and continue with conviction.

Collaboration is working with others toward the achievement of a mutually desired goal. It requires a collective willingness to listen to divergent views or even constructive criticism. It is the ability to decipher important contributions others may make and align those contributions in a manner that achieves the organizations long- and short-term goals. A collaborative leader is able to build healthy working teams and empower others to use their gifts to serve at their highest potential. Collaboration needs a self-confident individual to espouse shared values and responsibility. Ultimately, an inability to collaborate with others, will compromise opportunities to maximize an organization's strengths through the talents of its members.

Leadership selection in theological institutions can be driven by social capital, political alignment, and professional achievements. However, the selection process can be significantly improved if other factors are also used to elect the best candidates. The factors that should reasonably be considered are a candidate's ability to conceptualize solutions, to view God's domain holistically, to be creative, expressive, and tolerant with a sense of stewardship, to have good judgment, passion, and courage.

Selection committees should also consider a candidate's ability to collaborate. An individual does not necessarily need to have all these characteristics to be selected but must possess a good number of them in large doses to succeed as a leader. Naturally, only the candidates meeting the primary requirements of academic qualifications, Christian faith and character should be considered eligible. Social capital, political alignment and professional achievement are added advantages if even deemed necessary at all.

LEADERSHIP TRAINING

There are countless ways leaders develop. Some practical steps an organization can use to help a leader mature could include the nine areas of Yukl's developmental activities. These steps are as follows: defining multisource feedback; using developmental assessment centers, and assignments; implementing a program of rotating jobs; action learning; mentoring; executive coaching; and involving leaders in outdoor challenges and personal growth programs.[7] However, in a theological institution development can be too simplistic to the extent that core leadership characteristics which actually shape leader behavior could be missed. So, among Yukl's list of nine, there are actually five essential activities theological institutions must incorporate into their leadership development programs. Specifically, these essential activities are multisource feedback, developmental assignments, mentoring, executive coaching, and personal growth programs.

Multisource feedback (often referred to as 360-degree feedback) is an approach whereby leaders are observed, then receive feedback from supervisors and colleagues inside and outside their work environments. Participants complete standardized questionnaires with feedback regarding a leader's skills and behaviors. Sometimes, there are options for augmenting

7. Yukl, *Leadership in Organizations,* 397.

standardized responses with comments and additional information. However, in all cases, the primary purpose of this approach is to assess strengths and developmental needs of a leader. The effectiveness of this approach to a leader's development largely depends on who is giving the feedback and the freedom they have to be objective in their assessments and comments.

In cultures where providing candid responses to such questions are considered offensive, respondents will be unwilling to offer frank observations. In all likelihood, feedback will instead be vague and noncommittal. In this case, the leader has the additional task of assuring participants that their feedback will not be used for retaliation, but will be treasured as gifts benefitting everyone in the organization. In many cases, this assurance must be given repeatedly to everyone, or perhaps, to specific individuals. Yet, even with such repeated assurances, discounting every possibility of any backlash or victimization resulting from the feedback exercise, leaders should actually start the activity by choosing those whom they consider to have the courage and confidence to provide objective, candid feedback to make the exercise worthwhile.

Many theological institutions will seldom apply this approach to internal leadership development programs because of the assumption that feedback is tantamount to being judgmental. This however, is a clear misunderstanding of the value of feedback, because in reality feedback can complement the prayerful selection of a leader by helping a candidate fully and effectively use God-given talents. Helpful feedback will save a leader many headaches and the institution many problems.

A good feedback instrument should provide participants with a level of anonymity that ensures each person can respectfully express what they might not say in a face-to-face meeting. This will help colleagues to stop avoiding communicating from diverse perspectives, about the health of an organization and its leadership cadre. Any lack of freedom and transparency to help leaders know their strengths versus areas of improvement is most needed in cultures where feedback must be equated with a deep sense of love and concern for one's leader to succeed in their assignment. Such love and concern will override every fear and possible backlash that could result from candid completion of any such feedback instrument.

Similarly, leaders must be willing to receive feedback as a kind of gift rather than outrights attacks from disgruntled or envious colleagues. Just as colleagues and others find it very difficult to provide feedback; it is equally difficult for leaders to receive feedback. It takes a lot of self-confidence, security, and humility to accept feedback. This is especially true if leaders have never been involved in any structured feedback process.

It may be difficult to know how to accept and then respond to feedback. The developmental benefits of this kind of approach will only be effective if every response is evaluated and seen as an opportunity to refine leadership skills. This is most powerful when an institution makes it an optional approach to development but leaders nevertheless voluntarily take the initiative to enroll in the program.

It is not enough to select the right participants to give and receive feedback. There must also be a plan in place as to how to utilize the information for leadership development. Otherwise, this process can lead to frustration and self-doubt. Yukl noted that leaders are often left to interpret the results alone. Still others receive the report (compiled feedback) followed by a one-on-one meeting with a facilitator or in a group workshop led by a facilitator.[8] Having participated in all three ways of using feedback report both as a leader and facilitator, I have found that the one-on-one meeting with a facilitator is the most effective means of interpreting the results.

The one-on-one meeting affords the leader an opportunity to ask questions and seek clarification on specific comments on a report. The facilitator is able to explain the difficult areas of the report while helping the leader to see the value of the feedback and outline a plan for personal development. This approach for leadership development is critical in a sense that if this process creates self-awareness, feedback within a context can be useful for development. As earlier mentioned, leaders in theological institutions will benefit greatly from feedback exercises; however, this is only helpful if combined with other approaches, the information complements results from other developmental exercises.

Although there are no programs or institutions geared toward preparing people to lead theological institutions, creating opportunities through developmental assignments can equip leaders in ways we least considered possible. Developmental assignments are additional responsibilities given to a leader to help build certain skills and enhance leadership behavior. These may range from leading a new project; chairing a task force to plan a major change; dealing with a serious operational problem; developing and training others in the institution; or deputizing other senior leaders, among other plans.

These assignments have great impact on leaders because they stretch them beyond their regular duties forcing them to fully embrace and flourish in the leadership role by using principles that can only be gleaned on-the-job. These additional responsibilities can test the capacity of a leader by nurturing them into bigger roles. This is a practical application that helps

8. Ibid.

leaders exercise the energy needed to cope with the associated stress that comes with the role.

The assignment of these developmental tasks must be commensurate with the leader's abilities so that the individual is not overwhelmed and fails with disastrous, costly results. The capacity of a leader to handle tasks can either be underestimated or overestimated, and achieving the balance here is more of an art that comes by experience than a science. Developmental assignments need to be incremental beginning with relatively basic tasks to more complex responsibilities as one successfully accomplishes each task. The process can ensure that supervisors (or mentors) meet with leaders-in-training to debrief as well as reflect on lessons learned from the assignment. The discussions with supervisors/mentors must transcend the actual outcomes of a task. These interactions are sessions that shift from lesson learned to how the lessons are shaping one's perspective, changing behavior, and approaches to leading.

Supervisors must invest time and energy in this particular area of the leader development to get the full benefit from the exercise. It is the supervisor's experiences in the institution that will empower a leader in training to develop confidence and skill in making effective decisions. Learning how to lead by doing, especially at a high level is critical because there are no customized training programs to simulate such experiences. The cooperation of a leader in training and a supervisor is paramount to the success of the program because it clarifies organizational goals and expectations.

Mentoring is an employee training system in which a more senior colleague invests time to oversee and advise a colleague with less experience in a particular role in an organization. In a leadership development program, mentoring can build a protégé's capacity to function in more complex leadership assignments. Whereas developmental tasks emphasize completing assignments, mentoring focuses on relationships as the context for training. It is a one-on-one or group investment, which lasts for a specific period of time.

Mentoring is a powerful way to develop leaders because it is based on nurturing mutual understanding and support from all parties involved. Mentors often play multiple roles as encouragers, sponsors, coaches, guides, models, counselors, and teachers depending on the need and the circumstances. Institutional leaders need mentors; however, it is critical that they select the mentors themselves since mentoring is a voluntary relationship. Any attempt to assign mentors who are incompatible with the leader's desires, aspirations and personality will only lead to frustration and difficult relationships. Many well-meaning mentoring programs have faltered because neither the mentor nor the person to be trained had appropriate opportunities to express their preferences before the assignment was made.

Institutional leaders can best benefit from mentoring when four conditions exist in that relationships. There has to be willingness, compatibility, accountability, and empowerment. The demanding role of institutional leaders makes it very difficult for them to devote time and effort on any other thing if there is no willingness to be paired with a specific individual. This willingness motivates participants to make the sacrifices and changes in personality, character, values, and other areas necessary to sustain a working relationship. A forced mentoring relationship between individuals who do not want to work together will lack the enthusiasm that must characterize a successful training experience. A willing student will demonstrate an attitude to persevere and succeed.

The mentoring relationship needs to be molded into a mutually beneficial learning experience. As expressed in 2 Timothy 1:2, and Philippians 2:19–22, it takes time and resources to build a relationship. There can be no mentoring if the parties are not willing to be friends, because it is within the context of friendship that learning occurs for many adults. The process is effective because the need to preserve the relationship can override the sacrifices that will inevitably need to occur to adjust to new circumstances in a routine life.

A well-grounded relationship soothes the delivery of difficult corrections, and gives added joy to victories which can transcend the initial reason for the mentoring. Institutional leaders often are placed on pedestals by followers, but mentoring helps initiate meaningful that can sustain a willingness to give and receive useful feedback in a loving and safe place. Good relationships often enhance effective mentoring while strained relationships can hamper the achievement of mentoring goals.

Accountability in a mentoring relationship ensures that motivations are not one-sided. Those in training are accountable to their mentors and vice versa. This reciprocal engagement places responsibility on both parties to faithfully work toward the achievement of shared goals. Leaders of theological institutions are more vulnerable than one can imagine to exploitation. It is therefore important that as they seek help through mentoring, they are safeguarded under responsible relationships. Accountability ensures that commitments are adhered to and when it is not possible, reasonable explanations are provided to avoid rifts in the relationship. (2 Tm. 2:2) When the mentoring process is undergirded by accountability, the relationship can remain strong as mutual goals are achieved. Institutional leaders are therefore motivated to invest more into the relationship for their growth and effectiveness in their tasks.

Empowerment is the ultimate goal of a mentoring relationship and enables institutional leaders to achieve desired goals. Our Lord Jesus Christ was very intentional about empowering his disciples and did so through his mentoring presence and later under the Holy Spirit to carry out the Great Commission (Mt 28:18–19; Acts 1:8). Jesus therefore empowered his leaders, and that made a big difference in their ministries wherever they went during the era of the early church. Similarly, mentors need to be intentional about different ways they can empower their mentees by coming alongside them to make changes in the areas of character, skills, and values.

Mentors are able to instill, correct and affirm traits by providing helpful perspectives that allow leaders to make good choices. Mentors have the power to affirm a leader's giftedness, which in turn will help develop the confidence needed to excel in their areas of strength. Mentors model values by explaining their actions and the rationales supporting those decisions. This level of empowerment ensures that institutional leaders are attuned to their God-given abilities as well as their weaknesses as they make countless leadership decisions. Different mentors may empower leaders in different areas and it is advisable to have more than one mentor so that the confluence of gifts can strengthen a developing leader to lead effectively.

The wealth of knowledge among former institutional leaders is too often under-utilized. This treasure trove of experience is a needed resource in mentoring programs. Unfortunately, former leaders are kept at arm's length from their former institutions and have no opportunity to share information that could empower developing leaders in their new roles. Sometimes this snub is due to the circumstances surrounding the exit of a former leader or simply a "changing of the guard" mentality. The mistakes as well as the successes of former leaders are priceless experiences that could help transform a developing leader into strong leader. However, the desire to reinvent the wheel with each new leadership era is an exercise in wasted time and talents.

LEADERSHIP DEPLOYMENT AND TRANSITIONS

Leadership enables one to assign new responsibilities to leaders who have been selected and trained. On the other hand, selecting and training leaders without a clear plan for how to deploy them once training ends will only create frustration. Frustration arises from a confusion in duties, which often leads to sudden departures and loss of human resources. Although this subject is also tied to succession planning, it is broader than succession. Succession planning is helpful for any organization but it gives the impression that one must train others to assume their position only when an office opens.

Deployment and transition involves the training of leader and the change of assignments from one position to another commensurate to new abilities and competences, including for the very top position in the institution.

The intentional development of leadership skills and competences must always be coupled with opportunities for utilization of those skills. This provides a road map for senior institutional leaders to know when and how an investment in skill development will be utilized. It also enables the current leader to plan their exit long before they are actually ready to leave their positions. Many leaders dread the discussion on training and deployment, let alone planning for it when they are still a leader. It takes courage and immense confidence to bring up the matter for discussion and to map out the intricacies of how it needs to be carried out. Before we discuss the factors that must guide leadership training and deployment, it is essential that we explore why the subject raises a red flag for leaders.

Many leaders have been caught in the midst of political storms during a season of transition. Those who brave the subject to start training their successors found themselves fighting for their positions because their successors could not wait to assume office. Many successors in training have often maneuvered and applied all manner of dirty tactics to get rid of their mentors. As a result, leaders have found themselves undermined and their good intentions compromised. The effort to train in order to transition should be a safeguard of an institution's future. Yet, unexpectedly it is now a bone of contention. This is why a clear and definite deployment strategy during transitions is critical for all institutional leaders.

Deployment plans should be introduced during a training program. This is so the trainee is very clear regarding the next assignment when training is completed. If deployment to the next demanding task follows immediately after training, the transition creates room for an up-and-coming leader to implement principles and lessons. This will reduce any tendency to usurp a current leader's position or to stagnate over a long period of time waiting for another assignment. Loyal up-and-coming leaders will even opt to leave an institution in search of new assignments, should they find themselves unassigned within a reasonable time to a leadership role.

Shared Values

Few factors are necessary in our institutions to ensure effective deployment and transition. The factors that are important are shared values, loyalty, and an institution's future. Deployment and transitions need to be perceived as positive activities within an institution and not a management gimmick to punish those who do not adhere to the status quo. This is only possible if deployment of trained leaders to other assignments becomes an important shared value within the institution. A shared value provides a platform for open discussions about how leadership training is to be carried out, deployment opportunities, and a list of individuals in top leadership positions who should be considered for these opportunities.

This means an institution should be constantly working on creating new opportunities to absorb its trained leaders. Open discussion in an institution improves transparency and removes the type of secrecy or suspicion that inspires destructive rumors. Open discussions allow for close scrutiny of organizational processes and procedures, integrating leadership deployment as a positive sign of growth and development within the institution. Shared values take time to entrench. Nevertheless, an institutional leader has a fundamental responsibility to ensure that shared values become a pervasive motivation. Consequently, a strong framework minimizes future operational obstacles. Deployment to new assignments becomes a means of rewarding hard working, progressive leaders.

Loyalty

It is important for leaders to have a sense of loyalty to their institution. In this way, both the institution and the leader can benefit from the training and development program. Shared values without institutional loyalty will result in high turnover as leaders move from one position to another. Institutional loyalty therefore acts as the glue that holds upcoming leaders together and motivates them to stay in an institution for longer periods. Loyalty must be nurtured through staff care, adequate compensation, and a sense of ownership. Staff in theological institutions need care as much as the students do. So, if staff feel neglected and abandoned, then staff motivation and loyalty are similarly diminished.

This is particularly important when an institution is going through a period of crisis. If staff feel cared for, individuals will strengthen the campus through support in numbers. Therefore, my general perception that an institution cares for my well-being and addresses my concerns is a powerful fuel for loyalty. An institution must do whatever it takes to help staff feel appreciated through executive action, because an organization's well-being is fundamentally tied to the well-being of its employees.

Compensation is an important factor in recruiting and retaining a highly qualified staff. This is especially true among theological institutions where compensation often falls below competitive salaries for the high caliber of staff desired. Compensation must fully assure and satisfy staff that better opportunities are not elsewhere and that an institution (employer) fully values them. It is not uncommon to hear leaders say that they are working in a particular institution as a service to God.

As true as this assertion may be, the impact of compensation on influencing loyalty to a theological institution (employer) cannot be ignored. There is a limit to everything and leaders can take so much pain and misery for a season but not forever. When leaders are unable to live in decent housing, pay children's school fees, and regularly provide for the livelihood of themselves and their families, these circumstances affect their loyalty to their institution. After children have been sent home several times for non-payment of school fees, one begins to wonder why they are serving God in such an institution that is unable to assist its scholars (employees) care for their families. A leader does not need to be highly compensated in order to be loyal to the institution; however there is a threshold at which personal considerations complicate workplace training and deployment.

Ownership is a process built over a long period of time. It is a sense of protecting feelings and attachment to an institution that motivates one to do whatever it takes to ensure that the core mission is safeguarded. The stronger an employee's sense of ownership, the deeper a sense of loyalty will be for an institution and all it stands for. Ownership separates the actions of a hireling from that of an owner in times of crises. Hirelings are often in an institution to merely earn a living. Whereas, staff who have a strong sense of ownership will be motivated to go beyond minimum duties to make sacrifices that ensure the well-being of an institution. Loyalty is significantly undermined when ownership flounders. Leaders must utilize the goodwill they enjoy among staff to build ownership so that the mission of the institution can be sustained through strong loyalty.

FUTURE OF INSTITUTION

Training leaders to serve should not only be tied to current needs but any future strategic direction of an institution. It fosters forward thinking and planning. Training ensures that the needs of tomorrow are provided for today. Institutions can only chart the right path if they intentionally assess risks in anticipation of potential future challenges. Sometimes this is difficult because of the tyranny of urgent issues; however, institutions must preempt future leadership crises with continuous risk assessments. Current institutional needs should inform leadership selections, the training mode and context, the scope of exposure, and subsequent deployment strategies.

Anticipated needs for future skills and competencies should inform the kind of training institutional leaders focus on and implement. However, candidate selection is critical and if that is compromised, then the entire process can be jeopardized.

Determining trends and factors at play in order to make strategic decisions is a core skill leadership candidates for the next generation should possess. After leaders have been selected and trained in core competencies, opportunities should be made for them to apply knowledge to practical experiences in the field. This will stretch their knowledge and confidence. There has to be calculated efforts to engage new leaders even during training and deploy them to certain strategic positions of the institution for specific periods in preparation for greater responsibilities. Confidence builds among candidates when they can test a number of leadership concepts and principles in safe but real working environments.

The deployment into future roles needs to be smooth and seamless, suggesting that current leaders must have clear exit plans from their positions in the institution. When a leader relinquishes a position in an institution, such a move does not necessarily require leaving an institution. Rather, stepping aside from an active leadership role can simply mean retiring from that role, but not entirely from friends and colleagues. Former leaders are still valuable assets who can continue to support current and future leaders by sharing insights and providing historic perspectives regarding the institution's legacy.

The shared values of an institution, the loyalty of its staff and a program to assess future needs are all critical components in training and deploying leaders in an institution. Shared values create the environment, loyalty and leadership competencies that should influence candidate selections, and eventual training, experience and deployment. Any institution that fails to intentionally train and deploy leaders is creating a vacuum that will complicate leadership selection in the future.

SURVIVING THE PERILS OF INSTITUTIONAL LEADERSHIP

Institutional leadership is often characterized by certain challenges that transcend the institutional make-up. They are deep rooted and call for a leader's honesty and ability to ask for assistance. These challenges are varied and can include a number of issues. However, basic issues that may create an overwhelming state of affairs for an underperforming leader can include an inability to meet the challenges created by the position or the emergence of significant issues regarding personal health, family, or career development. Likewise, institutional politics, an inability to manage stress or even a lack of confidantes or trustworthy counselors can create an avalanche of unmanageable problems for a leader that he or she cannot overcome.

Personal Leadership Capacity

Personal leadership capacity is a condition that others can perceive but more importantly is well understood by an individual leader. It is the ability of an individual to carry out leadership responsibilities based on one's own assessment. Only a leader can tell whether he or she is comfortable with a particular assignment or not. It is not often when a leader can recover from underestimating significant problems and mismanaging the response to them. A leader's capacity is often informed by several factors such as successful planning and implementing of projects, strong character and practical experiences.

Additionally, a leader's ability to discern situations to make good decisions, while remaining positive in the face of failures or difficulties and be singularly devoted to a clear mission and vision, all contribute to one's personal leadership capacity. The complexity associated with knowing whether one is capable of handling a particular situation necessitates a regular personal evaluation in light of the responsibilities at hand. Sometimes feedback from close associates and senior leaders can shed light on one's own capacity to perform at certain levels. Such feedback should be subjected to the leader's own evaluation and should not be strictly followed as the true representation of one's capacity.

There is nothing as difficult as leading based on unrealistic assessment of one's capacity by others. Contrarily, living in denial that one can perform certain tasks without the requisite abilities only aggravates the challenges of performance resulting in frustrations. Taking all the factors of personal leadership into consideration, a leader should assess their own capacity and only use the attributions of others as confirmation or critique of their conclusion. The final decision to accept a leadership position should be based primarily on a leader's confidence and awareness of personal abilities to provide the needed leadership. Boards and leaders of theological institutions must respect the decision of a leader being considered for a position and refrain from pushing leaders into roles for which they are ill-prepared. Personal leadership capacity should be factored into leadership selection, training and deployment to ensure that every leader has every opportunity to be successful.

Imbalanced Life

Institutional leadership transcends the charisma of inspirational speeches and glamour of cocktail parties. It is hard work and sometimes this takes a toll on a leader's personal health, family, and even career development. The demands of leadership responsibilities often require that leaders work long hours in order to move the agenda of an institution forward. These extended hours are spent at the expense of maintaining good health through regular exercise and rest. These essential activities are often ranked very low on the priority lists of leaders. Sometimes, they are considered a waste of time if not a distraction. Regular health examinations are even ignored. Although leaders are fully aware that these activities are important, they do not devote time for them until their health is in crisis. Many leaders have cut short their leadership tenure because of health ailments requiring early retirement or untimely deaths because they did pay due attention to their health.

Evidently, leaders cannot lead effectively if they are in poor health and therefore need to balance work with the care for their personal health. An institution suffers if a gifted leader leaves a position for health reasons; a situation that is often preventable. Consequently, an executive board and all the people associated with an institution must hold leaders accountable for balancing work with attention to personal health and social relationships, like family. Sacrifices for an organization at the expense of one's health should be discouraged at every level of institutional leadership.

Families suffer when leaders spend extended hours away from home or carry work home. Children grow up without the attention, love and care of their mothers or fathers because of leadership responsibilities. Many marriages have fallen apart and others have lost their zest to become only shells without substance. The marriages of leaders are the first relationship to suffer if the leader is unable to balance his or her life with leadership responsibilities. It is therefore important that leaders create an accountability group to help him or her maintain a balanced lifestyle especially in the area of marriage and family. Long after leadership responsibilities are over, one's spouse, children and loved ones are the enduring relationships in a person's life.

In the thick of things, leaders are inclined to put their personal development at the back burner while attending to pressing needs of an institution. It is therefore common for many leaders to be so absorbed in their responsibilities that they have little time for reflection or career development. Many leaders ascended to the heights of their careers because of their expressed leadership capacity and career achievements. However, once serving in the highest levels, personal efforts for professional development slow down.

In this way, leaders eventually plateau in their growth and development. Although individuals gain exposure and experience through leading, these seldom add significant professional contributions to their fields of academic discipline. Unless one is able to take periodic sabbaticals for reflection and writing, one loses any motivation to contribute to their fields of discipline.

Institutional boards must insist that leaders take sabbaticals for the sake of their health, family and professional development. More importantly, leaders have the primary responsibility to ensure that they create opportunities for themselves and guard against other intruders likely to snatch time and resources away. Leaders need support groups who will encourage them to make bold decisions with the clear knowledge that institutional challenges will not all be solved even if the leader's nose is to the grindstone for 24 hours a day, seven days every week. Financial sustainability, though important, will be worthless if by achieving it a leader forfeits a marriage, or the closeness of children and loved ones. An institution's financial sustainability must begin with the sustainability of a leader's personal life with family. Only then will organizational issues fall into proper perspective.

Political Pressure

Many leaders struggle with financial sustainability not because they are poor leaders, but because they underestimate the pressure of politics on their decisions. Political pressure in theological institutions comes in all shapes and forms. It is the influence certain individuals or groups with authority have on an institutional leader to make or change certain decisions in their favor. Every institution has its unique political structures and avenues of pressure to influence the overall agenda of the school. Sometimes these may be a mission agency that owns the institution or influential individuals representing a mission agency. Other times it may be denominational leaders or a board that owns the institution, and so on.

At the same time, these groups may not always be the sources of political pressure. The real agitators are often disgruntled and unsatisfied staff of the institution. It is typical that efforts toward financial sustainability will most often generate intense political pressure, especially regarding third stream projects, and other financial investments. Similarly, pressure becomes very intense with efforts to change the vision or mission of an institution. Political pressure cannot be completely avoided however hard a leader may try, but can be cunningly managed to strike compromises that allow a leader to deliver on his/her mandate while keeping the main stakeholders somewhat satisfied.

However, even with diligent management of such pressures, a time comes when a leader needs to decide whether to go along with a decision influenced by these avenues or pursue his convictions and face the consequences. Blatant disregard of these avenues for personal convictions should only be the last resort after every effort to negotiate and convince the powers that be fails. Moreover, a leader must always have a back-up plan before embarking on a decision based on reason and conviction, especially if the decision is contrary to the prevailing political pressures. It is always helpful for leaders to learn from others who have weathered such storms under different circumstances.

There is really nothing new under the sun and therefore the current challenge however complicated they may appear have occurred before elsewhere and lessons can be drawn for these decisions. Identifying a leader outside the institution with expansive experience as a mentor will provide opportunity to explore various options on how to manage the pressures. Political pressures can weigh heavily on institutional leaders with severs negative impact on their health, families and performance of their roles. The impact of political pressure is especially grave if the leaders love and respect the individuals and groups from which the pressures emanate. One does not need to lose their lives under political pressures, instead one must make decisive decisions on when to continue in their roles under the pressures and when to seek other responsibilities elsewhere.

Safe Places

Places where leaders can go and empty themselves of their frustration, hurts and pains are in limited supply. A safe place is not the counselor's clinic but an occasional time and space devoted exclusively for leaders to meet other colleagues and mentors for an unhurried time of physical, emotional, spiritual and mental healing in the presence of the Lord without any fear of disclosure. It is a place to cry or laugh as loud as you want to and for as long as you want; confess your sins and failures to the Lord in whichever manner you want; listen to God, the counsel of mentors, and the life stories of other fellow travelers; receive healing from God; and rest in the presence of your heavenly father.

The fear that true honesty will result in judgment and condemnation has been repressive. The repression has given rise to other negative manifestations in the typical life of leaders. It is not only safe places that are in short supply but experienced leaders in these places who will listen and provide helpful feedback to other leaders. The path of financial sustainability is often

a lonely road, tedious and difficult to travel. The pains and hurts in this journey are too heavy to be carried alone. Therefore, leaders need occasional
breaks to offload the burdens so they can travel lightly. More importantly,
the baggage has ways of taking both an emotional and physical toll on leaders' health—leaving him or her feeling burnt out.

Many leaders are still in their positions but have no emotional energy
to make the bold decisions they know will transform their institutions. They
are keeping their institutions afloat with the barest of emotional energy left
in their tanks. Definitely, if nothing changes with time, the leader burns
out and develops a chronic health condition that makes him or her unfit
to lead any longer. Or, a leader can simply suffer an untimely death from
complications that could even puzzle medical workers. This has been the
trend for decades. Yet, it need not continue if we develop more safe places
for institutional leaders to get away to reflect, rest, and refresh themselves as
they unload all the burdens they have been carrying for years.

Safe places are partly in limited supply because those who could create
them are plagued with the same problems. Moreover, it is expensive to do
so. Financial sustainability must inherently take into consideration the cost
of safe places for its leadership, if they are to last long on the job. The rate of
institutional turnover of leaders could be significantly reduced if budgeting
for safe retreats for leaders were a common line item. Safe places are a necessity just like the very pursuit for financial sustainability. Therefore, organizations should consider this a feature of growth and development programs.

Leadership is critical to the whole discussion on financial sustainability. It is the cog in the wheel that gets the wheel moving and holds
everything together. The selection of leaders is critical to the leadership
question whether for today or for the future. However, equally important is
the leadership training program and what it attempts to accomplish. Training for the sake of it only leads to frustration and high turnovers, therefore
there has to be an intentional strategy for deployment that allows trainees
to utilize their newly acquired skills and competencies in the institution.
Transition of leaders from one position to another is a good way of providing broad exposure for promising leaders who will likely to assume higher
critical positions in an organization. Of course, it is always helpful to be
aware of the challenges leaders face in leadership positions, in order to help
leaders find effective ways to address and solve them.

Chapter 10

The Wheels of Financial Sustainability

MOVING THE WHEELS OF financial sustainability is at the heart of our entire discourse. History indicates that churches, mission agencies and individuals have always supported theological education in Africa. Efforts directed at moving the wheels of sustainability are not meant to exclude the continuous involvement of churches, mission agencies or individuals whose contributions over the decades have sustained theological education. Instead, the drive toward sustainability is meant to find ways of augmenting existing support by exploring additional ways to fulfill the mission of an institution.

Since the establishment of Sierra Leone's Fourabay College in the 1800s, the very first Sub-Saharan African theological institution, there have not been many situations in which theological students have paid the full cost of their education. In the beginning, theological education was one hundred percent free for students who were supported by scholarships. After more than two hundred years, tuition still only covers an average of thirty per cent of the entire cost of training. Consequently, it would be impossible for partial tuition to generate enough revenue to fully meet the budgetary needs of a campus. Until that happens, theological institutions must explore ways of staying in business by moving the wheel of sustainability to fill the shortfall not covered by tuition. As might be imagined, this is an enormous task that requires many approaches and strategies.

Contextually, the outlook for financial sustainability among African institutions is not as optimistic as administrators would like. The playing field is littered with casualties succumbing to the consequences of insufficient financial resources. Yet, although the apparent factor is insufficient revenue to balance operational budgets, many other problems plague

African theological campuses. These problems range from a lack of faculty development, inadequate administrative staff, and limited learning resources, crumbling physical facilities, low student enrollment and high institutional leadership turnover. Although our focus in this discussion is financial sustainability, all of these challenges are issues tied to limited finances and insolvency.

Both clergy and laity are called by God to ministry. In preparation, training is needed for these ministry workers to effectively discharge the duties of their call. Since God will continue to call individuals to serve in ministry, many approaches have been explored to equip them. In addition to a sole dependence on the Holy Spirit as teacher, Theological Education by Extension (TEE), and residential Bible college education have been familiar avenues of training. Yet, these and other alternate training methods are filled with challenges that must be addressed.

Apart from the call and training, graduates of theological institutions traditionally enter the ministry being offered low wages to support them. For this reason, students are becoming increasingly reluctant to invest in theological education as the cost of living rises across global economies. A degree from a theological institution is becoming less attractive. With regard to alternate training options, many programs lack requisite accreditations. Hence governments do not always recognize the degrees awarded from these domestic programs. Without accreditation, graduates cannot work for the government as religious educators, chaplains, or in any other role certified by unaccredited programs. The call to ministry is important, but one must seek ways of acquiring accredited training to be equipped for the task. This is where theological education becomes an inevitable option. So, in spite of the challenges that saddle theological education, the need to perpetually ensure that it functions optimally cannot be overemphasized.

Stakeholders of a theological institution play a significant role in ensuring that the training of ministry workers continues. Churches, mission agencies, donors, governments, and local communities are the stakeholders and in one way or another influence a school's financial well-being. Denominational and non-denominational theological institutions receive assistance from churches in many forms that support overall operations. Mission agencies send workers to serve in administration and on the faculty. These agencies also regularly give financial support. Donors provide on-going charitable contributions that facilitate training workers to serve in church and society.

Although governments are not often considered stakeholders in theological institutions, yet without their involvement institutions would not exist. This is because government agencies provide permits and regulate all learning environments. At the same time, government agencies are not direct beneficiaries from their support in the same sense as a church. However, governments do benefit when society is transformed and social ills are reduced through the ministry of graduates.

The communities in which theological institutions are situated are also stakeholders because they provide the basic amenities from which the institution operates, and the lives of the people in these communities are sometimes interwoven with students and staff. Ultimately, stakeholder roles vary with each party depending on the nature of the relationship with the institution, location, and influence on local culture. Nevertheless, these roles are critical if institutions are to fill shortfalls in their operational budgets.

Theological institutions by virtue of their name have biblical and theological justifications for all they do. It is not that reflections on biblical or theological dogma will automatically resolve challenges, but both of these do provide a framework for sound decision-making. Since institutions exist to train men and women for service in church and society, it is imperative that the Bible and theology inform a school's activities. For instance, Pauline descriptions of missionary support through tentmaking activities to generate revenue are derived directly from the Bible.

Apostle Paul indicated that missionary support is always preferred, but in situations where donations would compromise the bold declaration of God's truth in correcting and rebuking evil, Paul voiced a preference to instead earn his support through providing for his own livelihood. Consequently, for as much as charitable donations to support missionaries were the norm in the early church, Paul distinguished tentmaking activities as equally sacred ways to support a ministry. However, he did not boast that tentmaking made him financially independent from the local congregations. Likewise, Paul did not encourage anyone to boast about how their charity supplied his needs. Rather, Apostle Paul was content with both approaches, and did not reveal a preference. Rather, either was a credible support system, as long as the end result was the advancement of God's call.

Apostle Paul's experiences with tentmaking in Corinth and the generous giving of the Macedonia churches offer us a broad framework to carefully examine. What cannot be overlooked is that neither of these approaches to funding became Paul's main focus but instead remained a means to accomplishing his ministry. Similarly, neither donations nor tentmaking of any form of fund raising should be the primary mission of ministry. Rather, each of us must keep our call to disciple making as the primary motivation and endeavor to accomplish it.

Likewise, for practical purposes, theological institutions must utilize God-given seed in all manners possible and not confine themselves to a few select financial options to resolve sustainability issues—as long as available options do not contradict Scriptures. Like Paul, schools must explore various opportunities available to them in the context of their current resources. Then, the on-going effort to secure other options is justified for the sake of the well being of their institutions.

MOVING THE WHEEL OF FINANCIAL SUSTAINABILITY

The act of moving the wheel of financial sustainability is determined by how the spokes are aligned. The six spokes in the wheel of financial sustainability as discussed in this book are church ownership, institutional governance, third stream projects, strategic collaboration, modes of delivery, and leadership development. These spokes individually and concertedly drive the agenda of financial sustainability discourse in theological institutions in Africa. Different conditions in an institution call for different configurations of the spokes to ensure that the wheel moves in timely fashion, in the right direction. The process is more of an art than a science; although, there are certain fundamental considerations that are scientific to every art. This may include for instance, understanding why an institution exists and the challenges associated with fulfilling its mission.

Church Ownership

Theological institutions exist not only to train leaders called to ministry in the church, but also to serve all of humanity. This is also the responsibility of the church, and the people serving in leadership create initiatives and programs to accomplish this goal. Theological institutions must exist with, within, and for the church. These positions reflect the ownership relationship between a church and an affiliated theology institution.

Theological institutions can exist with the church as an extension of its ministry to strengthen leadership capacity within its ranks and to deliver its core mandate. This is how a school complements a church's ministry. A church might be helping those who are not involved with any church to understand its mission. Likewise, an institution must exist within the church by allowing students to serve with church leaders to gain practical experience outside of the classroom. Theological institutions must exist for the church by being the voice of the church on matters that require complex biblical scholarship. This strategic role facilitates continuous engagement with the church in order to clearly articulate its political and philosophical position in society.

Church ownership is critical because it addresses issues of accountability along with church responsiveness toward the institution. Accountability means that the church ensures the institution is fulfilling its organizational mandate. This is a reciprocal activity that requires the church to also makes itself accountable to an institution. In this way, leadership can review how closely aligned operations are to fundamental principles of the Scriptures.

Because responsiveness is reciprocal, it enhances mutual benefits for all parties involved with an organization. If a church neglects a theological institution under its care, its own leadership and subsequently the organization's health will decline. It is self-defeating to ignore the motivations and philosophies that shape leadership who are daily attempting to accomplish organizational goals.

Institutional Governance

An institution's appointed board of executives is the primary governing body over a theological school. The appointment of governing board members for African theological institutions has followed various patterns through the years. The planning of some were clearly systematic. Others appeared to have been haphazardly appointed, so that member talents do not align with the needs of an institution. The responsibility of institutional governance is to grow vested trust. A governing board has formal authority to make decisions that impact the policies of the institution. It must also function with courage and foresight to approve activities that can advance an institution's mission and vision.

The ability of governing boards to ensure financial sustainability is dependent upon how effective they have been in their primary functions. Institutional leaders have a responsibility to ensure that their boards receive the training they need, so they can be the necessary support for an institution. Jason Ferenczi theorized in his study of theological institutions in Asia, South America, Eurasia, and Caribbean that board effectiveness can be defined by the following five principles: community of trust, strong alignment with the organization, shared commitment to responsiveness, strong leadership by a CEO, and adequate preparation for transition.[1] Although the study focused on institutions in other countries outside Africa, these principles are applicable to almost every institution in Africa.

1. Ferenczi, *Serving Communities*, 2–3.

A governing board has the primary responsibility to ensure that the financial outlook of an institution is managed well and that it has enough resources to carry out its duties. The board must therefore have within its membership, people who are knowledgeable in all of the areas of financial management. An African governing board must work passionately to place their institutions on the path of sustainability. This cannot be achieved with an emotionally detached or indifferent board. Rather an active, engaged and competent institutional governance team is the best kind of team to lead a theological institution.

Third Stream Projects

Third stream projects can generate revenue for theological institutions apart from revenue generated by tuition and donations. Since donations to theological institutions have been plummeting steadily in recent years, schools have created new revenue streams for the sole purpose of fulfilling their core mandates. Of course, charitable fundraising is often the first revenue-generating strategy for many theological institutions in Africa. In reality, many theological schools first opened their doors to students because of generous donations from a specific church or mission agencies. Missionary staff and denominational leaders spearheaded those fundraising initiatives. Today, it is critical that we do not underestimate the important role of an institutional leader in coordinating and sustaining donor relations.

Funding sources for many African theological institutions differ depending on a variety of factors. So, even though tuition might be a second stream of revenue, it is not enough to meet budgetary needs for most schools. According to an OCI survey, tuition only covers 25 percent to 30 percent of total operating expenses, on average, of most institutions. It is fallacious therefore to hope that tuition will increase revenue as student enrollment rises, since a majority of students are not paying the full cost of their education. In such situations, the more students using a school's facilities and resources, the greater the financial burden on an institution—provided all other variables remain constant. The challenge of operating in the red is not solved by tuition and donations alone. For this reason, third stream projects have been introduced as a creative way to fill budgetary shortfalls and achieve long-term financial sustainability.

"God-given seed" is a coined phrase that describes a unique resource or opportunity placed within every institution to develop third stream projects and leadership development. Theological institutions must trust God to open their eyes to identify and explore their divine seed gifts for the benefit of the institution. God-given seed can be tangible resources such as land, buildings, or intangibles such as any talents found among the student body, faculty, alumni or administrators. Seed resources can also be partnerships and networks with organizations, businesses, churches and political entities. Leadership's ability to identify these divine resources is the first most important step before engaging in third stream projects.

There are many examples of third stream projects. They include engaging in different forms of collaborative research, consulting services, agricultural projects, leasing facilities, and so on. These are not exhaustive examples but provide a conceptual reference to the possibilities depending on a school's context. A governing board also has an opportunity to manage risk when an appropriate resource has been identified around which to develop a third stream project befitting a school's context. A strong institutional capacity to manage tuition, strengthen an organization's donor base, and grow profitability through third stream projects will set theological institutions on the path to financial sustainability. Like Apostle Paul's perspective on missionary support and tentmaking, the pursuit of third stream projects should only facilitate a ministry without competing with the school's core mission. All stakeholders must work to guard against drifting focus, lest the good intention of a third stream project muddles a theological institution's core mission.

Strategic Collaborations

In an ever-changing environment, strategic collaboration is important among theological institutions because it allows partnering organizations to leverage their strengths for cost effective and sustainable outcomes, while minimizing their weaknesses. There are different ways institutions could greatly benefit from collaboration: academic programming, accreditation processes, financial and administrative services, faculty development, and acquisition of library resources, physical facilities, and many more essential services. Deliberate efforts to collaborate in these areas may significantly reduce costs and improve outcomes to help organizations thrive.

As an example, institutions can work together to design creative solutions for academic programs that will fit current and future needs across campuses. This would include identifying and hiring qualified faculty. Collaborations would help schools fill positions and simultaneously mentor and develop future faculty members (i.e. graduate students). Although staff development is encouraged, it is difficult to fill all positions while faculty is training. However, through collaboration, staff can be shifted or shared to meet staffing needs—even as academic programs are revisited and revised to reflect current African realities. The advantage of collaboration with other institutions is in how qualified human resources can be strategically deployed and associated costs shared among campuses.

Stockpiles of outdated resources have consistently prevented African students and faculty from staying current on relevant global issues. This defect robs them of the opportunity to contribute to global scholarly debates. Few new books are added from year to year unless there are big donations from Christian book drives. Therefore, institutional collaborations would help by making a wider variety of materials available through interlibrary loans and electronic databases, bearing in mind the challenges of available connectivity. The costs of these materials could also be allocated in a manageable way.

Institutional and program accreditation is an influencing factor on African education, because of the priority that people assign to certification—even over factors like formation, skills or competencies. National and regional accreditations are not cheap and even at times simply force conflicting agendas on schools seeking certification. Apart from academic programs, faculty and library resources, accrediting agencies are very particular about physical facilities because of the importance of the learning environment in education. Through collaborations institutions can partner with others to offer courses in the same facilities and share learning resources.

Another expensive requirement is insurance. Schools must create a financial shield for themselves in the event of accidents arising from human or property failure. Likewise, employers offer medical insurance to employees as a competitive salary package to attract the best candidates. However, insurance is a tremendous operating expense but could be purchased for a much cheaper price when secured as a group otherwise known as a cooperative. For example, individual small theological institutions in the Eastern African region could form a cooperative and purchase faculty pensions for a much larger network of people at lower rates.

Modes of Delivery

Theological education has traditionally been offered in lecture halls and classrooms with students as an audience to an instructor during a specific window of time when attendance is required. The cost of maintaining schools with this style of residential instruction has been growing over the years. However, if institutions are to be financially healthy over the long term, campuses must change the residential model into something that is equally effective but cheaper to operate. As with every change process, there has to be dissatisfaction with the status quo and willingness to embrace new ways of achieving the same goal. As institutions seek to be financially solvent, viable alternatives should be considered to still deliver first-rate instruction but at manageable costs. Alternatives include open and distance learning modes, church-based instruction, and integrated learning, among others. Institutions seeking alternative ways of delivering instruction must work with others to improve their approaches.

Every decision regarding the mode of delivery—whether it be open or distance learning or church-based instruction, is very important in determining the overall cost of education. Approaches to open and distance courses (e.g., online, mobile phone, blended, church-based and integrated learning) will require investment. Therefore institutions need to select the most effective approach based on available human and financial resources.

Leadership Development

Central to financial sustainability of theological institutions is leadership development. Training candidates to develop into mature wise leaders means showing individuals how to conceptualize solutions, then plan and implement strategies to initiate projects for an organization's long-term financial sustainability. Leadership development for theological institutions is a critical component because it is the cog that holds all other factors influencing financial sustainability together. Although theological institutions train leaders to serve church and society, the focus of that leadership development is not to address leadership needs of an institution.

A church body, mission agency or a governing board depending on how institutional governance is structured, often does the selecting of leaders for theological institutions. Each entity has the responsibility to recruit suitable candidates to take over the reins of an institution whenever the need arises. Social capital, political alignment, and professional achievements are three influential factors—apart from any primary qualifications—that influence the ultimate appointment of a candidate.

There are countless ways leaders can be developed to lead theological institutions; however, the process can be idealistic to the extent that core practices needed to actually shape leader behavior can be missed. Yukl is an authority on leadership development and has identified essential activities that should be part of any such training program: multisource feedback, developmental assignment, mentoring, executive coaching, and personal growth programs. These areas are critical for leadership development including programs sponsored by theological institutions in Africa.

Leadership deployment enables one to assign new responsibilities to leaders who have been selected and trained. Selecting and training leaders without any clear plan for deployment only creates frustration among one's leadership team. This often leads to sudden departures and loss of human resources. In particular, deployment and transition involve the training of a leader. Commensurate to new abilities and competencies, a transition is simply a change of assignments from one position to another, including promotions to executive positions in an institution.

The intentional development of leadership skills and competences must always be coupled with opportunities for the utilization of those skills. This provides a road map for senior institutional leaders to know when and how the investment in their skill development will be utilized.

Many leaders dread the discussion on training and deployment, let alone planning for it when they are still in leadership position. It takes courage and immense confidence to bring up the matter for discussion and to map out the intricacies of how it needs to be carried out. After leaders have been trained, they must be deployed to serve in requisite positions. Deployment plans must start at the same time as a training program so that by the time training is coming to an end, the trainee is very clear regarding the next assignment. If deployment to the next higher responsibility follows immediately after the training, it creates room for the upcoming leader to implement principles and lessons learned thereby reducing the temptation to undercut a current leader's position or lose motivation through a long waiting period without any challenges to stay sharp.

Institutional leadership is often characterized by certain challenges that transcend the institutional make-up. They are deep rooted and call for a leader's honest cry for help if they are to be addressed. These challenges include inadequate personal leadership capacity; sacrifices of personal health, family, and career development; ability to survive the pressures of institutional politics; lack of a safe place for rest and counseling. The selection, training, deployment and any transitions all focus on the skills and competencies of institutional leadership. Therefore, there has to be a program to cater to the physical and emotional needs of a leader so that he/she can weather the storms that occur in leadership.

Financial sustainability is possible but it takes more than and individual leader to accomplish the goal. It is not an individual affair, however gifted that individual might be, rather it takes the concerted effort of many leaders with various in an institution to achieve the goal. It is a community affair that draws wisdom from churches, mission agencies, governing boards, faculty, administrators, students, alumni and the wider society to safeguard what really matters, the mission of theological education. One can be skeptical of a gifted leader's drive to ensure financial sustainability but it is difficult and almost impossible to stop a concerted effort of committed leaders purposefully working to achieve financial sustainability of their institution. It is even more impossible if their strength and trust is in the Lord whose mission they endeavor to fulfill.

Fundamental to the journey of financial sustainability of theological institutions is the historical and contextual factors that impinge on institutional performance. The factors may vitiate the efforts of leaders if not carefully examined to establish their alignment with the efforts directed at financial challenges. History of an institution matters, and the context in which it operates cannot be ignored. The spokes of financial sustainability continuously interact with these factors; hence leaders must adopt a learning posture that allows them to carefully navigate the changing course of history and emerging contextual challenges that might circumvent their efforts to achieve financial sustainability.

Bibliography

Aleshire, Dan O. *Earthen Vessels: Hopeful Reflections on the Work and Future of Theological Schools.* Grand Rapids: Eerdmans, 2008.

Andringa, Robert. "Governance and Board Relations." In *Christian Leadership Essentials: A Handbook for Managing Christian Organizations,* edited by David S. Dockery. 65–85. Nashville: B. & H., 2011.

Barnett, Paul. *The Message of 2 Corinthians.* Bible Speaks Today. Downers Grove, IL: Intervarsity, 1988.

Barnett, P. W. "Tentmaking." In *Dictionary of Paul and His Letters,* Gerald Hawthorne and Ralph P. Winter, 926–27. Downers Grove, IL: InterVarsity, 1993.

Bellon, Emmanuel O. *Transforming Leadership through Values-based Training.* Orlando: International Leadership Foundation, 2011.

Bernard, J. H. *St. Paul's Second Epistle to the Corinthians.* In *The Expositor's Greek New Testament,* edited by W. Robertson Nicoll, 3:27–119. Grand Rapids: Eerdmans, 1979.

Bowers, Paul. "Theological Education in Africa: Why Does It Matter?" Lecture at the AIM-SIM Theological Education Consultation, Honeydew, South Africa, 19–23 March 2007.

Bruce, F. F. *1 & 2 Thessalonians.* Word Biblical Commentary. Waco, TX: Word, 1982.

Calvin, John. *The First Epistle of Paul to the Corinthians.* Translated by John W. Fraser. Calvin's New Testament Commentaries, edited by David W. Torrance and Thomas F. Torrance. Grand Rapids, MI: Eerdmans, 1960.

Carver, John. *Boards That Make A Difference.* San Francisco: Jossey-Bass, 1990.

Clinton, J. R. *Leadership Emergency Theory.* Altadena, CA: Barnabas Resources, 1989.

Coe, Shoki. "In Search of Renewal in Theological Education." *Theological Education* 9, no. 4 (1973) 235.

Cole, Victor Babajide. *Training of the Ministry: A Macro-Curricular Approach.* Bangalore: Theological Book Trust, 2001.

Collins, Jim. *Good to Great.* New York: HarperCollins, 2001

Conn, Harvie. "Theological Education and the Search for Excellence." *Westminster Theological Journal* 41, no., 2 (1979) 311–63.

Craigie, Peter. *The Book of Deuteronomy.* New International Commentary on the Old Testament. Grand Rapids: Eerdmans, 1976.

Danker, William J. *Profit for the Lord.* Grand Rapids: Eerdmans, 1971.

Eadie, John. *Thessalonians.* Greek Text Commentaries. Grand Rapids: Macmillan, 1979. 58, 68, 201.

Elliston, Edgar J. *Home Grown Leaders*. Pasadena, CA: William Carey Library, 1992.

Farley, Edward. *Theologia: The Fragmentation and Unity of Theological Education*. Philadelphia: Fortress, 1983.

Ferenczi, Jason. *Serving Communities: Governance and the Potential of Theological Schools*. ICETE. Carlisle, PA: Langham Global Library, 2015.

Ferris, Robert. *Renewal in Theological Education: Strategies for Change*. Wheaton, IL: Billy Graham Center, 1990.

Figel, Jan, ed. *Higher Education Governance in Europe*. Brussels: Eurydice Education Unit, 2008.

Findlay, G. G. *St. Paul's First Epistle to the Corinthians*. In *The Expositor's Greek New Testament*, edited by W. Robertson Nicoll, 2:729–953. Grand Rapids: Eerdmans, 1980.

Frame, James E. *A Critical and Exegetical Commentary on the Epistles of St. Paul to the Thessalonians*. ICC. Edinburgh: T. & T. Clark, 1979.

Freedman, Mike. *The Art and Discipline of Strategic Leadership*. New York: McGraw-Hill, 2003.

Gilliland, Dean S. *Pauline Theology and Mission Practice*. Eugene, OR: Wipf and Stock, 1996.

Godet, Frederick L. *Commentary on St. Paul's First Epistle to the Corinthians*. Vol. 1. Clark's Foreign Theological Library, new series, 27, 30. Grand Rapids: Kregel, 1977.

Gordon, R. P. "Philippi." In *New Bible Dictionary*, edited by J. D. Douglas, 928. Leicester, UK: InterVarsity, 1982.

Grubb, Kenneth. *The Need for Non-Professional Missionaries*. London: World Dominion, 1931. 11.

Guinness, Os. *The Call: Finding and Fulfilling the Central Purpose of Your Life*. Nashville, TN: W. Publishing Group, 1998.

Guthrie, Donald. *New Testament Introduction*. Downers Grove: InterVarsity, 1990. 432.

Harrison, Everett F. *Introduction to the New Testament*. Grand Rapids: Eerdmans, 1964. 245.

Hiebert, D. Edmond. *The Thessalonian Epistles*. Chicago: Moody, 1980. 11.

Higher Education Governance in Europe: Policies, Structures, Funding and Academic Staff. Brussels: Eurydice, 2008. Print.

Hock, R. F. *The Social Context of Paul's Mission*. Philadelphia: Fortress. 20–21, 67.

Houston, B. "Missiological and Theological Perspectives on Theological Education in Africa" in Handbook of Theological Education in World Christianity. 715–270. Oxford: Regnum, 2010.

Hughes, Philip. *St. Paul's Second Epistle to the Corinthians*. ICNT. 1962. Repr., Grand Rapids: Eerdmans, 1979.

Judge, E. A. "Macedonia." In *New Bible Dictionary*, edited by J. D. Douglas, 721. Wheaton, IL: Tyndale, 1982.

Keil, C. F., and F. Delitzsch. *The Pentateuch: Deuteronomy*. Vol. 1 of *Commentary on the Old Testament in Ten Volumes*, 1:269–517. Grand Rapids: Eerdmans, 1980.

Kelsey, David. *Between Athens and Berlin: The Theological Education Debate*. Grand Rapids, MI: Eerdmans, 1993.

Kemper, Robert. *What Every Church Member Should Know about Clergy*. New York, New York: Pilgrim Press, 1985. 65.

Kittel, Gerhard, and Gerhard Friedrich, eds. *Theological Dictionary of the New Testament*. Abridged-in-one-vol. ed. Translated by Geoffrey W. Bromiley. Grand Rapids: Eerdmans, 1992.

Kouzes, James M., and Barry Z. Posner. *The Leadership Challenge: How to Make Extraordinary Things Happen in Organizations*. 2nd ed. San Francisco: Jossey-Bass, 1995.

Le Cornu, Alison. "The Shape of Things to Come: Theological Education in the Twenty-First Century." *British Journal of Theological Education* 14.1 (2003): 13–26.

Leith, John. *Crisis in the Church: The Plight of Theological Education*. Louisville: Westminster John Knox, 1997.

Lenski, R. C. H. *The Interpretation of First and Second Corinthians*. Minneapolis: Augsburg, 1963.

Lowery, David K. "2 Corinthians." In *Bible Knowledge Commentary*, edited by John F. Walvoord and Roy B. Zuck, 551–86. Wheaton, IL: Victor, 1983.

Luck, Donald G. *Why Study Theology?* St Louis: Chalice, 1999. Print.

Mabuluki, Kangwa. "Theological Education by Extension in Zambia." In *Diversified Theological Education*, edited by Ross Kinsler. Pasadena: William Carey, 2008.

Martin, Ralph. *2 Corinthians*. Word Biblical Commentary. Waco, TX: Word, 1986. 344.

Marshall, Howard. "1 & 2 Thessalonians." *The New Century Bible Commentary*. Grand Rapids: Eerdmans, 1983. 72.

McCauley, Cynthia, Russ Moxley, and Ellen Van Velsor, eds. *The Center for Creative Leadership Handbook of Leadership Development*. San Francisco, CA: Jossey-Bass, 1998. 4.

Mike, Freedman. *The Art and Discipline of Strategic Leadership*. New York: McGraw-Hill, 2003. 24–25.

Morris, Leon. *1 & 2 Thessalonians*. New International Commentary on the New Testament. Grand Rapids: Eerdmans, 1977. 71, 251.

Mugambi, J. N. K. "Christianity in Africa, 1910–2010." In *Atlas of Global Christianity*, edited by Todd Johnson and Kenneth Ross, 111. Edinburgh: Edinburgh University, 2009.

Mwesigwa, F. "Modern Religious and Ethnic Conflict in East Africa: Religious Education Curriculum Review: A Requisite Response." Lecture, The Joint Conference of Academic Societies in the Fields of Religion and Theology, Session B3, University off Stellenbosch, Stellenbosch, June 22, 2009.

Neill, Stephen. *A History of Christian Missions*. Middlessex: Penguin, 1975. 263.

Ostrom, Elinor, and Larry D. Schroeder. *Institutional Incentives and Sustainable Development: Infrastructure Policies in Perspective*. Boulder: Westview, 1993.

Plummer, Alfred. *A Critical and Exegetical Commentary on the Second Epistle of St Paul to the Corinthians*. Edinburgh: T. & T. Clark, 1978.

Report from the Theological Education Fund, 1958–1963. New York: Theological Education Fund, 1963.

Robert, Dana. "Promotion of Missions." In *New 20th Century Encyclopedia of Religious Knowledge*, edited by J. D. Douglas, 563–64. Grand Rapids: Baker House, 1991.

Robertson, Archibald, and Alfred Plummer. *A Critical and Exegetical Commentary on the First Epistle of St. Paul to the Corinthians*. Edited by Samuel R. Driver, Alfred Plummer, and Charles A. Briggs. Edinburgh: T. & T. Clark, 1950.

Rolston, Holmes. *Stewardship in the New Testament Church*. VA: John Knox, 1959. 85.

Sanneh, Lamin O. *West African Christianity: The Religious Impact*. U.S. ed. Maryknoll, N.Y.: Orbis, 1983.

Snook, Stewart. *Developing Leaders Through Theological Education by Extension*. Wheaton, IL: Billy Graham Center, 1992.

Snow, Douglas. "Microcredit: An Institutional Development Opportunity." *International Journal of Economic Development* 1, no. 1 (1999) 65–79.

Stewart, John. *The Nestorian Missionary Enterprise: A Church on Fire*. Edinburgh: T. & T. Clark, 1923.

Stogdill, Ralph M. *Handbook of Leadership: A Survey of Theory and Research*. London: Collier MacMillan, 1974.

Swanepoel (UNISA), Francois, Ezra Chitando (AIC Leader), Paul Mwuara (Kenyatta University), Archbishop Mofokeng (AIC Leader), and T. Mushagalusa (Univ. of Goma, DR Congo). "Panel Discussion on Theological Education, Session A6." Lecture, Joint Conference of Academic Societies in the Fields of Religion and Theology, University of Stellenbosch, Stellenbosch, June 22, 2009.

Thompson, J. A. *Deuteronomy: An Introduction and Commentary*. Vol. 5 of Tyndale Old Testament Commentaries. Downers Grove, IL: InterVarsity, 1974.

Toussaint, Stanley D. "Acts." In *Bible Knowledge Commentary*. Wheaton: Victor, 1983. 414.

"USP WSSD Team Report: Johannesburg World Summit on Sustainable Development." The University of the South Pacific (USP). 2002. Accessed 2014. http://www.usp.ac.fj/pace.

Vine, W. E. *Vine's Expository Dictionary*. Nashville, TN: Nelson, 1997. 81, 127.

Wahl, W. P. "Towards Relevant Theological Education in Africa: Comparing the International Discourse with Contextual Challenges." *Acta Theologica* 33, no. 1 (2013) 266–93. doi: http://dx.doi.org/10.4314/actat.v33i1.14.

Webster, Douglas. *Survey of the Training of Ministry in the Middle East*. Geneva: Commission on the World Mission and Evangelism, 1962. 4.

Wigram, George V. *The Englishman's Greek Concordance*. Grand Rapids: Baker, 1979. 166.

Wilson, J. Christy, Jr. *Today's Tentmakers: Self-Support: An Alternative Model for Worldwide Witness*. Wheaton, IL: Tyndale House, 1981.

"World Study Report." *Challenges and Opportunities in Theological Education in the 21st Century: Pointers for a New International Debate on Theological Education* 14: 17. *Edinburgh 2010–International Study Group on Theological Education*. Web. 9 Mar. 2012.

Yukl, Gary. *Leadership in Organizations*. 6th ed. Upper Saddle River, NJ: Prentice-Hall, 2006.

Zmijewski, Josef. In *Exegetical Dictionary of the New Testament*, edited by Horst Balz and Gerard Schneider, 2:247–79. Grand Rapids: Eerdmans, 1991.

Zorn, Herbert. *Viability in Context*. Bromley, Kent: Theological Education Fund, 1975.

Index